THE CAMBRIDGE ILLUSTRATED HISTORY OF

France

THE CAMBRIDGE ILLUSTRATED HISTORY OF
France

COLIN JONES

CAMBRIDGE
UNIVERSITY PRESS

For Kelsey and Blanche, affectionately

Published by the Press Syndicate of the University of Cambridge
The Pitt Building, Trumpington Street, Cambridge CB2 1RP
40 West 20th Street, New York, NY 10011-4211, USA
10 Stamford Road, Oakleigh, Melbourne 3166, Australia

First published in 1994
First paperback edition 1999

This book was laid out and produced by
CALMANN & KING LTD
71 Great Russell Street,
London WC1B 3BN

Project editor: Damian Thompson
Picture research: Susan Bolsom-Morris
Layout: Andrew Shoolbred
Cartography by Hardlines, Charlbury, Oxford

Typeset by Wyvern Typesetting Ltd., Bristol
Printed in Hong Kong

A catalogue record for this book is available from the British Library

Library of Congress Cataloguing-in-Publication Data

Jones, Colin. 1947–
    The Cambridge illustrated history of France / Colin Jones. —
1. ed
        p.   cm. — (Cambridge illustrated histories)
    Includes bibliographical references and index.
    ISBN 0 521 43294 4
    1. France—Civilization.   I. Title.   II. Series.
DC33.J66   1994
944—dc20   94-19310
                                                            CIP

ISBN 0 521 43294 4 hardback
ISBN 0 521 66992 8 paperback

Contents

Preface

With the explosion of historical knowledge in this century, professional historians have rarely been rash enough to try to cover the whole of the history of France in a single volume, and have largely abandoned the field to amateur historians and professional writers, who have had few of their qualms. As I explain in the Introduction, I have tried to dodge the pitfalls and embrace this Cinderella among historical genres with some warmth. My aim has been to provide an accessible account that is more than a chronicle of the political history of the social and governmental elite; that gives economic, social and cultural history their due; that respects the regional as well as the national framework; and that gives full weight to questions of gender, class and race.

As Richard Cobb – the greatest British historian of France this century – has put it, history contains "a wide element of guesswork. It is like attempting to sound the unsoundable, and to penetrate the secrets of the human heart". The amount of guesswork is all the more extensive for the historian roaming well outside his professional area of scholarly expertise, not to mention approaching the history of France as a foreigner. How well I have come to terms, first, with national preconceptions and misconceptions, second, with my inevitable deficiencies of specialized knowledge over much of the historical record, and, third, with the challenge of writing a new sort of national history will be for readers to judge.

It remains to thank most warmly those colleagues and friends who have helped by reading drafts of various parts of the typescript and saved me from more egregious errors than I care to relate. Fellow historians at Exeter University – notably Jonathan Barry, David Braund, Bryony Coles, Julia Crick, John Critchley, Robert Hudson, Linda Hurcombe, Nicholas Orme, Tim Rees and Peter Wiseman – were especially helpful. My thanks, too, to Roger Chartier and Emmanuel Le Roy Ladurie. Numerous other friends and colleagues – including those at Stanford University, where I spent 1993–94 as Visiting Professor of European History – helped too, in all sorts of ways. All should be absolved from blame for any problems that remain, which are my responsibility. On the production side Rosemary Bradley, Melanie White and Damian Thompson provided advice and support, and Susan Bolsom-Morris was a superb picture researcher. Finally my thanks go to Josephine McDonagh, for being there.

Colin Jones

Foreword
by Emmanuel Le Roy Ladurie

In its way, *The Cambridge Illustrated History of France* is a striking example of the seductive yet thorny topic of Anglo-French or Franco-English relations. It is a topic about which much could be said.

In Carolingian times, while "France" and "Germany" were central to the immense and fragile European state constructed by Charlemagne, England kept itself to itself, with the Continent – to adopt a famous phrase – "cut off". From 1066 and throughout the Middle Ages, William the Conqueror and his successors controlled from Normandy an England that was not always appreciative of contacts, though it would be churlish and anachronistic to see this in terms of occupation, collaboration and resistance . . . The Plantagenets brought British influence down to the Garonne before the Hundred Years War, that stunning and long-lasting catastrophe. Contacts between the two countries subsequently became less explosive. Despite religious differences, most cultivated French people valued contacts with the English. Every period of intellectual and political openness from 1595 down to 1925 was marked by a dose of cultural and diplomatic anglophilia. Henry IV counted on his "good sister Elizabeth"; Mazarin was Cromwell's ally; the ministries of Dubois and Fleury marked a period of cross-Channel friendship, coinciding with the impact of Newton and Shakespeare on the French Enlightenment; and in the nineteenth century, too, numerous economic and political models (parliamentarism, free trade and press freedom) came from England.

The obverse of this relationship, however, was conflict. From the time of Richelieu France was generally on top, but this changed dramatically from the Seven Years War onwards. A period of nearly two centuries had opened up in which France would be constantly defeated, at first by the English (along with the Prussians), subsequently by the Germans (now enemies of the English). The 1914–18 war was in theory a French victory; but the million-and-a-half French deaths made it a disaster all the same – and one followed by an even greater catastrophe, 1940.

One can understand why, following these disasters, the French proceeded to a national stock-taking after 1945–50. They came to seek reconciliation with Germany and threw themselves unconditionally into the European adventure. Post-war Britain, in contrast, retains a certain distance towards, even a suspicion of, the Continent.

Colin Jones' work is of course utterly antithetical to such an approach. His *Cambridge Illustrated History* is a book which should allow his compatriots to become better acquainted with their neighbour. The French past, which Jones explores using the techniques of the New History, reveals unexpected riches and highlights material overlooked by the old school of event-oriented, positivist historians (both French and English). Authoritative, well written and solidly thought through, this book, which has no recent equivalent in writing about French history, should reach out beyond the British Isles to the English-speaking world in its entirety.

Introduction

We can draw a line, roughly from north to south, across the middle of the department of the Hérault, on the Mediterranean coastline in Lower Languedoc, dividing the area into eastern and western sectors. In the east, soccer is played as the first winter game (Montpellier fields, at the time of writing, a first-division team in the national soccer league); in the western half, rugby has the same role (in the 1970s and 1980s Béziers was the premier rugby club of France). This bifurcation of the department – roughly along the line of the Hérault river valley – corresponds, broadly speaking, with a split detectable throughout the long history of the region. Predominantly left-wing voters to the west have traditionally been distinct from right-wing supporters in the east; supporters of the Revolution of 1789 in the east could be distinguished from dissidents in the west; sixteenth-century Protestants in the east, from Catholics in the west; late medieval Cathars in the west, from orthodox Catholics in the east. The division recurs in the diocesan framework created in the early Middle Ages. And it probably dates back to pre-Roman times; archaeologists confirm the presence of a cultural frontier here, with one grouping, the Volcae Arecomici in the west, having a different material culture from the Volcae Tectosages in the east.

Such stories could be told about a great many regions within France. If we are not generally aware of them or have lost them from sight, this is partly because professional historians tend to work in relatively short time-periods, eschewing the broadest angles of vision. It also owes something to the fact that most multi-period histories of France prefer to commemorate national unity rather than exploring division, divergence and variety within French borders. Such histories have tended to be written as if the frontier separating the French from undifferentiated "Others" was the only cultural boundary worth investigating. In this, they remain true to the penchant of national histories for blatant, often flag-waving chauvinism.

Historians in the nineteenth century – when national histories came into their own – conceived of the French nation as comprising a group of men with a common language, common racial features and a common culture that distinguished them from their neighbours. In so far as these characteristics were not shared in the past within the boundaries of the present-day state, then the historian's task was to show, through the prism of the nation state, how men came to possess a common ethnic, cultural and political heritage. The common identity was often viewed as being centred on Paris and its environs: "The real France," Michelet (a Parisian) had announced, "is northern France" – a phrase echoed in the doubtless apocryphal remark of Charles de Gaulle (a northerner), that "Africa begins at Lyon". It was in the Paris region, declared one of the most prestigious of these national histories at the turn of this century, "where national history essentially took place".

Yet, as the example of the Hérault department suggests, if we stick to this increasingly outdated model, then we miss a lot. If we want to understand what motivated

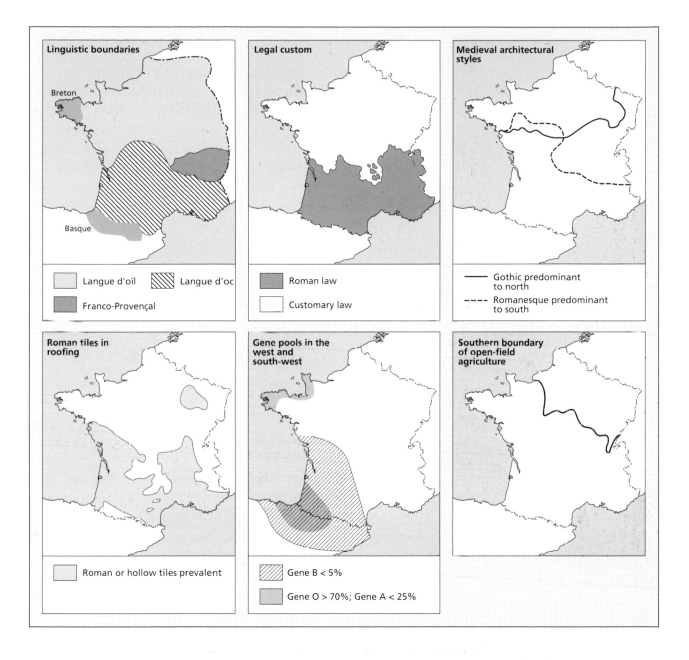

people in the past, it is as rewarding and helpful to examine the major internal, cultural frontiers as the political boundaries defining the limits of national territory. Even at the very end of the twentieth century identity in France is local and regional: in certain respects, many individuals still count themselves as much Auvergnats, Bretons or Basques as French. This testifies to the enduring character of regional divisions.

The long-term persistence of linguistic frontiers within France mocks the assumption that the French nation has ever been linguistically unified in any meaningful sense until very recently. The major division – between the *langue d'oc* in the south and the *langue d'oïl* in the north – is only one of a range of important dividing lines. In the

Cultural boundaries. Deep internal boundaries highlight differences in everything from language to building style. The lines of division cut different ways – the genetic geography, for example, seems quite distinct. Overall, an anthropologist would have little difficulty positing a strong north–south profile.

middle of the nineteenth century a quarter of the French population did not speak French, and another quarter understood it very imperfectly. Many of these were located in the north: fifty kilometres outside Paris, peasants spoke Picard as their first language; and we may also note northern cohorts of Breton speakers in the Armorican peninsula, Germanists in the east and a smattering of Flemish speakers on the Belgian frontier. The bulk of those resistant to the French language, however, were situated in the Midi, the area of the *langue d'oc*.

The line of cultural demarcation between north and south occurs remarkably frequently in France's history. The map distinguishing a north, where customary law obtained, as against a Midi, where Roman law was the basis of local legal codes, is an extraordinarily important one linked to the transmission of property. The line also broadly corresponds with differences in more everyday material culture: as for example, types of roofs and water-mills. It is interesting, too, to compare this with a rather different medieval boundary – that marking the areas where Gothic and Romanesque architecture was prevalent in the Middle Ages.

One could draw other important lines of division besides the north–south one. In genetic terms, for example, there is a strong case for seeing the Basque area and southwest Gascony as very different from the rest of France (and indeed most of western Europe), and this forms a boundary which has had other significant cultural expressions. So too in many respects – such as style of farming and social structure – a line running from the Channel coast to Geneva has constituted a marker of difference.

It should not, however, be imagined that cultural boundaries are solely geographical, and that only localism counts. Although I have placed particular emphasis on geographical factors to illustrate a point, gender and social class are every bit as crucial areas of demarcation, difference and identity as region. Much of the finest work in French history in recent decades – notably that in the tradition of the so-called *Annalistes* – has sought to uncover the worlds of workers, peasants, marginal groups and women, and it has striven to extend the boundaries of the past to include private as well as public life. Drawing on these rich sources, we can now, for example, incorporate women into French history as more than queens or royal mistresses. Peasants may now be viewed as more than brakes on "Progress"; marginal groups as more than threats needing to be repressed; colonial societies as more than "primitives" awaiting the metropolitan civilizing mission. French history now appears more complex – and more interesting – than the chronicle of the achievements of a limited group of, we might say, Dead White Northern Elite Males.

The *Cambridge Illustrated History* format lends itself particularly well to an analysis that gives due attention to questions of locality, class, gender and other principles of difference. Cartography allows many of the regional distinctions to be highlighted and explored. In addition, the illustrations allow us to portray diversity at all levels of French society. Representations of royal coronations stand alongside primitive contraceptive devices. The Gothic cathedral is juxtaposed with the mass-produced Citroën car (post-structuralist Roland Barthes, as we shall see, actually compared the two).

Opposite The ceremony of healing the "King's Evil" (scrofula), as practised by Henry II (r. 1547–59). The belief in the divine power of the "royal touch" dated from the eleventh century, and the Capetians exploited the ritual for propaganda purposes. As the king touched the sick person, he would say, "The king touches you; God cures you." By the eighteenth century, this formula had changed to: "The King touches you; may God heal you" – a shift to the subjunctive which reflected a scepticism on the part of the toucher, if not the touched. This example comes from a sixteenth-century illuminated manuscript, *Les Heures de Henri II*.

CHAPTER 1

France Before the Romans

The human species tiptoed imperceptibly into French history. Although Europe cannot compete with the archaeological record of Africa, where hominid remains four million years old have been discovered, the ancestors of *Homo sapiens sapiens* were already to be found in France two million years ago. Notable here was *Homo erectus*, whose physical remains have been found dating to approximately half a million years ago. Then came the Neanderthals, who were present from about 100,000 BC, and who were characterized by a short, stocky stature and a large, rugged, deep-featured head. Only from around 40,000 BC did these begin to be replaced – for reasons which remain entirely unclear – by modern humans (*Homo sapiens sapiens*), in whose more conventional bodies we recognize ourselves.

These developments took place in the context of huge environmental changes wrought by the Ice Age. Geologists distinguish four periods of glaciation, or freezing, in the far-distant past: ice-sheets reached down from the north into England, northern Germany and the Low Countries; a smaller icecap centred on the Alps; glaciers spread far out from the Pyrenees and Massif Central; and conditions of permanently frozen soil prevailed as far south as the Loire valley. Phases of ice advance were, however, interspersed with times of thaw – and it was during a warmer, interglacial phase of the Würm period, which lasted between roughly 90,000 and 9,000 years ago, that *Homo sapiens* appeared.

For the little we know about these early humans we are dependent upon the archaeological record. Archaeologists divide this prehistoric past into periods characterized primarily by the type of tools which societies employed. The Stone Age, in which stone-based tools were used, is divided into two distinct eras: the Old Stone Age, or palaeolithic period (from earliest times to *c.* 6,000 BC in France) and the New Stone Age, or neolithic period (*c.* 6,000 to *c.* 1,800 BC), in which polished stone tools were used. The transition from Old to New Stone Ages was one of the most crucial in human history, namely, the shift from hunting and gathering lifestyles to those characterized by more settled communities practising farming. The Age of Metal began in roughly 1,800 BC, when societies began to employ copper, then bronze, in their tool-making. The Bronze Age (1,800 to 700 BC) was followed by the Iron Age (*c.* 700 BC to the time of the Romans), so called because of the widespread use of this tough and resilient metal.

Throughout this early period France was subject to migratory movements, especially from the east, whose rationale and extent remain clouded in mystery. Demographic pressure caused by population levels outstripping food supplies may well have been the major factor in making peoples mobile. Ecological deterioration – changes in animal populations on which peoples depended for their foods, for example – may also have played a part. New peoples brought new cultural patterns and modes of behaviour, which could then be adopted and further spread by indigenous peoples. The Romans, who arrived and settled in France in the first century or so before

Christ, brought with them not only a relatively complex and sophisticated culture, they also introduced writing to France. With the Romans, pre-literate prehistory passes into the realm of history.

THE OLD STONE AGE

Early societies affected their environment less than they were affected by it, especially during the geological and climatic upheaval of the Ice Age. Glacial advance and retreat caused spectacular shifts in the native flora and fauna. While freezing, steppe-like conditions prevailed in ice-age periods, the interglacial periods could be hot, with tundra giving way to jungle-like forest. A surprisingly wide range of animals lived at some time or other over this early period, ranging from Arctic species (musk ox, reindeer) to carnivores more at home in subtropical climes (hyena, lion), temperate-zone herbivores (red deer, aurochs), mountain species (chamois, bear, ibex) and grassland grazers (bison, horse) – to say nothing of now extinct species, such as the mammoth (whose remains are found throughout France down to the Mediterranean coastline), the woolly rhinoceros and various types of hippopotamus. All these animals were at some time important food sources of early hominids.

This is a period frequently characterized as the "Age of Man the Hunter". Yet the label seems doubly inappropriate. Plants rather than game probably provided the bulk of the food of these prehistoric populations. Moreover, it seems likely that the

The Lascaux caves, from 16,000 to 14,000 BC, the most celebrated example of cave art.

The most ancient form of cultural expression to take place within French borders, far predating that of Greek and Roman civilizations, cave art has been recognized only very recently as a part of France's cultural heritage. At first archaeologists, used to thinking of prehistoric peoples as primitive savages, found it difficult to accept the authenticity of decorated prehistoric objects. Professional endorsement was swiftly followed by wider public interest, when some were shown at the Universal Exhibition held in Paris in 1867. Paradoxically, prehistoric art entered the public sphere only shortly before the advent of Impressionism in 1874.

The great Lascaux cave in the Dordogne was found as late as 1940, and discoveries continue to be made. The most striking recent find was in July 1991 by the diver Jean Cosquer, at Cape Morgiou, twelve kilometres south-east of Marseille. The paintings, engravings and daubings found in the Cosquer cave date from the Magdalenian period, between 18,000 and 16,000 years ago. The cave was probably ten kilometres from the coast during the Magdalenian period, but the rise in sea level by over one hundred metres at the end of the Ice Age sealed normal access, thereby reducing environmental damage.

The location of this cave, in Provence, is unusual. Though cave art is found over an area ranging from Paris and Rouen in the north to Gibraltar and Sicily in the south, most of it is located in south-west France (notably in the Dordogne and the Pyrenees) and in north-east Spain – indeed cave art is often called Franco-Cantabrian art. In other respects, however, the pictorial contents of the Cosquer cave are fairly representative of prehistoric parietal (or wall) art. Though cave art dates back to before 30,000 BC, the Magdalenian period saw a veritable artistic explosion.

Prehistoric art: the Cosquer cave

The most brilliant examples – Lascaux in the Dordogne, Altamira, near Santander in Spain and Niaux in the French Pyrenees – date from this period.

A host of different methods is evident at Cosquer as elsewhere: finger marks, stencilled hands, rock engravings and paintings. Charcoal and ochre were the preferred media. As is typical, animals make up the bulk of the subjects represented at Cosquer: of nearly fifty representations so far listed, horses, bison and ibex are the most common, but there are also chamois, felines, a megaceros and some marine species, notably seals and penguin-like great auks. (By contrast Lascaux, whose "Hall of Bulls" is a veritable Sistine Chapel of cave art, contains 600 paintings and nearly 1,500 engravings.) The Cosquer cave has not yet yielded examples of portable art. Elsewhere engraved, painted and sculpted objects are extremely numerous. The fifty prehistoric caves of the Dordogne region alone have produced over 2,000 objects:

carved bone, stone, antler, ivory objects, clay figurines and the like.

Though access to the Cosquer cave is now difficult because of the rise in sea level, there is every reason to believe it has never been easy. Cave art is frequently located in dark, secret places, usually far away from normal habitations and intended to be illuminated only by fat-burning lamps. In some cave sites paintings are over a mile from the cave entrance, through chambers that professional speleologists find challenging. In the caves at Lascaux, moreover, some of the paintings are fifteen feet from the ground, which would have necessitated the use of scaffolding.

The identities and intentions of the cave artists remain a profound mystery. Stylistic similarities between paintings in different caves suggest schools of cave artists, or systems of apprenticeship. It is conceivable that the artists served a magical function for the societies involved, and that the painted caves were sites for initiation ceremonies aimed at bringing good luck in the hunt. Cave art seems replete with meanings; yet we lack the codes for discovering what they were.

Auks, here depicted on the roof of the Cosquer cave (c. 16,000 BC), may have formed a part of the diet of the coastal cave-dwellers.

newcomers – they drove existing shepherd communities up into the Alps and the Massif Central, for example. However, the shift to the Chasseyan also operated through peaceful acceptance by existing groups, for it represented a new style of life in France as a whole, as much as a new layer of immigrants.

The shift towards a farming existence is conventionally identified as one of "Man's" greatest achievements. Yet a great deal of archaeological and ethnographic evidence suggests that the initial impetus came from women rather than "Man". Selecting and planting seeds seems a natural extension of the food-gathering activities in which women probably specialized. As long as farming resembled horticulture – that is, while it was close to human dwellings in which women attended to child-care – it probably allowed women to maintain a high status. At all events the impact of the transformation on the scale of human enterprise was dramatic: population increased, it can be surmised, ten-, then a hundredfold, reaching 100,000 by 3,700 BC, one million over the next millennium, and peaking at perhaps four to five million by the beginning of the first millennium BC. The phenomenon was at the same time cause and consequence of social change.

Statue menhirs from Filitosa, Corsica. The island contains more than one third of the total number of such effigies located on French territory. The Corsican standing stones are distinctive not just for having the rudiments of features (nose, eyes, mouth), but also for representing the paraphernalia of Bronze Age warfare (helmets, shields, daggers). They seem to be a commemoration of the heroic.

The area of France underwent a number of significant transformations in the six millennia before the modern era. The passage from hunting and gathering to pastoral and farming lifestyles (left) was diffused from two main centres – the Mediterranean in the south and so-called "Danubian culture" from the east. Megalithic culture (centre), which appears to have originated on the Atlantic seaboard, in time spread throughout France and beyond. Customs of urn/field burial, in contrast, originated in the east.

The slowness as well as the complexity of the cultural currents by which the shift to farming life was achieved makes archaeologists wary of using the term "neolithic revolution" to describe the process. After all, can any change which lasted three millennia – it was in place throughout France by 3,000 BC – seriously be considered "revolutionary"? In fact the so-called neolithic or Stone Age "revolution" was essentially evolutionary. It made, moreover, a major impact on the landscape: early farmers scooped out areas for cultivation from the primeval forest, using slash-and-burn techniques and often moving on to new areas within a generation or two. Grazing, too, affected the ecosystem, banishing forever forest cover on some highland areas with poor soils. The bare, goat-cropped flanks of Mont Aigoual and Mont Ventoux in the south are testimony in our own day to the impact of early farmers on landscape.

The relative homogeneity of cultural forms under the Chasseyan began to break down in the third millennium BC. In the Armorican peninsula a distinctive grouping developed, flourishing especially between 3,500 and 1,800 BC, whose most characteristic cultural expression was megalithic monuments. The so-called Seine-Oise-Marne (SOM) culture, originating in northern France, extended far and wide during the same period. In the Alps and the Jura a distinctive lakeside-dwelling civilization evolved, and from around 2,200 BC we begin to see traces of "Bell Beaker" culture, characterized by distinctively shaped pottery. The latter may have represented a new style of life, but alternatively it may have been brought by new, incoming groups originating either in Spain or in central and eastern Europe. Bell Beaker culture was especially important in its use of copper – for decorative ware, utensils, arms and armour. The Age of Metal was coming to supersede the Stone Age.

THE AGE OF METAL

The emergence of metallurgy highlighted growing social and economic complexity among early farming communities. Experiments with copper at the beginning of the second millennium BC led to the invention of bronze, a tough and resistant alloy of copper and tin. The new metalworking technology, adopted throughout France from around 1,400 BC, was passed on after 1,250 BC by populations practising "urn/field burial". This entailed cremation of the dead and and the interment of their ashes in urns that were placed in cemeteries outside the village. The practice of urn/field burial swept most of France, except the Atlantic seaboard. It reached the Rouergue, for example, by 950 BC, flourished there until 725 BC, and was still being practised on the Languedoc coast in the third century BC. By then, however – and notably from the eighth century BC – fresh migrant groups were already invading northern climes. Though these groups – the Celts – probably had much in common with the urn/field burial peoples, they were culturally distinct from them. They swept south and westwards and by 700 BC they were present in the Armorican peninsula. All of France north of a line between Carcassonne and Geneva bore marks of their presence by 400 BC.

This migratory phase had its roots in the east. The Scythian peoples of the Steppes, and societies in the Near and Middle East, seem to have been the epicentres of waves of turbulence which travelled outwards across Europe, triggering short- and long-term migratory waves over several centuries. Greek and Roman writers at first used the term "Gauls" to denote these restless and footloose Celts, who spread widely throughout Europe. Some pushed south-east as well as westwards, reaching "Galatia" in the Balkans and Asia Minor (hence the name "Gaul"). Another group, the "Cisalpine Gauls", had marauded into Italy, sacking Rome in 390 BC, before settling down in the Po valley. Others penetrated the Iberian peninsula. Still others had settled in Great Britain and Ireland by the third century BC: the Parisii tribe, based in the Paris basin, established a colony in Yorkshire. These mobile populations appear to have communicated exclusively in Indo-European languages, established from around 2,000 BC, on which the major European tongues would be based. They provided a dense cultural covering over France in which there were relatively few cracks: French placenames bear virtually no traces at all of pre-existent languages.

The Celts constituted a sprawling, untidy but powerful set of groupings whose area of influence far surpassed the frontiers of what would soon be Roman Gaul. Archaeologists classify the material culture of the eighth-century-BC Celts as belonging to the "Hallstatt" stage of Iron Age civilization (named after a site in Austria near Salzburg). The iron cutting-edges on their ploughs, for example, allowed them to extend cultivation on to heavy soils, while their weighty iron swords, stronger than defensive armour made of bronze, plus their mastery of horsemanship, made them formidable warriors. From the fifth century BC a variant form of Iron Age culture – the La Tène stage, named after a village on Lake Geneva, and characterized by distinctive styles of pottery, weapons and jewellery – began to predominate.

This terracotta representation of a Gaulish warrior, dating from *c.* 200 BC, was found in Lombardy, which Gaulish tribes had invaded several centuries earlier. This wild and valiant warrior was typical of a breed of foot soldiers that could be found from Britain to the Black Sea. By the time of Caesar's invasion of Gaul in 58 BC, more sophisticated military techniques were being employed, including chariots and cavalry.

The Celts came bearing ploughshares as well as arms. The Celtic warrior elite formed a landed aristocracy. They made use of a variety of tenancy arrangements and were based in large estates that were characterized by open fields. Their iron ploughs, sickles and reapers boosted agricultural production and stimulated demographic growth. Population, which had slumped dramatically under the impact of the warfare they had initially waged, increased from two to three million in 500 BC to probably between six and eight million at the time of the Roman annexation in 51 BC. This demographic expansion may have been accompanied by a deterioration in the position of women. Celtic warfare was largely man's work, while the heavy, iron-trimmed plough needed a masculine hand too, it would appear. Ploughing the fields became a male preserve, as did large-scale herding for milk, hides and other secondary goods besides meat. The status of Iron Age women was apparently in decline.

Opposite Constructed between 2000 and 1400 BC, the stone alignments around Carnac in Brittany cover several square kilometres, making it the largest and most concentrated site of its kind in the world. Whether they commemorate a cult of the sun and other religious rituals or whether they acted as a kind of astronomical observatory is unknown.

The martial Iron Age culture of the Celts was firmly hierarchical, with the warrior elite dominating subservient tenants, clients and maybe slaves too. Among some southern and central tribes, a powerful aristocracy had replaced the traditional Celtic system of a hereditary monarchy by one of annual elected magistrates – a system which seems better to have enshrined their power. In the new social order tribal units were broken up into a bewildering patchwork of lesser subtribes, each occupying a smallish natural unit. The Romans estimated that Gaul possessed some sixty tribes, which between them controlled some three hundred territorial entities, to which the Romans gave the term *pagus* (whence the later French term, *pays*). Roughly 1,200 to 2,000 square kilometres in size, these units constituted a crucial element of political differentiation and were destined for a long, if unsung, role in French history as the framework within which much local history would take place. As the conquering Julius Caesar was later sardonically to note, the region as a whole was "divided by language, customs and laws".

This bronze mask representing a Celtic god was discovered in 1839 at Montsière in the Hautes-Pyrénées, and dates from the second century BC. The eye-holes may have been filled with glass or ceramics.

The Celtic cult of the severed head, mentioned by a number of ancient writers, lies behind this ceremonial gateway from Roquepertuse, near Marseille, dating from between the third and the second century BC. Recent archaeological research suggests that the lintel between the pillars may have been longer, and that the skulls faced into the household rather than outwards.

Celtic Gaul

Scilly Isles

ICTIS (St. Michael's Mount)

MORINI
MENAPII
ATREBATES
NERVII
EBURONES
TREVERI
AMBIANI
CALETI
BELLOVACI
SUESSIONES
REMI
MEDIOMATRICI
ELIOCASSES
LEXOVII
Seine
EBUROVICES
Lutétia (Paris)
MELDI
TRICASSES
LEUCI
PARISII
Montereau
UNELLI
ESUVII
Agedincum (Sens)
Vix
RAVRICI
OSISMII
CORIOSOLIATAE
REDONES
AULERCI
SENONES
CARNUTES
LINGONES
SEQUANI
DIABLINTES
CENOMANNI
Genabum (Orléans)
Alesia
Vesontio (Besançon)
VENETI
ANDECAVI
TURONI
BITURIGES
AEDUI
Saône
NAMNETES
Corbilo ?
Avaricum (Bourges)
Loire
Bibracte (Mt Beuvray)
HELVETII
PICTONES
CUBI
LEMOVICES
SANTONES
Gergovia
SEGUSIAVI
Vienna
ALLOBROGES
Uxellodunum
ARVERNI
BITURIGES
VIVISCI
PETROCORII
VELLAVI
Bordeaux
HELVII
VOCONTI
NITIOBROGES
CADURCI
GABALI
Rhône
Garonne
RUTENI
Arles
Monaco?
VOLCAE
ARECOMICI
Agde
Marseille
Antibes
Nice?
TECTOSAGES
Narbonne
La Ciotat
Hyères?
Sanary
SALLUVII
Rosas
Ampurias

Prior to Roman colonization, the Celts had established themselves throughout Gaul, leaving only marginal areas in the south-east and south-west still dominated by indigenous peoples. Celtic Gaul formed a crazy-quilt of tribes and sub-tribes making shifting alliances and frequently resorting to war. Farming techniques were fairly advanced. In addition, the tin trade established currents of movement and exchange from the far west and centre, where the tin deposits lay, through to the Mediterranean coast.

Legend:
- Iberian and Ligurian peoples
- LEUCI Main Celtic tribal groupings
- - - - Frontier of "The Province"
- ● Main Gaulish town
- Tin mining area
- → Probable tin traders' route
- ○ Tin trading centre
- □ Colonies of Marseille

The Vix princess

In 1953 archaeologists discovered at Vix in Burgundy, just north of Châtillon-sur-Seine, the grave of what appears to have been an Iron Age princess or priestess buried in a ceremonial four-wheeled chariot and dating from around 525 BC. Pride of place among the artefacts uncovered, which rank among the richest aristocratic grave goods in prehistoric Europe, is taken by a massive bronze crater (or ceremonial vessel). Five feet high, and weighing over 440 pounds, the vessel is decorated with a bronze frieze showing a cavalcade of warriors, and there are elaborate handles supported by gorgons. The princess had been dressed in ceremonial finery, though all that remained were amber, schist, pearl and

The gold diadem of the Vix princess.

silver jewels, earrings, necklaces and other decorations. Around her head, which had been severed from her body, was an exquisitely elegant gold diadem.

The most exotic goods came from afar: coral from the Mediterranean, amber from the Adriatic, bronze goods with Etrurian designs from central Italy. The constituent parts of the crater appear to have been manufactured either in Corinth or in Greek colonies in southern Italy, transported to the Vix site and reassembled there. The diadem may hail from the Scythian peoples, who lived beyond the Greek world on the banks of the Black Sea. All highlight the strong currents of exchange in which Iron Age Gaul had begun to be involved. Vix was a key trading post in the tin market, linking sources in the south-west of England and the Armorican peninsula with bronze-smiths in the Graeco-Roman world. It was close to the end of the navigable part of the river Seine, and well situated at the head of passages towards the Saône and Rhône rivers – and thus to Marseille.

The Vix crater, bronze, c. 550–500 BC.

Bronze calendar from Coligny, near Bourg. Dating from the late first century BC, it constitutes the oldest and most extensive example of Celtic script. The Celts did not have their own alphabet – here they employed the Latin alphabet, but at other times used the Greek. The calendar was possibly consulted by Druids for calculating ceremonial days to honour the gods.

The *pays* formed, as it were, the building blocks from which political coalitions were formed. Certain tribal groupings were able to amass a good deal of power through a loose system of clientage and alliance. In the second century BC the Arverni, based in the Massif Central, imposed their will on smaller groups and forced them to submit hostages and pay tribute, building up an extensive "Arvernian empire" in the process. Loose political arrangements of this sort were fragile, however, and easily fell apart. Gaul as a whole was marked by profound political discord, only partly offset by the rough cultural unity inspired by their polytheistic religion. Tribes accorded importance to a special priesthood, the druids. Each year the druids of the whole of Celtic Gaul held a convention at a ritual location, possibly close to Orléans, in the middle of the forest of the Carnutes tribe. Impressive as a show of cultural unity, the druid convention had no broader political significance, however. Though Celts may sometimes have felt a crude sense of fellow-feeling, there was no "Gaulish nation".

A new element was introduced into the region when, in *c.* 600 BC, the Greek colony of Massalia (present-day Marseille) was established by the (now Turkish) city of Phocea. Massalia helped to create a web of similar Greek-based trading cities on and near the French coast and in the Rhône valley. Hitherto trade had not been extensive and was largely restricted to the coasts. Through greater involvement in the tin trade – tin for making bronze came notably from Devon and Cornwall, Brittany and Bohemia – Massalia developed as the hub of a trading network in which much of France came to be involved. The trade built up more land routes through France, partly to avoid piracy from the Carthaginians of north Africa. The routes developed for the tin trade became available for other commodities too, and trade broadened into a more general north–south trading pattern: northern goods such as tin, copper, iron, glassware, leather goods, cereals, salt, slaves and maybe charcuterie were exchanged against Mediterranean luxury goods – jewels, for example, decorative ware and wine. The birth of French wine-growing, as well as olive cultivation, probably took place under the auspices of the Massalia merchants. The widespread diffusion of Greek coins from this period throughout France testifies to the importance of the role of the Phocean colony in the development of the Gaulish economy.

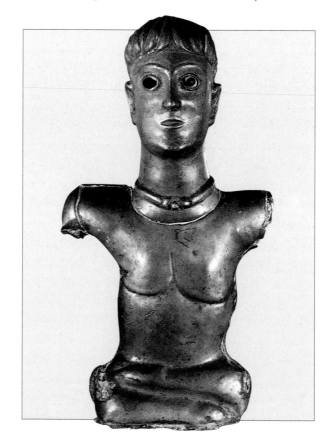

Gallo-Roman god with a torque. Dating from the first century AD, this bronze statue was found at Bouraye in the Paris region.

The growth of commerce and the development of agriculture boosted urban development. Small bourgs and embryonic towns emerged. Their material structures were unimpressive compared with what was going on south of the Alps; apart from stone-built defensive walls, for example, virtually all urban building was in wood. Yet some centres, such as Ensérune in Lower Languedoc, were impressive. And all contributed to the construction of an urban network which covered virtually all of France, except for the north beyond the Ardennes forest and the far west. The emergence within cities of neighbourhoods of traders and artisans and the appearance of separate areas for the town houses of aristocratic landlords signalled progress too. The archaeological finds in the princely tombs at Vix in Burgundy graphically illustrate the formidable extent of aristocratic wealth.

Economic growth was not, however, matched by greater political co-ordination. All roads might seem to lead to Massalia, but the Phoceans were merchants, not conquerors nor imperialists. They preferred to establish trading counters, not to impose new structures of political domination. Significantly, French words influenced by Greek are found predominantly in the fields of navigation, fishing and meteorology, while only a tiny number of Greek words remain in placenames.

Greek merchants did pave the way, however, for Roman legionaries and administrators. Massalia supported Rome in its struggle with Carthage and proved to be, as the Roman orator Cicero later put it, "the most faithful ally of the Romans". Rome valued such support. Its initial expansion towards the Alps brought the Italian city-state into contact with the Cisalpine Gauls based in the Po valley, while extension beyond the Alps caused potential friction with local Celts. The Romans sought friends and allies amongst the tribes – the Aeduans, based in Franche-Comté, were special favourites. The degree of support which tribes gave the Carthaginian general Hannibal, as he trudged Alpwards with his elephants in 218 BC, impelled the Romans towards closer control. From 125 to 121 BC Rome answered calls by Massalia for protection against hostile neighbours, plus an appeal for help by the Aeduan tribe against the Allobroges and the Arverni. The upshot was direct Roman control over the entire coastal strip. "The Province" (*provincia* – whence "Provence"), soon to be called Gallia Transalpina or Gallia Narbonensis, was to prove the springboard for the Roman annexation of the Celtic tribes to the north, and the establishment of Roman Gaul.

CHAPTER 2

Roman Gaul

The incorporation of the southern part of France into the Roman sphere of influence proved to be only the first act of a long-lasting saga in which France became the core of Roman Gaul – a province, or set of provinces, within one of the great world-historical empires. In acquiring Gaul, Rome increased the size of its empire by one third – an empire which, in time, would stretch from the Scottish borderlands in the north to the shores of the Upper Nile in the south, from Morocco and Portugal in the west to Armenia in the east. Roman authority brought in its train Rome's taxes, conscription, coinage, markets, officials, soldiers, language and writing. All in their different ways would immeasurably enrich the cultural fabric of a massive, sprawling area which included not only the whole of future France, but also all of Belgium and Luxembourg plus much of the Netherlands, western Germany and Switzerland and some Alpine fringes of Italy. Roman Gaul was far more than "France" under the Romans.

CONQUEST AND CONTROL

The Roman Empire was assembled by force of arms. Its rationale in Gaul as elsewhere was conquest, pacification and exploitation; anything else was a bonus. Like any imperial power Rome was sensitive to developments outside the immediate orbit of its control. Roman armies had, for example, beaten back an invasion of southern France by the Germanic Cimbri and Teutones from 109 to 101 BC. Alleged preparations for another such invasion in 58 BC – by the Helvetii, who were preparing to migrate from southern Switzerland into southern France – alerted Rome to the coming danger. This was combined with the threat of destabilization further north, where the Germanic chieftain Ariovistus had joined in a squabble involving the Arverni, the Sequani and Rome's long-standing allies, the Aeduans. To combat this politico-military threat Rome sent Julius Caesar.

"There was a time," Caesar later noted in his *Gallic Wars*, "when the Gauls were more warlike than the Germans." That day, he claimed, had passed, and Gaul required occupation and control if it was not to fall into the hands of the Germans, who would be unruly neighbours for Rome. Ambitious, already prominent in Roman domestic politics and seeking a wider stage for his talents, Caesar took on the task of subjugating Gaul with relish. It probably took longer, and needed more force – and more luck – than he had anticipated. The Gauls overcame their famed divisiveness and, under the Arvernian leader Vercingetorix, fought a relatively united struggle against the Roman armies. Caesar's victory in 52 BC at the siege of Alésia, however, forced Vercingetorix to yield. Mopping-up operations continued into 51/50 BC; but the back of Gaulish resistance had been broken.

Roman Gaul was thus a creature of the Roman army, and the threat of naked coercion was never far away. The legionary presence on the Rhine frontier stood permanently on guard. The fact that colonized settlements were staffed by army veterans also

Vercingetorix

The first move was made by Vercingetorix, a young Arvernian with very great power in his tribe ... He called his dependants together and had no difficulty in rousing their passions. When it was known what he intended to do, there was a rush of armed men to join him ... He (also) raised a band of beggars and outcasts from the countryside. Once he had recruited these, he brought over to his side all the Arvernians he approached, and he soon collected a large force of men, by urging them to take up arms in thecause of Gaulish freedom ...
He quickly won the support of the Senones, the Parisii, the Pictones, the Turoni, the Aulerci, the Lemovices, the Andes and all the other tribes of the Atlantic coast. By general consent he was given the supreme command.

Julius Caesar's *Gallic Wars* is a justification as well as an account of his conquest of Gaul between 58 and 51 BC, and we may reasonably suspect that this portrait of his most redoubtable Gaulish opponent inflates the Arvernian's importance, so as to make Caesar's victory over him all the more impressive.

Yet although there seems little doubt that Vercingetorix was a formidable opponent, it is altogether more questionable whether he was acting in the cause of "Gaulish freedom". An aristocrat from the powerful Arverni tribe, based in the Massif Central, which had quite recently switched from a monarchy to an oligarchic republic, he may well have been promoting his own cause. Caesar describes him as "a man of enormous

Gold coin, with the head of Vercingetorix.

energy" and "a very strict disciplinarian", using "savage means" – cutting off an ear or putting out an eye for even slight offences, for example – to put together a powerful army.

By this time, however, the wars were going badly for the Gauls. In 58 BC Caesar had dealt with the main causes of the wars, forcing the migrant Helvetii back into Switzerland and clipping the wings of the German leader, Ariovistus, who returned across the Rhine. The following year, he had brought the Belgi and north-western tribes to heel, then in 56 BC pacified the west and south-west, winning a naval battle over the powerful Venetii near Vannes. Sorties into England and across the Rhine in 55 BC and 54 BC were crowned with less obvious success, however, and though Caesar was establishing his position in 53 BC, the Vercingetorix coalition caught the Roman commander off balance.

The war was fought with great ferocity. The Arvernian leader enjoyed some successes, but in 51 BC was finally hemmed in with his troops at the stronghold of Alésia (near Alise Sainte-Reine in Burgundy). The conflict was effectively over. Vercingetorix was taken to Rome to appear in chains at Caesar's official triumph in 46 BC, and was then strangled.

Caesar's conquest was achieved with the loss of much Gaulish blood. Battlefield losses and civilian massacres amounted to over a million dead, and it seems likely that between half a million and a million Gauls over the next decade were exported to the Italian peninsula, where they flooded the slave-markets.

played a role in exerting authority. The network of Roman roads developed out of politico-military rather than economic motivation: troops could travel fast to any point where order had broken down. The symbolic language of Roman power had a strongly militaristic flavour which seemingly affected even Rome's Gaulish adversaries. Significantly, Julius Sabinus, leader of the most notable rebellion, in AD 69–70, postured not as the heir of Vercingetorix but rather as a descendant of one of Caesar's bastards. Overall Gaul was far less rumbustious and rebellious than the neighbouring

Iberian peninsula. The "Roman peace", or *pax romana*, won support from most Gauls, who perhaps felt that Rome had more to offer than their bellicose, barbarian neighbours in Germany.

The Gaul which stopped at or around the Rhine was only in certain respects a single area. Caesar remarked that it was divided into three parts, Gallia Belgica (in the north), Gallia Iberica (in the south-west) plus the sprawling trunk of Gallia Celtica. The list excludes, however, already Romanized Gallia Narbonensis, the firm springboard for Caesar's conquests – "more like Italy than a province," as the Roman first-century naturalist, the Elder Pliny, put it. In the administrative settlement of the region by Augustus in 13 BC, this four-part organization was retained – albeit with considerably reworked frontiers and different names (Aquitania, Belgica and Lugdunensis to the north of Narbonensis). With some minor retouching this structure stayed in place until the third century.

But although the region's administration was subdivided, the term "Gaul" did come to denote a certain cultural entity, at least as regards the three northern provinces. In 43 BC Lugdunum (Lyon) was designated the capital of the "Three Gauls". Its role as a

The sight of manacled Gaulish prisoners on the triumphal arch in Carpentras was a powerful reminder of Rome's martial superiority. After the fall of the Roman Empire the arch was converted into the porch of the city's first cathedral.

symbol of Gallo-Roman unity was endorsed by the construction in 12 BC of an Altar of Rome and Augustus at the meeting-point of the rivers Rhône and Saône. Representatives from the Three Gauls were permitted to hold an annual conference on the site, to discuss judicial and administrative affairs and formulate grievances to be passed on to Rome – as well as to participate in public worship of the Roman emperor. The high priest in these annual ceremonies of the imperial cult was, moreover, a Gaul.

Such measures formed part of a standard imperialistic strategy aimed at eliciting political consent without the need for coercion. The institution of administrative division within a vaguer cultural union typified a more general policy of divide and rule. The Arverni, for example, the leading edge of Gaulish resistance in the Gallic War, were divided up. Other tribal units competed against each other to gain tax and other privileges. Despite the massacres committed by him and in his name, Julius Caesar showed clemency to many of his erstwhile enemies, and incorporated them into his train of dependants. Caesar and Augustus liberally gave Roman status to magistrates – this long before the Emperor Caracalla (r. AD 211–17) made all free men within the empire Roman citizens in AD 212. In Gaul, moreover, this status could be inherited by children, thus increasing the spread of citizenship. The army too became an important career channel for ambitious Gauls, along with administration and local government. In AD 48 Emperor Claudius (r. AD 41–54) persuaded the Roman senate to admit Gauls among their number. This decision, part of broader moves to widen the Roman governing class, established a ladder of ascent which reached the very highest levels: the grandfather of Emperor Antoninus Pius (r. AD 138–61) had come from Nîmes.

The impact of the Gauls on Rome's central governmental apparatus was never considerable. Virtually all Gauls in the Roman governing class originated in more heavily Romanized southern Gaul, and their number in the senate was far exceeded by Africans, for example. Yet if Gauls made little impact in Rome, Romans were relatively few in administrative and governmental posts within Gaul. To a great extent, in fact, the Roman Empire in Gaul was administered by Gauls – and largely for Gauls too. Immigrants from the Italian peninsula seem to have been few, and one numerous category, military veterans, was clustered in southern Gaul. Generally the Roman authorities followed the inclination of Julius Caesar to graft local government on to pre-existing tribal forms. The Celtic tribe was transmuted – often literally – into the Gallo-Roman city-state, or *civitas*. Pre-conquest tribal groupings formed the basis of the sixty *civitates* of the Three Gauls, while the twenty-two administrative units of Gallia Narbonensis were also closely linked to pre-conquest divisions.

To most intents and purposes the *civitas* was the tribe in a toga. The Gaulish elites were allowed to dominate, if they submitted to Roman orders. Magistrates still often used the Gaulish title of *vergobret*. The *curia*, or city council, introduced in each local capital, owed much to pre-conquest forms. At village level no change was probably detectable. The new taxes may have been Roman in origin, but they were assessed and collected according to existing forms – and were still rather low. Not surprisingly Celtic tribal elites welcomed being refashioned into Gallo-Roman notables.

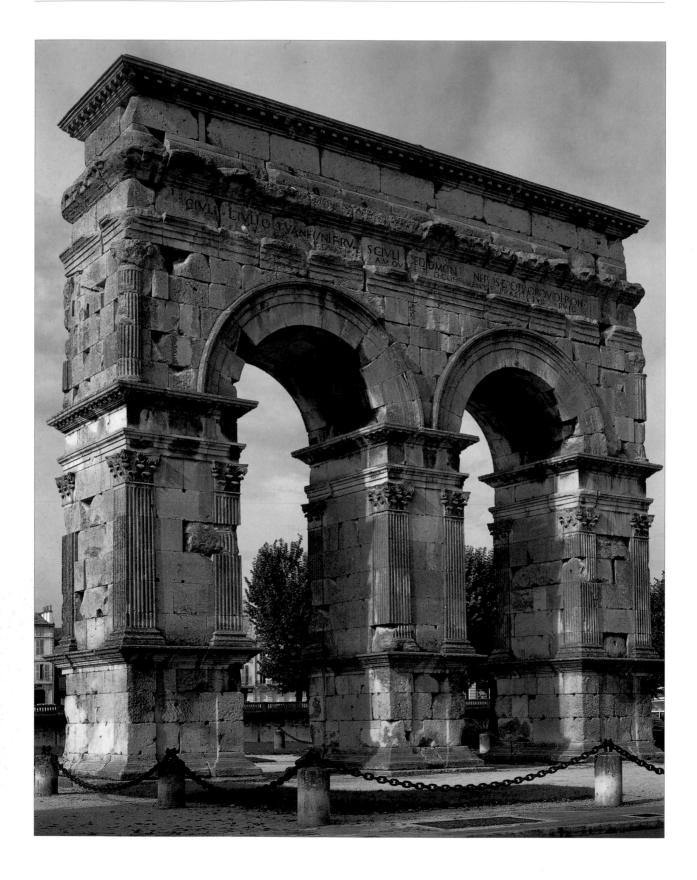

Was *romanitas* – Roman identity – more than skin-deep, however? Just as Roman political forms overlay older Celtic institutions, so Latin culture influenced, but never erased, the pre-conquest linguistic heritage. Latin replaced the Gaulish tongue as the language of written communication, but Celtic had in any case been an oral rather than a written language – the druids had been wont to educate the Gaulish political elite without the benefit of writing or even their own alphabet. Under Rome, Latin became the language of education for the elite: many towns – Marseille, Autun, Reims, Toulouse, Bordeaux and others – contained schools in which the Gallo-Roman aristocracy, by imbibing Latin, could learn the language of power, social ascent and cultural clout.

The imposition of Roman power was successful in creating a new, Gallo-Roman cultural amalgam. But the blend of Gaulish and Roman elements varied according to time, place and social level. It was in the interests of anyone who had dealings with political and cultural institutions to know Latin. In the towns potters dependent on wealthy clients learnt in time to put *fecit* instead of the Celtic *avot* on the bottom of their pots and vases. Yet even the heavily Romanized social elite never totally lost contact with its Celtic roots, while the further one descended the social ladder, and the further one moved from the towns, the more the balance between Celtic and Roman was weighted towards the former. The heavy concentration of Gaulish words in placenames, outliving Roman and later Germanic accretions, underlines this, as does the fact that many contemporary French words for agricultural implements and techniques have Celtic origins, for example *arpent* (acre) and *soc* (ploughshare).

The longer Roman occupation lasted, however, the more Latin penetrated and won over even backward rural areas. Rome's merchants, officials, labourers and soldiers acted as vectors of everyday Romanization. For some time bilingualism must have been the norm for many: one talked "up" in Latin, "down" in Gaulish. But in the long term a vulgar Latin far removed from the language of the rhetoricians prevailed. By the fifth century AD there is evidence that Gaulish was no longer understood in rural areas. Significantly, the Germanic invaders of the period called the inhabitants of Gaul "Romans". Even as Rome fell Latin was triumphing – and was to prove the basis for the development of the French language.

Evidence suggests that religion also evolved by cultural mixing rather than replacement. Roman government launched a campaign against druidism, whose secrecy, practice of human sacrifice and potential for subversion marked it out as dangerous. Emperors regulated the polytheistic cult that was to be followed in the empire, adding worship of themselves in the form of the so-called imperial cult. So closely was religion tied into the imperial system that it would have been unthinkable for the Gaulish political elite to shun the pagan and imperial cults, which appear to have prospered in Gaul. There were strong efforts to assimilate earlier beliefs within the accepted framework. Thus the annual religious ceremony at the Altar of Rome and Augustus in Lyon attended by representatives of the Three Gauls could be seen as echoing the annual druidic ceremony held in the forest of the Carnutes. It was held on 1 August, the

Opposite This arch at Saintes contains a Gaulish genealogy. The Roman-sounding name of the constructor, Caius Julius Rufus, contrasts with the semi-Romanized name of his grandfather Caius Julius Gedomo and his great-grandfather, the utterly Gaulish Epotsorovidus. In such ways the Gaulish elite assumed a Roman identity.

Statue of the god Mercury, from the Clermont-Ferrand region, dating from the late first to the fourth century AD. Mercury was one of the most popular Roman gods, probably because he corresponded fairly closely to a similar pre-Roman god. The horns represent virility, aggression and fertility.

ceremonial birthday of Emperor Augustus, but also the festival day of the Celtic god Lug, whose cult had given Lugdunum (Lyon) its name. In addition, despite official pressure towards conformity, many Roman gods were "gallicized". Roman temples too were often erected on Celtic shrine sites; while Roman thermal spas were built around the healing springs allegedly inhabited by Celtic deities. Gallo-Roman polytheism was thus a distinctive blend of two strong and resilient cultural forms.

The strength of the Gallo-Roman religious hybrid may also explain Christianity's slowness to penetrate Gaul. It was merely one of a number of usually Greek-speaking, Eastern mystical cults (worship of Isis and Osiris, for example, and Mithraism) that followed the lines of trade and administration into the province from the late second century onwards. Lyon seems to have harboured the first Christian community, and initially the cult was closely linked to the towns of the Rhône corridor. Only from the fourth century were the churches making efforts to organize rural parishes and to spread the cult into country areas – significantly, the Latin term *paganus* came to denote both "peasant" and "pagan". The sect's apparent secrecy triggered rumours of horrible and murderous rituals. Monotheistic, exclusive and intolerant – yet heroically committed to an interior ethic – Christianity seemed the polar opposite of Roman religion's open willingness to assimilate.

Diocletian (r. AD 284–305) stepped up the intensity of the persecution to which Christians had sporadically been subjected. Yet within a couple of decades Christianity had been transformed from a minor cult into the official religion of the Roman Empire. In the Edict of Milan in AD 313 joint-emperors Licinius and Constantine (the latter a Christian himself) restored freedom of worship to Christians. The earlier pattern was now reversed. By the end of the fourth century Christianity was the religion of the state and emperors were persecuting pagans and closing down their temples. The diocesan framework that developed in the fourth century underpinned the *civitates*, and closely integrated civil and religious power. Latin became the language not only of liturgy and theological dispute, but also of conversion. This was a tribute to how deep Roman culture had penetrated, and the Church acted as an important channel for the relaying of Latinate culture into rural areas.

PAX ROMANA AND THE "ETERNAL CITY"

The incorporation of Gaul into the Roman Empire not only created new political, administrative and cultural forms; the *pax romana* also transformed the region's economy. Julius Caesar had found Gaul politically anarchic, and the imposition of Roman authority allowed its economic potential to be realized. The effect of the Roman presence was that much of the wealth of the eastern Mediterranean moved west. The relatively underdeveloped Gaulish economy received a boost from Roman investment, immigration, urban building, road improvement, tax demands and military occupation. The prolonged period of internal security – both against incursions from outside the empire and from banditry within – plus the fact that Roman taxes were generally low and still collected by local agents also facilitated steady economic growth.

Nowhere was economic prosperity more in evidence than in the cities, where life blossomed under the Romans. Cities were constructed in stone rather than wood and wattle-and-daub, and were planned imaginatively. Sometimes laid out geometrically, their model was often "the eternal city", Rome itself, and many buildings were virtual replicas of Roman originals. Private dwellings coexisted alongside an impressive array of commercial and public buildings. Towns housed a colourful artisans' sector: besides the building trade, which employed large numbers, there was a whole range of urban trades and occupations. Lyon, for example, had guilds for shippers, rafters, wine importers, corn and oil merchants, cloak-makers, plasterers, silversmiths, glassmakers, potters, wool-carders, linen-weavers and soap-makers. Among public buildings there were the *forum*, market and meeting-place; the *curia*, or town hall; the *basilica*, or law courts; and sundry temples. These urban institutions, which beggared Gaulish precedents, were complemented by an impressive range of leisure facilities. Baths were a staple feature of the urban landscape. The cities of Gaul boasted no fewer than seventy-nine theatres, thirty-five amphitheatres and a score of other entertainment centres, including circuses and odeons. The logistics and engineering required to construct and maintain these edifices were immense: stone used in the construction of Lyon, for example, was hauled some 200 kilometres, while the city's water supply was brought from a distance of over seventy-five kilometres away.

Head of Venus, based on Greek models, found at Nîmes in 1853.

In towns material life could be good. Full participation in the public life of the city was, however, almost wholly male. Women had no place in decision-making in politics, law or in regard to questions of city defence. Roman law was sternly patriarchal: for example, fathers had the right to order the exposure of unwanted babies, and could make offspring stay minors, sometimes even beyond their marriage. It is difficult to judge how far social practice conformed with legal precept. Despite their saturation with patriarchal power, family relationships could be affectionate. The state, moreover, increasingly acted to bolster women's civic rights. Women could inherit, for example, they could initiate divorce; and, on getting married, their property was kept independent. They also played an important role in the clientage relationships on which Roman political and family life depended. Women of high social status also benefited from the considerable volume of trade in luxury goods – jewellery, gold- and silverware, fine cloth and cosmetics. How far such benefits reached down to women of lower social status outside the cities is, however, debatable.

A host of new towns emerged under Roman rule, and so, consequently, did a new urban network, which has endured astonishingly well: of 55 cities in France with a population of 100,000 in the late twentieth century, 37 had been Gallo-Roman cities, while out of 107 sites which served as capitals of *civitates*, 94 are towns today. Gaul lacked a monster city like Rome (perhaps 700,000 inhabitants); its biggest conurbations – Narbonne, Nîmes, Lyon, Autun, Reims and Trier – did not exceed the 20,000 to 30,000 population band. Most cities were far smaller, though they tended to look larger than they were. Indeed the monumentalism of gates and walls owed more to the desire to impress than to military needs. Leisure facilities were also designed on an

Roman Nîmes

Nîmes provides an excellent illustration of what provincial urban life must have been like under the Roman Empire in southern Gaul. It was one of Gaul's larger cities, with a population of perhaps 20,000. Located on seven hills, which gave it more than the usual claim to replicate the "eternal city", Rome itself, it was founded by Emperor Augustus in 16 BC as a military colony for his veterans. Several monuments are based closely on Roman models, notably the amphitheatre, based on the Colosseum, and the famous temple Maison Carrée. The latter closely resembles the Temple of Apollo in Rome. Constructed by Agrippa, son-in-law of Augustus, to commemorate Augustus' grandchildren, Gaius and Lucius Caesar, it was dedicated to the imperial cult.

Nîmes contained the full paraphernalia of Roman leisure. The 23,000-seater amphitheatre, constructed late in the first century AD, still stands, and is still in use, though a circus, a theatre and extensive baths have been destroyed. Before the arrival of the Romans, the city had been the capital of the powerful Volcae Arecomici tribe, and the focus of important regional trading links. On top of the Mont Cavalier, overlooking the city, sat a look-out tower which the

Coin with crocodile motif minted at Nîmes, or COL(onia) NEM(ausus).

Romans built over and renamed the Tour-Magne (again still in existence).

The city had a cosmopolitan reputation. The military veterans attached to the city by Augustus hailed from Egypt, following Augustus' capture of Alexandria in 30 BC, and early coins minted here depict a crocodile chained to a palm tree, a design which passed into the city's arms. Nîmes was also a key staging post on the Domitian Way, the main economic and administrative artery connecting northern Italy

with Spain (which had been a Roman province since 202 BC). Hence the city must have witnessed the passage of large numbers of travellers, merchants, soldiers and administrators, as well as pilgrims.

Nîmes was very much a city of waters. The sacred spring of Nemausus had long given the settlement some repute. Pre-conquest Celtic religion had set great store by springs, wells and caves, which were viewed as housing deities and serving as thresholds to the underworld. By naming the new city "Colonia Augustus Nemausus", thereby associating himself, as a deity within the Roman pantheon, with a pagan god, Augustus showed characteristic Roman pragmatism. Rather than obliterating the Celtic gods, the Romans preferred to assimilate them.

Water was also provided in abundance from outside the city walls. The Romans created a hydraulic system which transported 20,000 cubic metres of water per day from Uzès, a distance of fifty kilometres away. The aqueduct across the river Gardon at the Pont-du-Gard, constructed in 19 BC, is the highest surviving bridge structure from the Roman world, and (as one of the most impressive pieces of civil engineering in France until the reign of Louis XIV) a visible link with the past.

The Maison Carrée at Nîmes, first century BC: a perfect example of classical style.

extravagant scale: Lutetia (Paris) boasted a population of some 8,000, yet its arena contained 15,000 places.

The urban network was created remarkably swiftly. Massive building programmes in Gallia Narbonensis and some other sites (notably Lyon) were instituted by Augustus, using booty acquired from his victories in the east. Emperor Claudius' preparations for the invasion of Britain in AD 43 were important in filling out the urban and communications infrastructure of northern Gaul. But the rage for building also testified to the growth of indigenous urban prosperity and civic pride among local elites. The Gallo-Roman elite drew much of its wealth from the business and administrative networks into which cities were plugged. Roman roads, replacing the winding Celtic pathways with rectilinear masterpieces of civil engineering, may have been built for armies, but they also stimulated and facilitated economic exchange. Similarly the presence of troops could boost trade and wealth – the development of Trier as a major imperial city in the third and fourth centuries owed much to its strategic position close to the Rhine armies. Those cities did best which were able to turn this communications network to their advantage: with security less of a problem in the *pax romana*, fortified hill-towns either were left to rot, or else adapted and slid down the hill towards road and river junctions.

If towns derived wealth from their position on the networks of trade and administration, they also drew heavily on their surrounding countrysides. To be a city, chronicler Gregory of Tours was later to note, one required "walls, an imperial edict, and a rural hinterland". Town and country were locked into a symbiotic relationship, with the towns providing the markets and the commercial skills which rural inhabitants required. Many rural workers actually lived in towns, and would set off for the fields at dawn. Urban growth demanded a degree of efficiency in agricultural production and distribution: it was asking a great deal of any pre-industrial economy to feed the 6 to 7 per cent of the population who lived in towns. The achievement was all the more important because it was made without any major breakthroughs in agrarian productivity. The growth in production came from the extension of cultivable land, greater use of the sturdier wheeled ploughs already widely used before the conquest, crop diversification and vast improvements in distribution and exchange.

The backbone of Gallo-Roman agriculture was the villa economy. Villas were often continuations of pre-conquest Gaulish estates and the standard operation was large-scale farming on open fields. In time they spread to even apparently inhospitable localities such as Brittany. Villas tended to be farmed for their owners by individuals working under various kinds of contract and tenancy arrangements, plus some slaves. Many villas were large, factory-like complexes, with buildings set aside for agricultural and manufacturing functions (weaving, brewing or basket-making). Some may have contained as many as 400 individuals and been potentially self-sufficient.

In general, however, in the period of the *pax romana*, the triumph of large property stimulated not self-sufficiency but rather a willingness to enter into commercial arrangements. Villa owners were excellently placed to commercialize their production,

This poignant and evocative second-century funerary monument from south-western Gaul depicts a ten-year-old child holding its toys: a cat and a tame cockerel – also a symbol of resurrection – who nibbles the cat's tail.

squarely on Romans. The Roman tax system was regressive, which placed a heavy burden on peasants, many of whom were already living close to the breadline. The problem was aggravated when, from the third century, taxes began to be imposed individually rather than collectively. Severe inflation and outbreaks of epidemic disease only made matters worse. Many peasants were forced to sell up to big property-owners. Others abandoned their small-holdings to migrate to towns, which offered public assistance – everything from bread to circuses – and in which employment possibilities were more varied. There are signs in some areas of a return to mesolithic-style cave occupation. Some peasants chose to take to the woods, to live a shadowy life of banditry and highway robbery. The so-called Bagaudae movement of rebellious peasants grumbled through Gaulish agrarian history from the third quarter of the third century onwards. Shortage of labour led villa owners to tighten up the regulations tying their peasants to the land – a process supported in Rome; yet one effect of this was to create a wave of resentful refugees from the fields, who swelled the ranks of the Bagaudae.

The shift of large numbers of peasants out of productive employment into service-sector work or economic dependency increased the strain on an arguably over-urbanized empire. Given stable levels of agrarian productivity, prosperity had been ensured only by the excellence of Rome's distribution and exchange networks. That these were breaking down was signalled by the appearance of large-scale famines, even from the late second century. The Bagaudae aggravated rural insecurity; so, on a much larger scale, did the migrations of the Germanic peoples, who wreaked damage not only on property and persons but also on the smooth operation of the systems of exchange on which prosperity had been built.

There had been Germanic incursions beyond the Rhine in AD 162 and 174 in the Strasbourg region, but it was from the second third of the third century that the phenomenon began to assume a more consistently threatening form. In 253 the Rhine legions marched to Italy to sustain the claim of Valerian to the imperial title, leaving the frontier undermanned. Two tribes, the Franks (situated on the lower reaches of the Rhine) and the Alamanni (based on the river's upper reaches), punctured the security cordon, the former even reaching Paris and causing the Lutetians to cower on the Île de la Cité. Gaulish coasts also began to be harassed by Frankish and other Germanic pirates. In 260 the Roman general Postumus declared himself emperor and, with the support of the Rhine legions, established a Gallic empire independent of Rome. Significantly, most of northern Gaul, no doubt feeling that he would exhibit more commitment to the Germanic problem than a remote and insecure emperor in Rome, supported him. Postumus did indeed check the barbarian advance, though following his death, the Roman emperor Aurelian (r. 270–5) brought Gaul back under the Roman aegis. Almost at once – in 275 – the continuing nature of the threat was highlighted by a further attack by the Alamanni and the Franks, who sacked between sixty and seventy cities.

Roman emperors finally began to give higher priority to problems on the Rhine, and sought to find more appropriate administrative structures for coping with social, economic and political difficulties. Diocletian (r. 284–305), in particular, completely reorganized the structures of imperial administration. He divided the empire between east and west, each part to be ruled by an emperor ("Augustus"), assisted by a subaltern ruler ("Caesar"). This attempt at "tetrarchy" (rule by four) spawned imperial claims and counter-claims. Although Emperor Constantine (r. 306–37) temporarily united the empire under his authority and shifted its seat to the new city of Constantinople, this was a prelude to the definitive division of the empire into eastern and western halves in the year 395.

Diocletian also undertook root-and-branch reform of local administration in Gaul. His decision to create a more decentralized structure – two super-provinces centred on Trier and Vienne, including between them 17 provinces and 112 *civitates* – provided a more flexible and responsive apparatus. Military defences on the frontiers received particular attention. Diocletian also introduced important financial, currency and military reforms, in order to make the empire more able to resist incursions from outside. He offset the costs of maintaining a huge army by allowing troops to requisition more extensively for their requirements, and he also allowed taxes to be paid in kind. In this

Mosaic of bread-baking. Gaul was exceptionally fertile, and wheat and other grains were the most widely-grown crop. Caesar managed to survive the lengthy Gallic Wars without a serious food-supply problem.

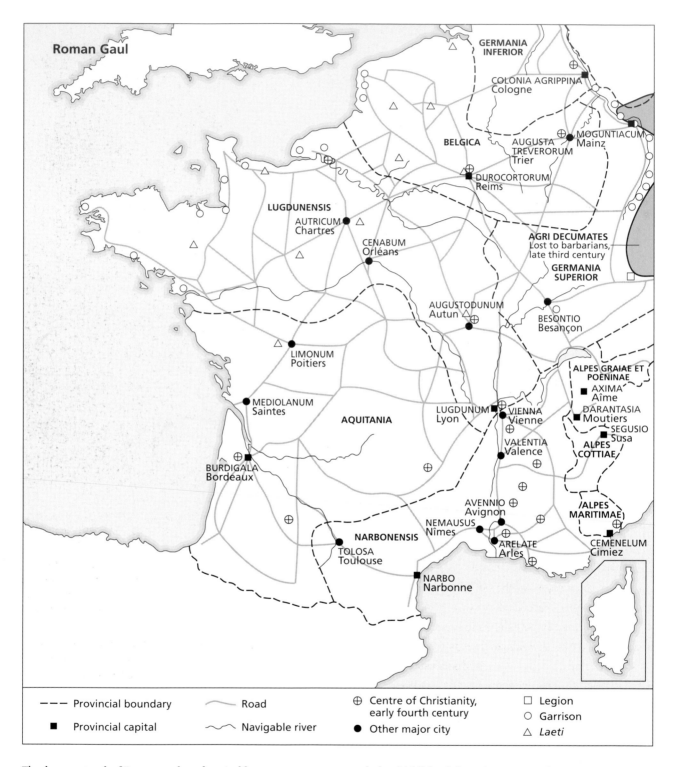

Roman Gaul

GERMANIA INFERIOR

COLONIA AGRIPPINA
Cologne

BELGICA

AUGUSTA TREVERORUM
Trier

MOGUNTIACUM
Mainz

DUROCORTORUM
Reims

AGRI DECUMATES
Lost to barbarians,
late third century

GERMANIA SUPERIOR

LUGDUNENSIS

AUTRICUM
Chartres

CENABUM
Orléans

AUGUSTODUNUM
Autun

BESONTIO
Besançon

LIMONUM
Poitiers

ALPES GRAIAE ET POENINAE

AXIMA
Aîme

DARANTASIA
Moutiers

SEGUSIO
Susa

MEDIOLANUM
Saintes

AQUITANIA

LUGDUNUM
Lyon

VIENNA
Vienne

VALENTIA
Valence

ALPES COTTIAE

BURDIGALA
Bordeaux

AVENNIO
Avignon

ALPES MARITIMAE

NEMAUSUS
Nîmes

ARELATE
Arles

CEMENELUM
Cimiez

NARBONENSIS

TOLOSA
Toulouse

NARBO
Narbonne

- - - Provincial boundary

■ Provincial capital

〜 Road

〜 Navigable river

⊕ Centre of Christianity, early fourth century

● Other major city

□ Legion

○ Garrison

△ *Laeti*

The dense network of Roman roads and navigable waterways combined military with economic functions. In the north and east in particular they serviced the military establishment required to keep the Gaulish provinces safe from Germanic attacks. In the south they highlighted the main commercial currents. It was along such trade routes that Christianity – an eastern import – penetrated the region from the second century AD.

way he had to raise fewer taxes. He struggled to control inflation, albeit at the price of a partial demonetarization of an economy whose strength had always lain in exchange.

In spite of these valiant endeavours to shore up a failing system, frontier violence continued to increase. In the fateful year of 406 a whole swarm of tribes crossed the ice-bound Rhine, forced their way into Gaul and settled where they pleased. Subsequently the Franks established a secure footing on French soil, the Alamanni settled in Alsace, the Vandals and Alans crossed Gaul and directed their footsteps into Spain and Africa, and the Burgundians established themselves in northern Gaul. In 412 the Visigoths set out from Italy and settled in the Toulouse area. In 416 an important page was turned, when the Roman authorities were forced to recognize the kingdom of the Visigoths as an autonomous mini-state – a move that marked the first serious tear in the fabric of imperial power.

Less conspicuously, however, the barbarian quest for land was dovetailing neatly with the empire's need for manpower: the Germanic tribes helped to repeople a society in the throes of depopulation. Though barbarians were moving in to settle in much larger groups than before, Rome had been sanctioning lesser settlements for some

The Porta Nigra, or "Black Gate", at Trier, now in Germany. The city was built up in the third and fourth centuries as the "Rome of the Gauls", and the centre from which the *limes* was controlled. From 460, however, it fell into Frankish hands. The gate, originally of bright sandstone, acquired its name from the build-up of grime over time.

Celtic deities were often associated with the figure three. Sometimes gods were represented in groups of three, and sometimes the gods were shown with three heads. This crude triad, dating from the third century, suggests a continuance of, or perhaps a revival of interest in, Celtic religion.

time. From the third century, in fact, the Romans had created *laeti* in depopulated areas, that is, settlements of refugees and barbarian prisoners of war. Gallo-Roman dealings with the barbarians took increasingly welcoming forms. In 358 the Salian Franks were accepted as military auxiliaries around the Rhine and Meuse estuaries: barbarians were now manning the *limes*. In 430 Franks occupying the region of Tournai and Cambrai were recognized as *foederati* ("federates"), or treaty-based allies. In 443 the Burgundians were established as "federates" in the Jura–Geneva region, and soon began to expand, taking control of most of the Lyonnais. Meanwhile the "feder-ated" Visigoths began to piece together a massive empire in the south-west. They annexed Provence between 470 and 472, the far south-west in 472, Auvergne between 474 and 475, and then set about forcing their way into northern Spain.

In these various ways the ethnic mix of the Gallo-Roman provinces in general, and the army in particular, was being transformed. Franks were particularly successful as soldiers – one Frankish general, Silvanus, had even usurped the imperial title (in 355) – and as military veterans they could retire to land-holdings within Gaul. In the 440s the Visigoths were used to put down a major rising of the Bagaudae in the south-west. In 451 Attila the Hun was defeated near Troyes by an army which included Franks, Visigoths and Burgundians. By that time, however, it seemed that even a barbarianized

Roman empire would find it difficult to resist further barbarian advances and internal dissension. The fall of the western empire in 476 had little impact on Gaul precisely because the processes of decomposition and restructuring were already far advanced.

With imperial power challenged both without and within, Gallo-Romans lived with a growing sense of anxiety. Long before 476, there had been warning signs of a loss of confidence in Rome's capacity to cope with barbarian raiding and peasant rebels. Effectively demilitarized during the *pax romana*, towns learnt the hard way that times had changed. The raid on Lutetia (Paris) in 258, for example, led to the rapid fortification of city defences. The city walls of a great many Gaulish towns had been for prestige and ostentation rather than defence, but all this now changed. Sometimes the size of the city needed to be reduced: defensible walls were too expensive to cover the entire living area, so cities determined to fortify only a central core. The fortified heart of Saintes covered 18 hectares where the city had formerly extended over 168, and at Amiens the reduction was from 100 to 10 hectares. At Sens, Tours and Périgueux, the authorities took stones from their amphitheatres and temples to buttress the inner defences. Now exposed, some of these massive leisure facilities were invaded by rats, weeds and squatters. Ominously, too, cities began to creep up hills again. In times of prosperity, under the *pax romana*, being close to roads and rivers had been seen as essential; now more remote, but more defensible hillside sites seemed attractive. The destruction caused by prolonged raiding was often too extensive to be properly repaired, so that the seductions of city life waned fast. Since barbarian raiders made a beeline for the concentrations of movable wealth in cities, many local notables shifted away from urban centres to newly fortified rural villas, less attractive, it was hoped, to the seasonal raider.

In this context it is perhaps understandable that Celtic language and culture enjoyed a renaissance. While Eastern religions, including Christianity, made progress in the towns, the Celtic pagan gods also made something of a comeback. The social elite was far from renouncing *romanitas*. But these developments signalled that the imperial cult had, it seemed, failed to make the "eternal city" eternal.

CHAPTER 3   *From Frankish Gaul to the Kingdom of West Francia*

Historians conventionally characterize the period from around 500 to the establishment of the Capetian dynasty in 987 in terms of the Frankish kingdoms formed after the fall of the Roman Empire. From the late fourth century a Frank, Clovis (r. *c.* 481–511), of the Merovingian dynasty, established a dominion which, under his successors, extended beyond Roman Gaul into Germany and north Italy. Although the Merovingian dynasty's political system was in clear decline by the seventh century, Frankish control was secured by the emergence of a Carolingian dynasty. This powerful family went on to establish a western European empire which was at its furthest extent under Charlemagne (r. 768–814). On Charlemagne's death, however, decline set in again. After a three-way division of the Carolingian inheritance in the Treaty of Verdun of 843, there emerged a new western bloc, "West Francia", which was to form the historical basis for the formation of France.

FRANKS, MEROVINGIANS AND OTHERS

The process by which the Frankish Merovingian dynasty came to prevail throughout Roman Gaul was a triumph for rude martial valour – though some might call it brutal thuggery. Frankish kings were above all great warlords, who enforced their power over their subjects by all means at their disposal. They maintained armed retinues, who swore an oath of allegiance to their chieftain in return for a place in his household and a share of plunder. King Clovis, said to descend from the legendary king-deity Merowech, rooted out rival Frankish rulers on the Rhineland with a brutality subsequently – and colourfully – recorded in Gregory of Tours' chronicle, *The History of the Franks*. He also pushed forward to defeat, in 486, Syagrius, king of Soissons, possibly the last commander of an outpost of the Roman Empire, before going on to crush the Burgundians and the Visigoths in the south. Clovis established the basis of Merovingian power by making Paris his capital (in 511); by converting to orthodox Christianity (around 500); and by issuing a fundamental legal code, the Salic Law.

Clovis' work was continued by his sons, who secured Burgundy in 536, wrested Provence from the Ostrogoths in 537 and expanded into south and central Germany and northern Italy. With the exceptions of Lower Languedoc and Roussillon, which remained in the hands of first Visigoths, then Saracens, and the intractable western tip of the Armorican peninsula, the Merovingian dynasty had by the mid sixth century conquered all of Roman Gaul, as well as much of central Europe.

Rulers came and went. The practice of subdividing the kingdom among heirs meant that political arrangements varied considerably, and that only very few Merovingian rulers – such as Dagobert I, sole king from 632 to 638 – reigned over all Frankish lands.

The Franks (5th-early 6th centuries)

Paris
Tours
Toulouse
Marseille

Neustria   Burgundy
Austrasia   Aquitaine

Other barbarians (5th-6th centuries)

- - - - Visigoths
———— Burgundians
· · · · · · Alamanni

Bretons and Basques (4th-6th centuries)

Bretons

Basques (Vasconi)

Area of Breton settlement
Area of Vasconi settlement

The Vikings (late 9th-10th centuries)

⟶ Viking incursion
■ Area of dense Viking/Norman settlement

Saracens and Magyars (8th-10th centuries)

- - -▸ Saracens (8th century)
· · · ·▸ Saracens (10th century)
⟶ Magyars (10th century)

Conceived of as a broad political and cultural entity, however, Frankish power dominated the former Roman provinces of Gaul, and indeed western Europe more generally, for two-and-a-half centuries under the Merovingians, and for much the same length of time again under their Frankish Carolingian successors.

The word "France" originates in "Francia", designating the kingdoms and cultural domain of the Franks; so etymology, if nothing else, seems to reserve for the latter a special place in the formation of France and French identity. It is best, however, to resist the temptation of treating this period as merely a Frankish chapter in the unfolding story of France. Historians have perhaps been too readily convinced by the propaganda

The age of invasions. The conquest of Roman Gaul by the Franks could not prevent repeated invasions and incursions between the fifth and tenth centuries. As a result, other groupings – the Visigoths, the Burgundians, the Bretons, the Vikings – made a lasting cultural impact in many regions.

Gregory of Tours

The author of *The History of the Franks* (593–4), Gregory of Tours (538–94), our most lively and penetrating source on fifth- and sixth-century Gaul, was not a Frank by birth, but an Auvergnat. He was born into an aristocratic Gallo-Roman family of the sort on whose active support the Frank invaders heavily relied. The "Herodotus of the barbarian world" witnessed political life at close quarters: from 573 he was made Bishop of Tours, and worked closely with Merovingian rulers. He was a quirky individual – in trying to clear up his infirmities, he apparently made himself ill several

Fourteenth-century illumination of bishops Gregory of Tours and Salvius of Albi chastising Chilperic, Frankish king of Neustria.

times by drinking potions made from the dust of saints' relics. But he proved a stubborn and individualistic prelate. He

keeps a pretty straight face throughout his chronicle of Frankish garottings, murders, deceit, duplicity, corruption and personal violence. While representing Clovis as "a great man [who] became a great soldier", and clearly stressing the importance of the king's conversion to Christianity, he does not shrink from depicting a lust for personal power of almost psychotic proportions. Only occasionally does feeling break through: recording the dysentery of 580, which was especially deadly for children, he noted, "and so we lost our little ones who were so dear to us and sweet, whom we had fed and nurtured with such loving care. As I write, I wipe away my tears ..."

of the Franks, by the military successes they enjoyed, and by the fact that they were the only invading group to establish a long-lasting and influential dynasty. As a result many have overestimated the depth of Frankish influence. Significantly, it was the Latin-based Gallo-Roman language spoken by the bulk of the population, rather than Frankish German, which was the foundation of the French language. Furthermore, the character and experience of power had shifted appreciably with the fall of the Roman Empire. Roman Gaul had been an integral part of a broader imperial system, and this had had repercussions on political and cultural identity. The very phrase "civis romanus sum", available after AD 212 to every citizen of the Roman Empire, had evoked a varied set of rights and entitlements for all under Roman dominion. From the late fourth century onwards, in contrast, there was no such close association between individual identity and wider power structures. Roman Gaul was no longer part of a wider state. On the contrary, it was honeycombed by a bewilderingly diverse set of local identities, surprisingly few of which were profoundly "Frankish" in any way at all.

National histories which conflate the history of France with the chronicle of the Franks also undervalue non-Frankish barbarian and external influences. The history of the far south-west in the centuries following the fall of Rome is less the story of Frankish invasion than of the establishment of Gascon power structures; and that of Brittany, of immigration from southern England by Breton groups. Parts of what had been Roman Gaul were invaded, first time round, by Burgundians, Visigoths, Alans, Alamanni, Saxons, Huns and others, and in a second spate of invasions from the late eighth century, by Saracens, Magyars and Vikings. Each of these groupings left its own particular cultural mark, which highlighted the diversity of political and cultural identities in France in the post-Roman period.

Furthermore the Franks and the other immigrant groupings were less numerous than is often assumed. The "barbarian invasions" failed to register a seismic shift in the genetic make-up of Roman Gaul. Frankish newcomers numbered between 150,000 and 200,000 – perhaps 2 to 3 per cent of a population of maybe six to seven million. Other groupings counted even smaller contingents. The Franks were also unevenly spread throughout the country. Their influence was strongest in the north and north-east – indeed it was stronger in Belgium, the Netherlands and Luxembourg than in France. Placename evidence suggests that the further one travelled west and south from the region between the Rhine and the Somme and Meuse rivers, the less concentrated Germanic presence was. In the Midi, it was minimal. The dominance of the Franks was not based on population numbers nor on genetic impact, but was essentially political. Even then, moreover, it was limited.

The Franks' value-system was not totally alien to Gaul's erstwhile *romanitas*. As we have seen, the *limes* marking the border of formal Roman power had not been a *cordon sanitaire*, keeping Germanic and Roman cultures uncontaminated by each other. It was more akin to a garden fence, facilitating exchange and reciprocal influence. The Franks had been established on both sides of the frontier even before the "invasions". Population pressures from the east had helped force together what had formerly been a cluster of minor tribal groupings – the Salians, the Chamavi, the Bructeri, the Chattuari and others – into a kind of defensive league ascribed the title "Frank". They were easily enticed as military auxiliaries into defensive duties along the *limes*.

Roman influence on the Franks was apparent long before the period of the invasions. Roman luxury items were sought after by the Germanic tribal aristocracies. Roman political forms had also made themselves felt: the Frankish lawcode, the so-called Salic Law, was influenced by Roman precedent and composed in Latin (as were similar codes drawn up by the Visigoths and the Burgundians). This contained punishments for individuals attacking their neighbour's vines (showing that the quintessentially Roman taste for wine, rather than Germanic beer, had established itself

Far left Merovingian gold coin showing Romulus and Remus, suckling at their wolf mother. It was struck in the early seventh century at Toulouse, capital of Aquitaine, where Roman cultural influence was particularly long-lasting.

Near left Early seventh-century coin of Dagobert I, who reconstituted Frankish unity and proved to be the last Merovingian to rule personally over all Frankish lands. Mounted to be worn as a medallion rather than used as a unit of exchange, this coin testified to the post-Roman decline in mercantile activity.

The monastery of Saint-Guilhem-le-Désert

In the year 804 the Benedictine monastery of Gellone was founded at Saint-Guilhem-le-Désert in Lower Languedoc by the Austrasian aristocrat, count of Septimania, Saint William of Gellone (c. 755–812). Later *chansons de geste* were to call him William of Orange and depict him as one of Charlemagne's paladins, the heroic victor over the Saracens, who captured Nîmes by bringing in his troops hidden in wine-barrels. The founder retired from the world to his monastery, and when he died there it was said that the bells of the surrounding province rang without any hand on their ropes. The monastery became a stopping-place on the pilgrimage route to Santiago de Compostela in northern Spain. Wealth from this source led to extensive rebuilding from the thirteenth century, with a great deal of impressive decorative work.

Saint William was a convert to the Benedictine form of monasticism, which had originated in the work of Saint Benedict of Nursia (c. 480–547).

Reformed by Saint Benedict of Aniane (c. 750–821), and formalized in Louis the Pious' decree of 817, the rule was to be followed in all monasteries throughout the empire. It emphasized poverty, celibacy, obedience and stability – the monk was to be attached to his house as a serf to his land, and to lead his life as a full member of the community. Monks divided their day between prayer – the demands of worship were extensive – and labour (Saint Benedict of Nursia had recommended seven hours' manual work).

The cloister – an open courtyard surrounded by covered passageways – was the centre around which monastic life revolved. The main rooms and chambers of the institution led off from it – refectory, chapter-house, library, workshops and so on. Here monks walked in meditation, had their schooling, studied and perhaps copied manuscripts.

Purchased by a stonemason in the Revolution of 1789, when all Church lands were nationalized and much monastic property sold off, the monastery's buildings were pitilessly ransacked for construction materials. Elements of the cloister were found in the nineteenth century serving as vine supports in the garden of a magistrate in nearby Aniane, and they have since been reassembled in the grounds of the Metropolitan Museum of Modern Art, New York. Only the abbey church of the original institution still remains in place.

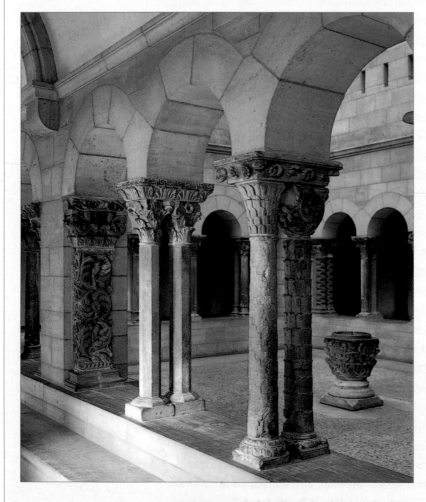

Reconstituted cloister of the abbey of Saint-Guilhem-le-Désert.

Saint Radegund (*c.* 518–87), queen of the Franks, depicted, in this tenth- or eleventh-century image, seated at the table of her husband, Clothair (r. 558–61), son of Clovis, before a table bearing bread, wine and fish. Radegund abandoned the court for an austere hermetic life.

the elbow. Yet this respect came mainly from the fact that women were viewed as prize possessions of their husbands, particularly as bearers of children. They enjoyed less legal autonomy than under Roman law, though they could control some forms of property independently. They were also more disposable now as marriage-partners: polygyny was well established – four Merovingian rulers, including Dagobert I, are known to have had more than one wife, and Charlemagne was to have four. Repudiation or divorce of a wife was easier. The Burgundian Code had it that women seeking a divorce were to be smothered in mire. Against this background of unreflective violence, women's lives could be tough. Only 40 per cent of women lived past forty, as against nearly 60 per cent of men.

The weakening of central power and the fusion of public and private spheres under the Merovingians – as under the later Carolingians – threw political power back into the lap of aristocratic families. The lack of formal state structures and the importance of the ruling family allowed women of strong character to make a real impact. One

tha
to
lar
Rh
Au
wh
ni
ch

in
be
cc
M
in

The Carolingian Renaissance

Like the later Italian Renaissance, the Renaissance which historians have located in the reign of Charlemagne and his ninth-century successors was characterized by an intense interest in the art and literature of classical antiquity. Classical Latin had to be relearnt as a language of expression, following its displacement by Germanic languages and by its evolution in West Francia into "rustic Roman". Yet whereas the Italian Renaissance was to be marked by fascination with non-Christian artistic and intellectual forms, the Carolingian Renaissance was soaked in ecclesiastical values, and was indeed largely conducted by self-consciously Latinizing churchmen.

The Carolingian Renaissance had its roots in Charlemagne's desire to act out the imperial role. Church and state overlapped very considerably. Carolingian capitularies (or edicts) multiplied the number of legal offences, and had much to say about the reform of morality. Law, it seemed, could Christianize and moralize the inhabitants of the empire, and the Church had a fundamental part to play in this mission. It provided the Carolingians with administrators, councillors, imperial agents, scholars, legal experts, teachers and ecclesiastical

This exquisite gold and bejewelled talisman, reputed to have belonged to Charlemagne, contained holy relics in its hollowed-out centre.

advisers. Churchmen were indeed the dominant figures in the Renaissance. The York-born ecclesiastic, Alcuin, who presided over the palace school – and who was noted for "anointing his throat with wine and beer to improve his teaching and make his song more melodious" – dreamt, it was said, of making the imperial court at Aachen (Aix-la-Chapelle) a new Athens.

The rescue of the classical heritage through the copying of Latin manuscripts was a central concern, and indeed most extant writings from antiquity were transcribed by the Carolingians. The codification of law, reform in handwriting and improvements in musical notation were further areas of interest. Apart from the construction of the imperial palace at Aachen – largely a copy of a church in Ravenna – few major artistic and architectural projects have survived. Carolingian art is distinguished by artefacts of a more modest scale, often displaying minute artistic workmanship. The wall paintings, jewellery, illuminated manuscripts and books that have came down to us combine classical models with the inheritance of late Roman, Byzantine, Celtic and Germanic art forms.

by the turn of the century built up a massive European empire extending over all former Frankish domains and spreading into south-eastern Europe and Italy. By entering the Italian peninsula to defeat the Lombards in 774, and assuming the mantle of king of the Lombards, Charlemagne made the Carolingians the dominant power in Europe, and he followed this up by pushing towards the Elbe and the Baltic in savage campaigns conducted against the Saxons.

The Carolingians prided themselves on campaigning with the cross as well as the sword – this was made all the more possible, because Arab power was now bottled up within the Iberian peninsula. Charlemagne also forced defeated pagan peoples to convert to Christianity. The missionary zeal of Saint Boniface in the conversion of the Germans was the velvet glove around an uncompromising iron fist: the defeats of the pagan Saxons in 782 were followed by near-genocidal massacres. In 785 Charlemagne

Opposite Detail from Louis the Pious' psalter, dating from the second quarter of the ninth century. Louis' reign was closely associated with the move for religious reform, notably of monasticism.

decreed that any Saxon refusing to be baptized or indulging in behaviour insulting to the Church was to be executed. Victor over the pagan and the infidel, the Carolingian dynasty also offered firm support to the papacy. Charlemagne's triumphs in the Italian peninsula allowed him to stabilize the position of beleaguered Pope Stephen II, as well as to carve out for him the papal states. These would remain the temporal base of the papacy right through to the nineteenth century. It was against this background that one should see the events of Christmas Day 800 when, in a ceremony in Rome which Charlemagne himself claimed not to have anticipated, Pope Leo III placed a crown on Charlemagne's head. He was thus consecrated as Emperor – the first emperor in the West since 476. Papal anointing helped to add a theocratic tinge to Carolingian power.

Charlemagne took religion seriously within his empire as well as without. He extended a strong measure of protection to the Church. Bishops played a major part in local administration, often outweighing the influence of counts. Charlemagne was also an important patron to monastic houses – not least because he saw them as counterbalancing the considerable secular power of the bishops. Of 304 major building projects undertaken in his reign, 232 were monasteries (as against seven cathedrals and sixty-five palaces). The dynasty made enormous gifts to the Church: from the years 751 to 825 Church lands in Christendom appear to have tripled, growing from 10 to about 30 per cent of the total cultivable area. The tithe, regulated by the emperor in a series of measures from 779 to 801, was to constitute a major element of Church income down to the French Revolution.

Generosity, to favoured laymen as well as to the Church, was thus a crucial ingredient of Carolingian power. It had a number of sources. The constant inflows of booty and tribute from wars were essential. There were military campaigns every year from the time of Charles Martel to Charlemagne's coronation. The treasure of the Avar Kingdom in Hungary, which Charlemagne brought back with him in 796, was fabulous. Land was a currency of power as much as gold, silver and jewellery. Territorial expansion provided new sources for giving property. The later Carolingians' capacity for generosity, notably towards the Church, had been partly based on Charles Martel's earlier confiscation of huge tracts of Church lands. After the last of the Merovingian *rois fainéants* had been deposed in 751 their confiscated lands placed huge resources at the disposal of the Carolingians. Rulers were also wont to distribute tax immunities.

Carolingian prodigality stimulated something of an economic revival. With plague dying out from the late seventh century, population grew – perhaps from 7.5 to as much as 9 million between the mid seventh and the mid eighth centuries. Monasteries which had benefited from Carolingian largesse were in a strong position to profit from the continuing eclipse of the urban sector. Indeed they often came to act as surrogate towns in their own right, amassing capital, organizing labour and facilitating exchange. Certain fairs run by monastic houses – such as those at Saint-Denis (near Paris), Corbie (near Metz), Saint-Riquier (near Amiens) and Saint-Vaast (near Arras) – achieved international prominence. Those associated with monasteries located in the suburbs of a

Purse reliquary of Pepin of Aquitaine (r. 817–38), son of Louis the Pious. Allegedly donated by Pepin to the abbey church at Conques, it shows the Virgin Mary and Saint John flanking Christ.

town – as was the case with Saint-Germain-des-Prés in Paris, Saint-Rémy at Reims and Saint-Sernin at Toulouse – even helped to revive the fortune of the adjacent town.

Economic revival could not, however, lessen the fragility of Carolingian power. It proved difficult to convert additional wealth within Carolingian society into major sources of income for the royal treasury. The monarch, who, as Christian warlord, dispensed favours with a liberal hand, still needed to secure new sources of income to operate as a generous provider of tributes. It would appear that this problem was becoming acute for Charlemagne in the last years of his reign. By about 800 he had reached a "plunder frontier" – campaigning abroad was replaced by more defensive operations to secure loyalty and conserve possessions within an already oversprawling empire. Other methods of securing support within his dominions were required.

The development of a bureaucratic style of government was a potential answer to the problem of making the empire cohere in a period when booty was in short supply. Carolingian administration had a strongly ecclesiastical flavour. Missionaries were used in Germany as the ideologists of Carolingian power, and they were quick to equate sins against God with crimes against the imperial person. But Charlemagne also viewed churchmen as able and literate administrators. The so-called Carolingian Renaissance – the revival of arts and learning – had a strongly religious flavour, and served the interests of the state bureaucracy. An innovation from 775, for example, was the systematic appointment of roving imperial administrators, the so-called *missi dominici*, on top of the routine administrative network of counts and bishops. Usually

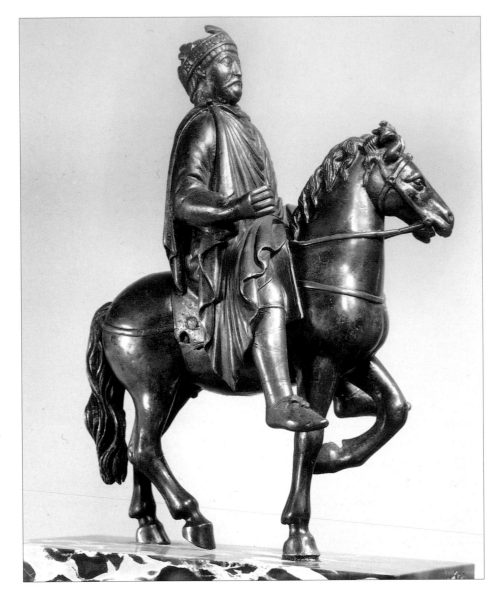

This idealized bronze horseback figure of a Western emperor (860–70 AD) may represent Charlemagne, or else Charles the Bald, under whose reign it appears to have been made. Frankish in many attributes – long moustache, clothing, hairstyle – the figure also recalls Roman equestrian statues.

sent out in pairs, one of whom was an influential churchman, these officials were entrusted with administrative surveillance. They judged, punished, redressed wrongs, received oaths and, on occasion, raised armies. A particular responsibility was to announce and put into effect Carolingian edicts, known as capitularies. These, made at the annual assemblies of free men, were written down and formed a body of imperial statute extending to religious, moral and secular concerns. The role of the *missi dominici* was complemented by Charlemagne's own tireless travelling. Oaths of loyalty to himself, introduced from 789 and required of males over twelve years old, also had a unifying function. So, too, did acts of commendation, the special oaths of fealty which he imposed on his most powerful subjects, theoretically making them royal vassals.

The oaths, the capitularies, the *missi dominici*, the imperial tours and the use of the Church as a dynastic agent and ideologist could temporarily hold in check, but proved unable to eradicate, powerful centrifugal forces. Rulers could posture as Rome's heirs or as Christian theocrats. By the end of Charlemagne's reign, however, it was becoming increasingly apparent that the prime political cement was still booty, essential for keeping the ruler's powerful subjects and their followers happy. The shortage of scope for plunder and booty posed a problem which was to become even more acute for Charlemagne's successors.

AFTER CHARLEMAGNE

The essentially unitary nature of Carolingian power had contrasted forcefully with the weak and divisive authority of the *rois fainéants*. After Charlemagne's death, however, a new phase of dynastic division damaged the already fragile mainsprings of imperial power. In 817 Charlemagne's successor, Louis the Pious (r. 813–40), declared that on his death the empire would be split up among his heirs. This caused a wave of resentment among his children, who from 830, with the support of magnates, waged civil war – first, against their father and then, after his death in 840, among themselves. In 843 the Treaty of Verdun made formal a division of the great Carolingian empire into three parts. The imperial title resided with Lothair, who was accorded a bloc of territory, Lotharingia, stretching from the Italian peninsula to the Baltic, and containing both Aix-la-Chapelle and Rome. This was squashed between an "East Francia" under Louis the German and a western bloc, West Francia, which was placed in the hands of Charles the Bald, who ruled as king from 838 to 877 and as emperor from 875 to 877.

The term "Francia" was still sometimes given to the area from the Seine to the Lotharingian frontier, but more generally the title "West Francia" began to be used for the western chunk of the old Carolingian empire. As time went on, it became apparent that this area had clearly floated off from the more Germanic, eastern part of the dominion of the Franks, and that the rough, unfashioned trunk of future France was becoming dimly discernible. It would be quite wrong of course to read too much into this. At the level of political geography, about one-quarter of present-day France was in the late ninth century in Lotharingian or German hands, and this changed only very slowly. The division enshrined at Verdun had nothing to do with ethnic groupings. (If it had, it would presumably have separated the Basques and the Bretons, the most clearly defined ethnic groupings in the western empire, from the mixed Germano-Gallo-Roman stock prevalent elsewhere.) Rather, Verdun marked political and hence highly fragile borders, following the courses of the Meuse, Scheldt, Saône and Rhône rivers, with splendid disregard for ethnic or cultural boundaries.

Nevertheless Verdun did help to constitute a new, broader cultural division. In the Oath of Strasbourg of 842, which Charles the Bald and Louis the German had sworn just prior to Verdun, Louis the German's army had to have the oath explained to them in German, Charles the Bald's in "rustic Roman" – that degenerate form of Latin which was the basis of the French language. The dominion which the Franks had established

Carolingian France

Cologne AUSTRASIA
Ghent
St. Omer
Nivelles St. Trond Stavelot-Malmédy Andernach
Lobbes Celles Prüm Altmunster
St. Amand St. Hubert Echternach
St. Riquier Péronne Trèves Mainz
Corbie St. Quentin Mettlach
Fécamp Hornbach
St. Wandrille Rouen Barisis au Bois Reims Gorze
Jumièges St. Denis Hautvillers St. Mihiel
Chelles Orbais ALAMANNIA
Mont-St-Michel NEUSTRIA Argenteuil Rebais Moutier en Der
Faremoutiers
Landévennec Murbach
Dol St. Mesmin Sens Remiremont
BRITTANY Ferrières Fontaine Annegray
Fleury Tonnerre Luxeuil
St. Nazaire Blois Flavigny
Tours Besançon
Noirmoutier Loches RAETIA
Bourges St. Maurice
St. Maixent d'-Agaune
Nouaillé BURGUNDY
Mazerolles Nantua SAVOY
AQUITAINE Lyon Novalese
Vienne Moûtiers
Sarlat
Embrun
Altaripa PROVENCE
GASCONY Arles Aix-en-Provence
Auch SEPTIMANIA Lérins
Narbonne

_____ Division of Carolingian empire by the Treaty of Verdun, 843   ▨ West Francia   ▧ East Francia   ● Episcopal seat   - - - - Boundary of ecclesiastical province

▨ Lotharingia   △ Carolingian palaces   ● Archiepiscopal seat   ● Other principal monasteries, c. 817

The trunk of future France is evident in the western bloc of the Carolingian Empire, carved up in the Treaty of Verdun of 843. As well as marking out "West Francia" from an eastern, Germanic, "East Francia", the treaty also defined the profile of an indeterminate area into which both powers would penetrate over the next millennium. The Carolingian Empire was also important for defining and consolidating the ecclesiastical and administrative framework of France's later development.

in the sixth century was slowly coming to be divided by language: by the end of the tenth century, the term "Frank" (*francus*) meant French; "Francia" was routinely distinguished from the "kingdom of the Teutons" or the "kingdom of the Germans" in the east; and kings of West Francia and Germany themselves needed translators to make themselves understood to each other.

Wide cracks, then, were opening up within the Frankish domain. Dynastic wranglings further whittled away the prestige and authority of central power. Lothair's death in 855 brought a further round of territorial reallocation; and briefly, from 881 to 887, the feeble Charles the Fat (king of West Francia 884–7) enjoyed the imperial title and ruled its entirety. His political weakness led a group of aristocrats to elect as king one of their number, Odo, a "Robertian" (that is, a descendant of the powerful count Robert the Strong). On his death, the throne passed back into the hands of a Carolingian, Charles the Simple (r. 893–922). But for the last century of Carolingian power, the throne shuttled back and forth between Carolingians and Robertians, depending on the political complexion at the time.

These dynastic squabbles took place against a darkening political atmosphere. Carolingian domains were subjected to fresh waves of attacks and looting from outside, by Saracens, Magyars and, especially, Vikings. Raiding by Saracen pirates from North Africa had begun in 793 with attacks in the Lower Languedoc area. Corsica was devastated in 806, and the whole of southern France subject to brutal raiding between 838 and 842, when the Saracens pushed up the Rhône valley to Arles. They established a permanent base at La Garde Freinet, in the Saint-Tropez area, and they continued spasmodic raiding from here until their eviction in 972/3. It was in the tenth century, too, that the Magyar tribes from the east made destructive sorties into French territory. They had reached Germany and Italy by early in the century, and from 919 through to the late 930s made lightning strikes into France, causing widespread devastation.

The pagan Vikings, or "Norsemen", constituted by far the most serious and enduring foreign threat which Charlemagne and his successors faced. These Scandinavian seafarers had conducted piratical raids on the west coast of France and the south coast of England from the last years of the eighth century, and were soon exploring the French interior. In 844/5 they attacked cities as far from the sea as Toulouse, Tours and Paris. From 851 they wintered in France, conducting systematic raids in the southwest of the country.

The Vikings caused a great deal of destruction and economic dislocation. The Carolingians saw in them the cause of all the empire's ills: population decline, material destruction, economic disruption, a drop in political morale. Yet the empire's nobles could not really gripe, for the Vikings were only practising the arts of plunder in which the Carolingians themselves were past masters. The plunderer had become the plundered, the predator the prey. Perhaps, too, the fact that most chroniclers were clerics, and that churches and abbeys were among the pagan Vikings' prime targets for looting, has unduly prejudiced later views. The incidence of Viking attacks on most areas in France was, moreover, often highly sporadic. Picardy suffered seventeen

The Vikings

In 885 the inhabitants of Paris cowered nervously on the Île de la Cité awaiting the arrival of a massive force of Vikings, coming to sack the city and put its inhabitants to the sword. The Parisians already knew about the Danish seafaring pirates. In 845 the latter had brought their fearsome long-boats to the city, "laying waste everything on either side," a chronicler had noted, "and meeting not the least bit of resistance". Pausing only to refit their vessels with timbers hacked from the rafters of the abbey church of Saint-Germain-des-Prés, they had retraced their route up the Seine.

The exploits of these pagan seafarers – the French called them *normands* ("Norsemen") – had studded Carolingian history for a century by 885. After several decades of fitful coastal raids, from early in the ninth century they had begun to use France's extensive river system to carry plundering to the heart of the country. Emperors, then kings of West Francia, did their best to combat the scourge. From 845 Charles the Bald regularly paid out tribute to the raiders to make them withdraw. The Norsemen only came back for more. From 860 the king began a policy of barring rivers in order to inhibit inland raiding.

The Viking fleet eventually reached Paris in 885: 700 large vessels, it was said, plus a fleet of smaller craft, and an accom-panying army of 30,000 to 40,000 men either in the boats or marching along the banks. Small Parisian armed bands, led by the Robertian leader Odo, heroically defended the two bridgeheads to the island. A lengthy siege developed, with the Vikings using every form of offensive craft, including fire-boats targeted at the bridgeheads. To the Parisians, it seemed that the Christian God was on their side. A Viking warrior was struck dead on entering the tomb of Saint Germain in the abbey church. And the ghost of the saint was observed walking along the ramparts at night sprinkling holy water. The saint's relics were devoutly brought to the Parisian front line. Eventually Emperor Charles the Fat arrived with an army. He preferred to negotiate rather than to fight, and, their pockets swollen with ransom, the Vikings were soon proceeding back up the Seine.

Paris was fortunate. Rape, pillage and wanton destruction were the hallmarks of these sea-borne raiders. "There is not a road," recorded one Carolingian chronicler, "that is not strewn with the bodies of slain Christians." Yet within a few decades the Viking warriors were seeking to settle down. Under the chieftain Rollo, the "Norsemen" established themselves near the estuary of the Seine in 910–11, and within a matter of generations had transformed themselves into "Normans".

The seventy metres of the Bayeux Tapestry portray the Norman duke William's conquest of England in 1066. The Normans – "Norsemen" – are, interestingly, referred to as Franks ("Franci"). Acclimatization was, it seems, complete.

assaults between 835 and 925 – which meant that the region was without raids three-quarters of the time.

Furthermore, there is a case for arguing that the impact of the raids was sometimes positive. By plundering urban and monastic centres which had stockpiled riches, the Vikings released wealth on to the open market and stimulated the economy. As with the Carolingians who preceded them, moreover, looting was only part of wider patterns of trading, bartering and gift exchange. Viking raiding had, it might be argued, a far more destructive impact on the Carolingian dynasty than on most of its subject peoples; it is important to disconnect the fate of the population of France from the fortunes of its major dynasty.

The crisis of the central power within West Francia, and more widely within the empire, was, moreover, as much internal as external. It became particularly pressing during the reign of Charles the Bald (r. 838–77), who was powerless too against Viking raids. Wealthy and powerful subjects were increasingly slipping the reins of a central power unable to ensure protection to its peoples. The Carolingians tended to fall back – as had the Merovingians before them – on the heartlands of their power between the Loire and the Scheldt. Rulers in the tenth century rarely went outside this area – in sharp contrast with Charlemagne's restless travelling. Indeed the Robertians, chosen as monarchs by northern nobles to defend against Viking attacks, were not even recognized in Brittany or south of the Loire. The *missi dominici* system broke down by the middle of the century. Capitularies ceased from 884. No national assemblies were convened after 889.

The structure of delegated royal power was also changing. The post of counts, in theory revocable at the ruler's whim, became more and more a lifetime, then a hereditary, appointment. In 877 they stopped presenting their accounts to the central government, thus marking a change in their status from state official to hereditary territorial princeling. Many of these men had in the past been awarded royal benefices (possession of royal estates). In the early days such royal gifts could in theory be withdrawn – the idea was that the servants of the crown were allowed, in return for service, to have temporary and provisional enjoyment of landed revenues, but not possession of the land itself. This distinction was increasingly lost. Magnates with extensive landed possessions began to assume the title of duke and act as royal viceroys. Indeed some began to assume regal airs, even mimicking their ruler by building up private followings whom they rewarded in kind and whom they attached to their person by similar oaths of fidelity. These forces had once been kept in check, but monarchs found it difficult to resist them now, as they had so little left to give. Local potentates developed extensive patronage networks in administration and in the Church which the Carolingian dynasty could not suppress. Favours were now bypassing the court, whence all bounty had once flowed.

Local leaders had an appeal kings could not match. The defensive needs of the period led to local magnates building fortified castles, from behind whose walls they posed as defenders of the local population from outsiders. In time they came to regard

CHAPTER 4   The Middle Ages

There was nothing about the condition of West Francia at the turn of the millennium which suggested its future as one of the most important states in western Europe. The new Capetian dynasty had only a tenuous hold on the assemblage of peoples and political units within the borders of a West Francia riven by major cultural divisions, and increasingly pulverized into often tiny political units. The French state might have subsequently developed on the scale of a Bavaria or a Belgium, that is, as a minor and second-rank power. Alternatively, such was its evident weakness after 987, it might have disappeared altogether and been swallowed up into some larger unit. At one stage, for example, in the late twelfth and early thirteenth centuries, it seemed possible that much of West Francia would be incorporated into an English-based "Angevin Empire". Henry, count of Anjou, had vast holdings on the Continent and was also, from 1154 to 1189, Henry II, king of England. At best, West Francia looked more like a collection of potential future states than a single, unitary one.

That "West Francia" between the year 1000 and the early fourteenth century developed into "France", a potentially front-rank power, owed a great deal to its rulers. The Capetian dynasty, after a slow start, became exceptionally adept at aggressive statecraft, extending the boundaries of its rule and increasing its hold over subject peoples. The roles of Louis VI (r. 1108–37) and Louis VII (r. 1137–80) in building up the Île-de-France as the centre of dynastic power; of Philip II Augustus (r. 1180–1223) in breaking the Angevin grip on south-western France; and then of Louis VIII (r. 1223–6) and Louis IX (r. 1226–70) in extending Capetian power in the Midi were paramount in this process. "In all of Christendom," an Italian observer noted by the early fourteenth century, "the king of France has no equal."

Moreover, the Middle Ages marked the beginnings of "France" as an ideological construct. The Capetian dynasty in particular helped to establish an idiom in which people could talk about France as a territorial unit *and* as a political community. Roman Gaul had been geographically more than the future France, and politically it formed a small part of a larger unit, the Roman Empire. West Francia was similarly only one-third of the wider community of the Franks – and it was to boot smaller than future "France". In the twelfth and thirteenth centuries the latter established itself for the first time as a key concept of political and cultural identity.

The chronicle of how the Capetian dynasty achieved what it did is, however, one aspect of a far more complex story. We need to evaluate the context of their activity, the lives of groups and peoples still often outside direct Capetian control, who were embarking on a process which would lead to "Frenchness". To do this we need to understand the workings of the feudal system and to unravel the workings of the Church in what became an "age of faith". We need to explain the mainsprings of the great economic and demographic revival which France experienced during these centuries. And we need to comprehend something of the complexity of regional life within West Francia.

Enamelled grave plate of
Geoffrey, count of Anjou
(1113–51), father of Henry II of
England, architect of the
Angevin empire. The inscription
reads: "By your sword, prince,
the crowd of robbers is routed
and by your vigilance the
Church has peace." The motto
and the emblems of power
convey a prince's assumption of
royal attributes.

As a power base this was solid, but it made a poor showing compared even with other magnates within West Francia. When in 1052, for example, the counts of Poitou merged Gascony with Aquitaine, they created a unit far larger than the Capetian lands. When in 1154 Brittany and neighbouring Normandy were brought together with Aquitaine and England, the resultant Angevin empire was bigger than the lands owing allegiance to the Capetian kings of France. Closer to home, the Capetians could also, with some justification, claim to feel encircled in 1125, when the powerful counts of Blois acquired the important county of Champagne. In the Midi the counts of Toulouse also came to dominate a massive part of southern France, stretching in the early twelfth century from the Rhône to Angoulême and from the Pyrenees to the Auvergne.

If the geography of Capetian power was patchy, so too was its consistency. Scribes occasionally portrayed the early Capetians as being "emperors in their own country". Yet their claims to sovereignty were hollow; rulers no longer passed laws, delegated power through a revocable bureaucracy or obliged free men to take obedience oaths. Their monarchical powers were less significant than their seigneurial authority. There is indeed a case for arguing that Hugh Capet and his immediate successors – Robert II the Pious (r. 996–1031), Henry I (r. 1031–60) and Philip I (r. 1060–1108) – owed their survival less to strength than to weakness. Their virtual inability to threaten the local power of territorial magnates, or to prevent them from acting alone and building up loyal followings, made the "rulers" tolerable for those who were actually more powerful.

Political authority now took the form of a confusing welter of personal ties of dependence. In theory the Capetian monarch was at the apex of a pyramid of feudal power, and the great magnates and high churchmen of the realm bound themselves to him by links of personal loyalty as his vassals. Yet these ties were of varying degrees of closeness, they operated only in West Francia and were observed as much in the breach as in the exercise. The practice, developed under the Merovingians and Carolingians, of rooting dependence in land also made the exercise of power problematic. It was quite possible for a lord to possess lands under the authority of a number of other lords: the counts of Champagne were vassals of the kings of France, for example, but also of nine other lords including the German emperor and the duke of Burgundy.

The bonds of personal loyalty and dependence were increasingly grounded in honorary titles linked to property. The creation of these "investitures" acquired classic form in the act of homage. The vassal would kneel before his lord, place his hands in his and swear an oath of fidelity on holy relics or on the Bible, thus becoming his "man". Besides property, the lord provided protection over his vassal, who in return owed his lord *consilium* ("counsel") and *auxilium* ("aid"). As "counsel" the vassal undertook to attend the court of his lord, offer him advice and bring to him disputes for arbitration and settlement. As "aid" the vassal had to agree to follow the lord to war, possibly with a retinue of armed followers, and to provide occasional financial assistance, including payment of the lord's ransom if he were captured, gifts on the wedding of his eldest daughter and so on. The military dimension of the relationship was

The girding-on of swords, part of the increasingly formalized ritual associated with the making of a knight, is illuminated in a thirteenth-century manuscript.

highly important: the grant of property was viewed as a means of enlisting the armed support of the vassal on horseback, plus possibly a retinue of knightly retainers – from Carolingian times, cavalry had become a key battlefield arm.

This arrangement permitted central control only as long as the king's vassals had reason for gratitude and awe. Under the Carolingians property granted could theoretically be taken back and rights were not absolute. By the tenth century, however, property grants were hereditary and included the wholesale transfer of judicial and political power. Chains of dependency trailed, moreover, through the whole of society. Relations of loyalty extended downwards so that the king's vassals developed hordes of their own vassals, linked to the ruler only in the most tenuous way. The great territorial princes, rather than their ruler, now administered loyalty oaths to those within their jurisdictions. Inhabitants of Burgundy, for example, swore fidelity only to their dukes.

For most French men and women, the kings of France had simply vanished. Having parcelled out their authority, and lacking military might, monarchs possessed only limited powers over their vassals. They had far less effective purchase on their vassals than the latter did on vassals of their own. It was at the lower level that the relationship invited awe and subjection. "You are my man," Count William of Poitou informed one of his vassals in the 1020s, "and your duty is to do my will. If I were to command you to do homage to a peasant, it would be your duty to obey ..."

This parcelling-out of authority was taken further, moreover, because of the failure of the territorial princes to maintain power throughout their own lands. Although feudal decentralization had initially favoured the territorial princes, who shielded their dependants from direct royal power, in the ninth and tenth centuries they in turn

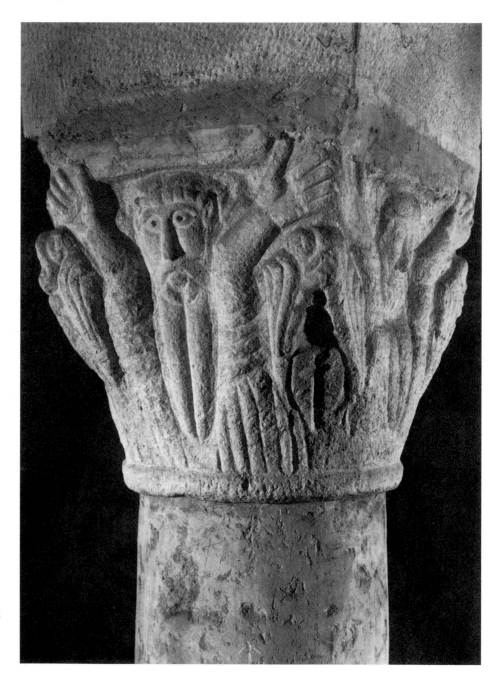

This eleventh-century figure from a column in the crypt of the Church of Sainte-Benigne, Dijon, shows one of the most widespread attitudes of prayer in the first millennium. It was gradually replaced by the more commonplace custom of placing the hands together – a gesture modelled on the seeking of feudal homage from a lord.

found it difficult to keep their own vassals in line. The creation of castles was originally part of the organized process by which royal authority was devolved. Once in place, however, they were used by truculent castellans and knights as a base. From there they could venture forth with gangs of mounted knights to impose their power willy-nilly on neighbouring peasants and to jostle against the power and prerogatives of their neighbours in private wars and pillaging expeditions.

The maintenance of law and order and the punishing of wrongdoers were thus becoming micro-events, far removed from the increasingly nominal authority of rulers and princes. Castellans and the knightly class in general had a good deal of leeway to impose forms of social and political organization on the land which were highly favourable to themselves. The lord's castle had provided welcome protection from the raiding of Vikings, Saracens, Magyars – and the aggression of petty seigneurs – but the price in the long run was that peasants had to accept greater subservience. The knightly class's superior military technology meant that peasants were almost powerless to resist the imposition of ever harsher feudal burdens.

As a result the legal status of the peasantry dropped. Free peasants holding land which was allodial (that is, free of seigneurial dues) became increasingly rare in the north. Most peasants were serfs who operated within the all-encompassing embrace of the manorial, or seigneurial, system. Slavery went into a slow decline; power was now lodged in land rather than bodies. Lords preferred a system whereby their serfs had their own plots of land (called tenures, or tenements), with which they could maintain themselves and their families. Yet, in return, the serfs were bound to the land and were obliged to do forced labour services on their lords' own property, known as the domain. This demarcation between domain and tenures predated Charlemagne, but developed quickly after the collapse of central authority. Peasants now took oaths which imitated vassalage. If called on, they were obliged to join their lord on foot in military expeditions or to keep watch in his castle over the campaigning months in the summer. There were other dues too, sometimes fairly eccentric, such as the obligation to beat pond-waters by night to quell the mating cries of amorous frogs, allowing their lord to sleep peacefully. Besides duties of labour, serfs also paid dues and taxes of various kinds. Lords enjoyed economic monopolies, too: they could force peasants to use the seigneurial wine-press, mill and bakery. Such rights were as remunerative to the lords as they were irksome to peasants. Lords also had judicial authority over tenements as well as domain, and could impose fines on a wide range of offences.

For most inhabitants of this France in the making, power was saddled on the horses of the knightly class. With central authority in decay from the ninth century, and with even territorial princes feeling the pinch in the tenth, the defence of the land and the meting out of justice had passed to local princelings, increasingly autonomous counts and hordes of truculent castellans. "You have so many partners and equals in the kingdom," Hincmar, bishop of Reims, had informed Charles the Bald in the late ninth century, "that you reign more in name than in reality." With power fragmenting fast, even below the level of the territorial prince, this remark was even more apt for the early Capetians.

Consecration of the main altar of the abbey church of Cluny monastery by Pope Urban II, 25 October 1095. The pope is shown to the left, while leading his priests on the right is the abbot, Saint Hugh, who in 1088 had begun work on what was then the most ambitious piece of ecclesiastical architecture in the Western world.

CHURCH AND CRUSADE

In many ways, European society in the tenth and eleventh centuries was a two-class society, formed of warriors and peasants. But when churchmen conceptualized society from the tenth century onwards, however, they added themselves as an additional order, or estate. Besides *bellatores* ("those who fight") and *laboratores* ("those who work"), they listed *oratores* ("those who pray"). The Church was thus viewed as a structural element of feudal society – and indeed it would remain one until the Revolutionaries of 1789 launched their all-out attack on feudalism. Churchmen enjoyed a place alongside the warriors rather than peasants. Only "workers" would pay taxes, and serfs could not aspire to the priesthood. The wealthiest families took the most prestigious Church appointments, which were in the gift of the great. Between one-fifth and one-third of landed property was in Church hands, and administered under feudal forms of land management. The Church collected its tithes on agricul-

"We who were Occidentals have now been made Orientals. He who was a Roman or a Frank is now a Galilean ... We have already forgotten the place of our birth". The mournful comments of a chaplain attached to the court of the kingdom of Jerusalem in the early twelfth century highlight the culture shock which many French knights experienced on their contact with the Holy Land in the Crusades.

They combated alienation in a strange land by bringing with them fragments of their own culture. In present-day Syria the mighty Krak des Chevaliers, the Parthenon of crusader castles, bears witness to this. The building of castles in stone had begun in Europe in the late tenth and early eleventh century, and the architectural lessons learnt in France – and added to by Byzantine and Arab influences – are

Krak des Chevaliers

evident in Krak's design. Some of the architectural features of the inner buildings also recall Gothic styles. In time, the architectural traffic would be two-way. The experience of the East strongly influenced European castle design.

Krak stands on a high spur and, with a network of similar castles, commands valley entrances to its south and east. Built on the site of a native fortress, which was captured in 1099 by the French knight Raymond de Saint-Gilles, the main work of fortification was done in the twelfth century, though the outer walls were completed only in the thirteenth. In 1142 the count of Tripoli handed it over to the Knight Hospitallers of Saint John, the crusad-

ing order whose members dedicated their lives to succouring the needy and fighting in the Holy Land.

"A bone in the throat of the Moslems," in the view of one Arab writer, Krak was a deterrent against Arab occupation of the region. Even Saladin forbore to lay siege to it. The castle was also – like its French parallels – a satisfying symbol of feudal power; it towered over a fertile valley "rich in every kind of produce", according to one French chronicler. The Knights constructed a windmill on its battlements, as an ostentatious reminder that it had the wherewithal to withstand any siege. Krak's eventual fall in 1271 was due to undermanning. A castle that had housed several thousand knights in the early twelfth century was defended by only a couple of hundred.

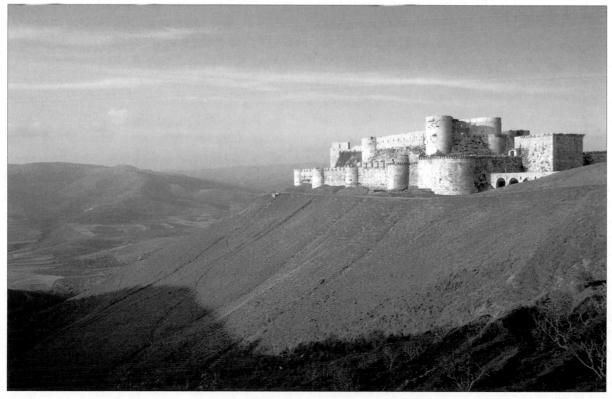

Krak des Chevaliers ("Krak of the Knights").

brought under crusader control, and though in 1192 Saladin agreed to allow Christian pilgrims free access to Jerusalem, the city stayed out of crusader hands.

With the exception of the Fifth Crusade (1218–21), when Jerusalem was partially reoccupied – through negotiations rather than by feats of arms – the city remained tantalizingly out of reach. Moreover, material motives, never far distant from the heart of the crusading movement, became increasingly important in strategic planning and execution. The Fourth Crusade (1202–4) ended in utter fiasco, because the crusading force was wrongly rerouted towards Constantinople, which it proceeded to put to fire and sword. The last century of the Crusades saw more and more desperate attempts to deal with the problems in the Holy Land by attacking the power-base of Egypt: "The keys to Jerusalem," it was said, "are to be found in Cairo." The campaigns ran into the sand on reaching the North African coast.

Crusading served Capetian dynastic interests well. It channelled knightly energies away from France, thereby reducing levels of internal violence. The spirit of plunder could be exercised at the expense of infidels rather than Christians, foreigners rather than the French. "Before the Christians started for the lands beyond the seas," noted the Benedictine monk Guibert de Nogent, "the kingdom of France was prey to perpetual disturbance and hostilities." The movement also helped to develop solidarity and shared values among the feudal class, and accustomed even the greatest feudal lords to a Capetian leadership which was becoming a tangible reality.

Saladin (1138–93), sultan of Egypt and Syria, from a Persian painting of *c.* 1180. Perhaps the most formidable of the crusaders' enemies, he preached a holy war against the infidel in order to unite the Arab peoples, but combined this with a chivalric generosity towards the weak.

THE RISE OF CAPETIAN KINGSHIP

By the end of the thirteenth century the French monarchy had come a long way since the days of the first Capetians, who had seemed at times the playthings of their more powerful magnates. Unable to count on naked coercion to have themselves obeyed – in 1100, for example, the counts of Flanders could field an army of vassals 50 per cent larger than that of the kings of France – successive Capetians were obliged to play to different strengths. In particular, they focused on one of the principal differences between them and even their most powerful subjects, namely, the sacral character of monarchy. Kings and churchmen used this as a propaganda weapon for dynastic prestige. They cleverly yoked together Merovingian and Carolingian traditions, to make of a Capetian coronation something similar to a bishop's consecration. It was a sacramental event marked – following the precedent of Pepin in 751–4 – by the monarch's anointment with holy oil. Not only did they thereby rule "by the grace of God",

The flower of French chivalry, commanded by Saint Louis, attacking and taking the Egyptian city of Damietta, during the Seventh Crusade in 1249. The crusade foundered in 1251, when Saint Louis was taken captive. He was not ransomed until 1254.

Reims cathedral

The famous "smiling angel" greets the entrant to the cathedral at Reims, generally acknowledged as one of the finest Gothic monuments of the French Middle Ages. Constructed from 1211 onwards, it is a typical product of the great period of cathedral building. Chartres might have more impressive stained glass, and the architectural merits of a number of other cathedrals may surpass Reims, but Reims' profusely abundant statuary – the other main component of the Gothic style – is particularly outstanding. The product of a number of sculptors' workshops, it influenced ecclesiastical buildings from Assisi to Westminster, and from Burgos to Strasbourg.

The Capetian dynasty was closely associated with the Gothic style – and with Reims in particular. The style's

innovator and champion, Abbot Suger of Saint-Denis, was a particularly potent and imaginative propagandist of the Capetian line. The style was widely referred to as *opus francigenum* – "Franks' work". The Gothic's conquest of Europe enhanced the dynasty's ideological lustre.

Reims was, along with the Abbey of Saint-Denis and Notre-Dame cathedral, one of the three key symbolic sites associated with the Capetians. Saint-Denis was where the kings of France since Dagobert I had been buried. Paris was the home of the living monarch, who took mass at Notre-Dame. Reims, in turn, was where Capetians were made kings, and were infused with divine grace. Clovis, the first Frankish king, with whom the Capetians were proud to claim continuity, had been crowned here by Saint Rémy, archbishop of

Reims. From the ninth century, it was claimed that a dove had descended from the heavens bearing in an ampulla oil for sacred unction. Miraculously, the oil never dried up, and successive kings of France were anointed with it. At Reims, too, the king became a miracle-worker: by receiving divine unction, he could henceforth cure by his touch individuals afflicted with "the King's Evil" (that is, scrofula).

By the reign of Saint Louis, a complex web of symbolic acts and associations had hardened into a "timeless" tradition which no monarch would wish to break. Reims cathedral thus became a "site of memory" (Pierre Nora) for the dynasty and, by extension, for the king's subjects. It was to remain in use for coronations down to 1825, when the last descendant of the Capetians to reign, Charles X, was crowned here.

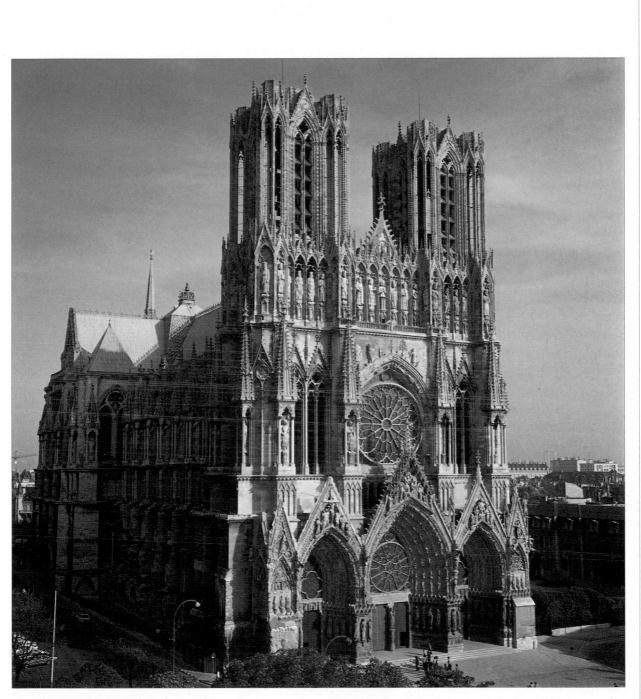

Left The smiling angel of Reims cathedral.

Above left This medieval illustration shows Clovis being at once baptized and anointed as a ruler, as a dove descends from heaven bearing an ampulla of sacred oil. As a result of this sacramental event at Reims, the monarch acquired the power of the "royal touch".

Above Reims cathedral, coronation church of the kings of France.

Simon de Montfort (*c.* 1160–1218) had been a crusader in the East before leading the internal crusade against the Albigensian heresy in the Midi in 1209. Killed while besieging Toulouse, his tomb is located in the cathedral of Carcassonne.

Lionheart (king of England 1189–99) in the Third Crusade, he returned early from the East to stir up Richard's French vassals against him. Aware of the Capetian threat, Richard had the massive fortress Château-Gaillard built on the approaches to his Norman lands, and in 1198/9 joined forces with Baldwin of Flanders to bring Philip under control. Philip bounced back, however, against Richard's brother and successor, John (king of England 1199–1217). In 1202, over a petty feudal dispute, Philip invoked his authority as John's suzerain to declare him a felonious vassal for failing to answer charges made against him in his court, and ordered the confiscation of his lands. He moved militarily against John, overcoming resistance at Château-Gaillard and bringing Normandy under his control in 1204. By 1206, he had won Anjou, Maine, Touraine and Brittany, as well as Poitou and the Auvergne.

The English did not give in gracefully. Capetian expansion in northern France (notably in Artois and Picardy) had provoked local hostility, and John joined the counts of Flanders and Boulogne and the German emperor in an anti-Capetian coalition. In 1214, in the Battle of Bouvines, Philip defeated the allied forces, and in the subsequent Treaty of Chinon (1214), John was forced to accept Capetian gains. Fighting rumbled on during the thirteenth century under Philip's successors, Louis VIII (r. 1223–6), Louis IX or "Saint Louis" (r. 1226–70), Philip III (r. 1270–85) and Philip IV the Fair (r. 1285–1314). The pendulum continued to swing in France's favour. In the Treaty of Paris in 1259, Henry III of England formally recognized the Capetians' annexation of all former English possessions except the Guyenne, and this was largely ratified in the Treaty of Montreuil in 1299.

Philip Augustus had broken the back of Angevin power and increased Capetian territories fourfold. His successors not only continued his work but also acted to extend the dynasty's power in the Mediterreanean south. In the sprawling lands of the powerful counts of Toulouse, heresy had taken deep root in the twelfth century. The Waldensian heretics – whose name derived from their founder, the Lyon merchant Valdes – preached forms of apostolic poverty and attacked hierarchy and wealth within the Church. More widespread was the so-called Albigensian heresy of the Cathars, centring on lands between Albi, Carcassonne and Toulouse. The Cathars believed in a form of dualism in which the material world was intrinsically evil, and only an elite of "perfects" could aspire to a life of purity. This left little room for conventional Christian belief or for the Catholic clergy. The "perfects" were widely venerated among the peasantry, while the movement's anti-clerical strain won it support from an elite irritated by the presumptions of Church power. Cistercian preaching missions led by Saint Bernard of Clairvaux had failed to nip the Cathar movement in the bud. In 1208 Pope Innocent III pronounced the Cathars more dangerous than the Saracens.

Philip Augustus was too involved with the Angevin struggle to lend open support to moves against the Cathars, but he did give tacit encouragement to a warband of marauding northern knights led by Simon de Montfort, who in 1209 attacked the count of Toulouse for protecting the heresy. This internal crusade was waged with heartless ferocity – "Kill them all," a papal legate ordered the northern knights on taking Béziers. "God will recognize His own." De Montfort assumed provisional control over the lands of the count of Toulouse, but it was Louis VIII who reaped the fruits of this vicarious northern victory. In 1224, the king purchased rights to the countship from de Montfort's heir; then in 1226 he led an expedition southwards with papal blessing, capturing Avignon *en route* and forcing all of Languedoc to acknowledge his rule. Further hostilities led to a compromise peace in 1229, organized by the young Louis IX's regent, his mother Blanche of Castile. The Venaissin county surrounding Avignon was ceded to the papacy. The Capetians retained most of Lower Languedoc for themselves, while Poitou and Auvergne were ceded to Louis IX's brother, Alphonse of Poitiers. Louis IX secured his position in the Midi in the Treaty of Corbeil with the king of Aragon in 1258: Louis renounced suzerainty over Catalonia and the Roussillon in return for Aragon's renunciation of claims in Toulouse and Provence. The area of the Spanish march, a Carolingian before a Capetian possession, had been losing touch with the rest of France since the twelfth century at least. This agreement helped to fix the limits of Capetian power on the Iberian frontier.

STATE AND SOCIETY

Both the geography and the consistency of Capetian power had been transformed between the tenth and early fourteenth centuries. The territories directly administered by the Capetians had grown enormously. Hugh Capet had enjoyed prestige as the vessel of sacral power and as feudal overlord of West Francia; Philip the Fair, by contrast, was the proud, even arrogant monarch of the most important state in western Europe. This was especially true now that, after the death of Frederick Barbarossa (emperor 1152–90), the Holy Roman Empire in eastern Europe was fragmenting under internal and external pressures.

The star of kingship had risen immeasurably high in France. Rulers still accentuated both the sacral and seigneurial sources of their power. Renewed interest in classical antiquity in the twelfth and thirteenth centuries, moreover, had led to the development of Roman Law, and a growing elaboration of the concept of sovereignty. It made of the monarch not just a feudal suzerain but also an heir of Roman *imperium*, who, as "emperor in his own country", as the phrase went, was responsible for the common good throughout the realm. From Saint Louis onwards, this included the power to legislate. That Philip II took the assumed name "Augustus" was symptomatic of the shift in the base of monarchical power. So was the monarchy's concern with coinage. Efforts to reduce the legal status of coins minted by others were supplemented in 1266 by Saint Louis' introduction of the large silver coin known as the *livre tournois*, which was to be the basis of French currency thereafter. The circulation of images of royalty prevailed over those of their mightiest subjects and was closely connected with the realm's new-found prosperity. The development of a large royal court wedded to conspicuous consumption and display also underlined changes in representations of monarchical power. The court of Philip V (r. 1316–22), for example, numbered 5,000 individuals, making it as large as a medium-sized city.

The growth of the court was part of the more general progress in state formation. The expansion of Capetian power made new bureaucratic demands: crown tax revenue grew by 80 per cent under Philip Augustus between 1180 and 1203, and as much again once the dynasty acquired Angevin possessions. Saint Louis and Philip IV, in particular, helped to develop the state's bureaucracy. Accountancy and archival procedures were improved. Clerks of the royal household were grouped into a chamber of accounts, while others specializing in judicial affairs became institutionalized as the parlement, which served as the monarch's final court of appeal. The standards of justice which the university-trained legists offered within the parlement were widely viewed as superior to those of the feudal lords. The role of the parlement was supplemented in the provinces by the network of salaried royal judicial officials, known as *baillis* (the title *sénéchal* was used in the Midi). Such officials had long been sent out spasmodically, but from 1190 they were assigned fixed places of residence. In addition, their powers – notably in supervising local administration and legal process, in representing the king and in transmitting his orders – were more carefully defined.

The extension of Capetian authority was accompanied by a number of practices which set pragmatic bounds to central power. These included the custom of bequeathing territories to the control of close relatives of the monarch in the form of "appanages", as they were known. On his death in 1226, Louis VIII made his sons appanages of Artois, Anjou, Maine, Poitou and the Auvergne. Such cessions – continued by his successors – were usually made on the understanding that the territory would revert to the crown if a line became extinct. This meant a delay of variable length. The vast sprawling appanage of the Poitou, ceded to Louis IX's brother Alphonse of Poitiers, reverted to the crown when the latter died childless in 1271. In other cases the

Royal legislation, municipal regulations and cultural interdicts aimed to keep lepers at a distance. In this fourteenth-century illumination a leper, complete with clappers to warn of his presence and begging-bowl, seeks urban alms alongside a disabled beggar.

reversion could take longer: Artois and Anjou, ceded in appanage in 1226, only reverted to the crown centuries later.

The growth of royal administration was accompanied by the revived notion of the monarch as fount of justice. This was no longer merely a feudal justice benefiting only the great and the good, but a fairer, more accessible form of justice. The memorable (and probably apocryphal) story of Saint Louis, seated under an oak tree in the forest of Vincennes, dispensing justice to all-comers, was endlessly recycled after being cited in Joinville's idealized account of the king's life. Saint Louis owed much of his repute to his saintly qualities. As well as professing a personal piety, he also acted the part of the crusader monarch both in the East and at home, where he completed the rout of the Albigensian heretics.

As this example suggests, the rise of Capetian monarchy, and its increasing emphasis on the sanctity of centralized justice, was accompanied by a growing intolerance towards a wide range of forms of dissidence and non-conformity. Like his father (who had at one stage exiled all Jews from the kingdom), Saint Louis introduced stringent anti-Semitic measures. Coercive measures were taken against lepers, too, to ensure they were placed in leper-houses. The rituals of confinement condemned sufferers from the disease to a form of living death, shutting them away from the rest of society. Sexual deviance was frowned on too. Prostitutes were more or less equated with lepers, and formally banned. (Saint Louis' successors would take a different tack, subjecting prostitutes to religious surveillance and regulation, which sometimes led to their being confined to certain areas of the city, as Jews with their ghettos.)

Sex was a particular anxiety, and the tendency was to project that anxiety on to women. Reform of the Church – notably the growing emphasis on clerical chastity – contributed to a worsening of their status. The idealization of "Woman" in courtly love literature, and in the growing cult of the Virgin Mary, centred on sexual purity rather than indulgence, and related the exception rather than the rule. For clerics now obsessed with their own chastity, women were a danger to be avoided – "sacks of shit", as one cleric charmingly put it; "mad dogs," stated another. The male-centred stance of the clerical elite may have helped to drive some women towards religious hetero-doxy. Women were, it seems, particularly drawn to Catharism, which envisaged both men and women being able to achieve spiritual perfection, and a number of other, more sexually liberal sects and heresies. Women had always been excluded from war-fare and the priesthood – the *bellatores* and *oratores* were uniquely masculine. They were also now excluded from the literate elite who formed the state bureaucracy and the liberal professions: indeed, the professionalization of government severely reduced the influence of highly placed females.

Church and state had combined their forces in the eleventh and twelfth centuries to construct a new matrimonial order. Marriage was a sacrament and the regular civil means of contracting alliances. The rules of feudal property-holding increasingly made of women from aristocratic backgrounds pawns on the feudal chessboard – the dowries they brought with them were seen as components of the male-administered system of inheritance. On the other hand, those who did not fit well enough into family property calculations were dispatched to nunneries. In fact, some women from within the social elite were still able to use their powers as wives, widows and mothers within the public sphere. Many, for example, simply took over all the administrative aspects of property when their men went crusading. Blanche of Castile, the mother of Saint Louis, who stood in for her son on several occasions during his reign, is a case in point. Similarly, there were many aristocratic women who still turned disadvantage to their favour, making their vocation within religious orders a spring-board for religious and sometimes political power.

Women, then, were only rarely and exceptionally allowed a voice. This contrasted all the more strikingly with men; for one of the characteristic features of state develop-

Chartered towns had extensive rights of local justice. In this folkloric case from Toulouse a pair of adulterers, chained together by their errant members, walk the streets in shame to the sound of the trumpet.

ment in this period was the rise of new methods of consultation and representation. Rulers in the past had consulted with magnates and prelates on matters of state as part of the feudal rite of *consilium*. In 1302 Philip the Fair formally convened the three estates of the realm – clergy, nobility and "Third Estate," or town representatives – specifically for this purpose. The Estates General, as it became, was France's national representative body down to 1789. A sounding-board and intelligence-gatherer of some importance, the Estates formed a pragmatic means of consulting the wider (male) political community, in order to acquire – maybe even to manufacture – consent for royal policy.

Other measures highlighted the dynasty's willingness to seek accommodation with the constituent parts of French society. The practice of consultation in the Estates General was extended by the development of provincial Estates later in the fourteenth century. Monarchs also ratified local legal custom: the codes of the Vermandois region

King Philip the Fair, depicted taking counsel. This imperious monarch was the first to consult systematically with representative bodies throughout the realm as a means of gauging opinion and seeking community approval for his acts. The lords spiritual and temporal are shown, together with their coats of arms.

and the Beauvaisis were given the seal of approval in the late thirteenth century, for example. Even from the eleventh century, the Capetians had also been profligate in granting municipal charters. In return for receiving royal protection, towns were accorded financial and judicial privileges.

The monarchy's use of these political mechanisms testified to a perceived need to keep abreast of opinion throughout the land, not just the views of feudal leaders. In 1303, for example, Philip presented for approval to the Estates the first permanent taxes of the Capetian monarchy. Levied on merchandise, but also including a substitution tax for non-performance of military service, the taxes proved difficult to collect, but they did mark an important stage in the development of relationships between state and society.

Finance was also at issue in another matter which came before early meetings of the Estates, namely, religion. The "Most Christian Kings" did not take kindly to even a pope interfering with royal prerogatives. Even the saintly Louis IX had proved staunch in the defence of the French Church, and his own rights within it. The growth in the strength of the papacy in the late thirteenth century, after the collapse of the Holy Roman Emperor's power and the conclusion of the Albigensian crusade, brought fresh strains. Relations took a turn for the worst when an attempt by Philip the Fair to increase taxes on the clergy led to violent denunciation by Pope Boniface VIII (pope 1294–1303). National and provincial Estates swung dutifully in line behind their king. The dispute got out of hand when Philip seized Boniface at Agnani, and the pope died on his hands from shock. The election in 1305 of a French pope, who in 1309 established his residence in Avignon, tipped the balance in the dynasty's favour.

Finance and religion were also intertwined in the king's attack on the Knights Templar. This crusading order had developed a lucrative sideline as international financiers, and in order to secure their wealth and contacts Philip the Fair had their leaders arrested in 1307 on certainly trumped-up charges. After a sensational show trial, he had them executed and the order dissolved, with their property passing into the royal treasury. Royal power was certainly pragmatic; it could also still be brutal.

THE "NEW SPRING": THE MEDIEVAL ECONOMY

The period from the late twelfth to the early fourteenth century, which witnessed the growth of Capetian power, produced in France, as in most of western Europe, a phase of brilliant social and economic progress, a "new spring" (G. Duby). Indeed the rate of economic expansion from 1180 to 1220 was probably unsurpassed until the eighteenth century. Climatic improvement may have made a contribution to better harvests – a warmer, less rainy long-term phase set in after about 1160 – though it was hardly a determining factor. An increased injection of precious metals into the European economy may also have played a part – imports of gold and silver from West Africa and the Near East were accompanied by the growth of silver-mining within Europe, notably in Saxony, Bohemia, Spain and even France's Massif Central. The halting of Viking, Saracen and Magyar raids helped too, since the disruption these had caused probably delayed economic growth in many areas. The Auvergne, which had been spared such raids, enjoyed boom conditions as early as the ninth and tenth centuries, while the upturn was much slower in Provence, which had been particularly severely affected by Saracen raiding.

Technological improvements were a further spur to economic growth. Not only were new methods and techniques invented, but their use became more widespread more quickly. The spread of heavier wheeled ploughs, combined with more effective methods of harnessing draught-animals, improved the productivity of arable land, especially in the north. The introduction of triennial rotation of crops probably helped here too. Windmills, pioneered in Normandy in the late twelfth century, and watermills also became more common: there were 245 of the latter in Picardy alone by about 1175, and perhaps 20,000 in France as a whole. As well as processing food, water power was put to industrial use, driving hammers or bellows, for example. The spread

The public burning, after torture, of Jacques du Molay, master of the Knights Templar, in 1314. A crusading order, whose members took monastic vows and who lived as soldiers, defending the Holy Places and guarding the rights of pilgrims, the Templars had developed skills in high finance. Their wealth and influence attracted the wrath of Philip the Fair.

of the use of the domestic spinning wheel was another factor boosting manufacturing production. Better techniques in mining and metallurgy were introduced, producing not only better arms and armour but also stronger and more resilient ploughs, agricultural implements and tools. Incremental technological innovations – the compass began to be used from the twelfth century, for example – also made for more navigable and more capacious ships.

Economic growth and diversification were closely linked to a massive rise in population. France, in its present-day frontiers, had a population of perhaps 7.5 to 9 million under Charlemagne, though this had probably fallen to about 5 or 6 million by the time Hugh Capet came to power in 987. By the time of the last Capetians, in 1328, it stood at between 18 and 21 million, perhaps 15 million of whom were directly under French kings. These figures could be compared with England's 3 to 3.5 million, or the 8 to 10 million in the Italian peninsula.

This rough tripling in population over three centuries was bound up with changes in the organization of the economy. The links were complex and reciprocal. Extra mouths gave an incentive to produce more food to peasant farmers, who, as serfs, owned their land, albeit under feudal conditions. Meanwhile extra hands, in what was still a very labour-intensive economy, allowed more to be produced. Certainly a great deal more land was brought under cultivation. Perhaps half of France's total landmass had been forest in 987; this was massively reduced. French monarchs from Philip Augustus onwards introduced surveillance measures on royal forests, suggesting that land reclamation on such a scale needed some regulation. The forms that land extension took were manifold. Some monastic orders, like the Cistercians, were specialists in colonizing large tracts of wilderness far distant from civilization. Hence Saint Norbert, founding a house at Saint-Gobain in 1120, deliberately chose "a fearful

Blanche of Castile

The daughter of Alfonso VIII of Castile, and granddaughter of Eleanor of Aquitaine, Blanche of Castile (1188–1252) was married at twelve years old in 1200 to the future Louis VIII (r. 1223–6). Her husband named her in his will as guide and adviser to their son. She served as regent from 1226 to 1234 while Louis IX (r. 1226–70) was a minor, remained close to the centre of government through to 1244, and then stood in again for her son from 1248 to 1252 when he was on crusade. She frustrated repeated attempts to foment rebellion by powerful nobles, who held that "a woman should not govern so great a thing as the kingdom of France". On occasion, she placed herself at the head of royal armies. She also ensured governmental continuity and responsible support in all her son's major administrative reforms – a son whose political achievements have eclipsed her own.

Saint Louis' chronicler Joinville emphasized Blanche's bad relations with Louis' queen, Marguerite of Provence, so that she has been regarded as the classic difficult mother-in-law. In fact Blanche placed great stress on the religious side of mothering, and took personal charge of her children's education. That her eldest son was canonized, a daughter (Isabella) beatified, and that she herself was regarded as a saint augmented the lustre of the Capetian dynasty. The chronicler who commented that she ruled as well as a man was paying her the ultimate backhanded accolade.

Blanche of Castile, with the young Louis IX at his books. From a fourteenth-century manuscript.

solitude … a fetid marshland, sterile and uncultivable heath, the home of fevers and wild beasts". Much land reclamation, however, amounted to little more than the extension of cultivation to wasteland and scrub on the margins of the village. Five-sixths of land reclaimed in Picardy, for example, took this form.

The result was a transformation of the physical character of the landscape. Bread was the staple foodstuff of nine out of ten French men and women, and farming patterns reflected this. In the north and north-east, the open-field system of cereal cultivation firmly established itself. Dwellings were often clumped together around a central hub – a form of habitation favoured by new communities that were formed in virgin territories. About 500 *villeneuves*, as the new communities were called, were created in the Paris basin. In Aquitaine, where they were called *bastides*, 600 took root. France was also endowed with over 1,000 leper houses during this period, and these frequently took the form of agricultural colonies. Reclaiming land involved draining marshes as well as chopping down trees: the construction of dike-systems for this purpose developed in Flanders, and it subsequently spread to the lower Somme, the Seine, and the marshlands of Poitou, Brittany and the Camargue. These developments put the finishing touches to the creation of the network of 30,000-odd villages within which French rural history – and indeed French history full stop – has been lived out to the present day.

The vast extension of cultivable land was not a straightforward exercise in supply and demand of land and labour. Existing structures of feudal power loomed large in the initiation and conduct of these enterprises. The days of the booty economy were passing, for the Crusades had failed to provide a long-term theatre for military pillage. The costs of military hardware spiralled upwards – the sophisticated protective mail-shirt required by knights cost the price of a farm in the late eleventh century. Many a crusader had to sell up in order to afford to campaign in the Orient. Changes in aristocratic lifestyle also provided an incentive to adapt; the round of hunts, tournaments, feasts and courtly entertainments was becoming increasingly expensive. Seigneurs, then, were motivated to make their rural power pay more. Those who failed to adapt risked losing everything, and the period saw the decline, for example, of many petty castellans who, attached to the military aspects of their status, still held out hopes of living from plunder.

The growth of agrarian productivity in the medieval period owed much, then, to the pressure which the seigneurial class put on their peasants. Wherever one looked, feudal rapaciousness was close at hand. Seigneurs might agree to marginal extensions of land, for example, on condition that peasants paid them extra levies. The more ambitious among them invited peasants to reclaim land, offering them incentives, tax privileges and exemptions from seigneurial dues – even, on occasion, livestock and tools. The prosperous seigneur now not only collected dues and taxes on all aspects of the lives of the peasants within his domains; he also exploited his control of the local mill-house, bakehouse and winepress; pastureland and forest were often under his control, too; and he regulated all aspects of economic activity in the locality. Rather than using feudal labour services as a means of having his domain land farmed, he often preferred to lease this out to local peasants under sharecropping (*métayage*) or money-rent arrangements. Other seigneurial dues and levies might be commuted to cash too. As a result, feudal lords were changing from agricultural producers in their own right to *rentiers* – receivers of rents and dues. The extensive legal rights and judicial powers that they continued to enjoy helped to ensure that they creamed off the best part of peasant surplus.

Increased seigneurial rapaciousness acted as an incentive in peasant agriculture, too, spurring innovation and diversification. Cereal productivity registered real progress. Other sectors of the rural economy also benefited. Wool became a particular area of speciality, especially as the cloth trade expanded. Lay lords and bishops were also closely involved in the development of winegrowing. Salt and metal production

Illumination of the letter Q, from a Burgundian manuscript representing the life and activities of Cistercian monks, who are shown roughly clad in brown (they later switched to white). In the early days the monastic communities were entirely self-supporting.

boomed. Though the main beneficiaries of economic expansion were drawn from the social elite, many peasants, too, enjoyed an improvement in their lot. Those in particular who produced a marketable surplus benefited enormously. Village communities proved adept at winning privileges from their lords, so the seigneurial burden may have lightened in some areas.

With the raiding and pillaging of the ninth and tenth centuries at an end, towns too could now come out of their shell. The period from 1100 to 1300 produced an urban growth more dramatic than anything since Roman times. Whereas early medieval cities had been essentially religious and military centres, they now developed above all through their economic functions. They looked to river and sea for expansion and

The economy of medieval France

Bruges
Calais · Ypres · Lille
Arras · Cambrai
Amiens · St. Quentin
Rouen · Beauvais · Noyon · Laon · Verdun · Metz
Bayeux · Coutances · Lendit · Soissons · Reims · Toul · Strasbourg
Caen · Evreux · Senlis · Meaux · Chalons
Mt. St-Michel · **Paris** · Lagny · Colmar
Dol · Chartres · Provins · Troyes · Epinal
Quimper · Rennes · Le Mans · Orléans · Sens · Bar · Langres
Vannes · Angers · Blois · Auxerre · Semur · Besançon
Nantes · Tours · Dijon
Bourges · Nevers · Autun
Poitiers · Moulins · Chalon · Mâcon · Geneva
La Rochelle · Limoges · Lyon
Saintes · Angoulême · Clermont-Fd · Vienne
Périgueux · Le Puy · Grenoble
Bordeaux · Puy-St.-Front
Cahors · Rodez
Agen · Montauban
Bayonne · Albi · Pézenas · Nîmes · Carpentras · Aix
Auch · Toulouse · Montpellier · Avignon · Marseille
Orthez · Béziers · Narbonne
Perpignan
Barcelona

→— Main trade route	▓ Wine production	■ Champagne fair	• Main Gothic church outside Paris environs
▓ Cloth production	░ Salt production	▢ Other major fair	○ Town of Gallo-Roman origin
			● Town of medieval origin

The economic geography of medieval France highlighted the importance of the Paris region. Conveniently placed to benefit from the booming Champagne fairs and the cloth-making region of Flanders, it was an important grain- and wine-growing region and was also situated on major currents of commerce. The city of Paris was only the most important in a burgeoning network of medieval urban centres, most of which could trace their origins back to the Roman Empire or beyond.

wealth. Of the cities with more than 20,000 inhabitants in the thirteenth century, Paris, Ghent, Ypres, Toulouse, Strasbourg, Tours, Orléans, Lyon, Lille and Metz all commanded important waterways, while Bruges, Rouen, Saint-Omer, Montpellier, Narbonne and Bordeaux all turned resolutely towards the sea.

The feudal elite had such a powerful hold over the levers of economic power at the height of the Middle Ages that they inevitably influenced the development of towns. Lords, increasingly sensitive to market potential, realized that the presence of towns and fairs attracted wealth into the region which they could tap through tolls and other dues. The stone castles from which truculent castellans had defied authority and coerced peasants from the tenth century often came to house local markets. Patterns of castle building reveal a growing symbiosis between feudal power and mercantile exchange. Fortified walls were extended so that merchant houses and artisans' dwellings could nestle up against feudal keeps. Mercantile wealth came to be a kind of life-support system for a feudal nobility ever more alert to the high costs of the aristocratic lifestyle. Demand for luxury goods and services among the nobility also attracted many craftsmen to the towns that were growing up in the shadow of the castle. There, these artisans would transform the raw materials bought at the markets into desirable luxury commodities. Much the same was true in towns with resident bishops and monasteries. The upper clergy were among the most conspicuous of consumers, and made important contributions to urban development and diversification.

In this context, the old three way division of society into "worshippers", "warriors" and "workers" was beginning to look archaic even as it became fully established. The military and ecclesiastical elites still held sway within society, but the "Third Estate" label hid a wide spectrum of existences. Social differentiation on the land had given rise to a small elite of peasant producers who were doing well by marketing their surplus. Their status contrasted with the majority of rural workers, who hardly produced enough for themselves to eat. In the towns the arrogant disdain of lay lords and prelates now had to accommodate the presence of the wealthy merchant and manufacturer. The appearance of the grasping merchant as a stock figure in medieval sermons and literature reveals the growing importance of a social mobility which found no place within the fixed categories of feudal society. Other social groupings were also emerging. In particular, a strong service sector was making its presence felt: churchmen, scribes, judges, medical men, property stewards, notaries – all contributed to the diversity of the urban milieu, as did the growing numbers of state officials.

Public law could accommodate these emerging social categories through the extension of corporative privileges. Just as provinces were having their legal customs endorsed by the state, so towns and the economic and work-related groupings within them were accorded legal personality, and given extensive rights of self-regulation. In 1268 there were no fewer than 100 recognized guilds in the city of Paris alone. France was becoming – like its European counterparts – a *Ständestaat*, a "society of orders", in which the social tissue was composed of many corporative bodies, all with their own rights and privileges enshrined in public law.

Seal of the commune of Meulan, 1195. The collective portrait of the founding officials sits below the royal fleur-de-lis. The seal, the treasure-chest, the bell, and communal property (notably the town hall) were the four characteristic attributes of communal authority.

Although many towns had started life as the poodle of the local feudal lord, they were soon straining at the leash, and bidding to establish freedom and autonomy. Associations of town-dwellers, or "communes", bound together by an oath of frater-nity rather than an act of feudal homage, petitioned the monarch for rights of self-government. The city of Le Mans was the first to make such a bid, in 1070. Lay and Church authorities often looked askance at such movements – communes were "tur-bulent conspiracies" in the view of one churchman, "violent and pestilential" accord-ing to another – and towns did indeed sometimes harbour heretical religious movements. Yet the feudal elite soon discovered how to turn the communes to their own account. Thibaut IV, count of Champagne in the early thirteenth century, it was said, "established communes of burghers and peasants in whom he trusted more than his own knights". The Capetians were also especially adept at using the establishment of communes as a way of extending their own authority and at the same time disad-vantaging rival lords. Louis VI was known as "the father of the communes" in recogni-tion of the large number of such municipal franchises he granted, including Laon, Beauvais, Noyon, Soissons and Reims.

This development sparked some ferocious power-struggles. In Laon in 1112, the local bourgeois seeking a municipal charter even murdered their own bishop. A "battle of the bells" sometimes ensued, with the town-hall clock, which chimed out a "time of the merchants", competing with the "time of the church" struck out by church bells (Le Goff). Tension was less acute in the cities of the Midi, which already had strong tra-ditions of municipal institutions and where local nobles and bourgeois proved more compatible bedfellows. Brittany, in contrast, had no municipal institutions whatever before the fifteenth century. But, in general terms, such struggles demonstrated that the feudal nobility could no longer count on having everything their own way.

MONARCHY, CULTURE AND REGIONALISM

France's economic boom in the twelfth and thirteenth centuries made it seem a kind of terrestrial paradise. The country, noted the chronicler Philippe Mouskes, "abounds in woods, rivers and meadows, in virgins and in beautiful women, in good wines and in redoubtable knights". Capetian propagandists claimed that economic prosperity was a direct reflection of the new-found strength and prestige of the dynasty. They did the same for France's cultural prowess, which was increasingly expressed through the medium of the French language. Under the Merovingians and Carolingians, Latin had been the only written language of consequence in the West. As Latin ceased to be spoken, local dialects boomed. French, with its roots in Latin, was originally Francian, the popular language of peasants and artisans of the Île-de-France. Yet it came to gain a wider European significance because of Capetian power, though Latin stayed in place as the language of the Church, the law-courts and the universities.

The international standing of the French language never rivalled Latin. Nevertheless, it was the official language of the social elite in England from the Norman invasion of 1066 down to the end of the thirteenth century; and it served the same pur-

The troubadours

"It was in Languedoc", Dante later noted, "that the users of living languages were first to essay poetry." Indeed, from roughly 1100 down to 1300 (but particularly from c. 1130 to c. 1200), a vernacular lyrical poetry developed in southern France. Troubadours, who combined poetry with musicianship, were drawn from every echelon of society: from wandering minstrel-acrobats up to such nobles as William, ninth duke of Aquitaine, who was allegedly the first practitioner. There were, moreover, trobairitzes – roughly twenty female troubadours are known.

"My lady tries me and tests me so she can know how I love her." This dictum of William of Aquitaine is symptomatic of the quest of the lover and his "lady" celebrated in troubadour literature. Love is celebrated between a usually idealized woman and her champion and lover – a relationship, it has been suggested, which reflected a common social reality, what with large numbers of un-propertied knights swarming around the households of the nobility. The erotic element in the relationship evidently clashed with the ethic promoted in orthodox Church teaching. In poetry by trobairitzes, too, there is often an element of mutual sensual gratification – as, for example, with Béatrice de Die, who mourns the loss

of her champion, and who remembers when

> Naked-armed I held him tight
> And pillowed on my breasts at night
> I gave him joy with my caress.

The vibrancy and apparent popularity of this school of poetry testified to the dynamism of the *langue d'oc* culture of the Midi. In time, it would influence aristocratic circles in the *langue d'oïl*: Eleanor of Aquitaine and her daughter Marie de Champagne were notable channels for the lyricism of troubadour poetry into the north. They also helped to formalize it into the conventions of courtly love, which placed less emphasis on sexual gratification than on the quest for the favours of a distant, idealized lady.

The placing of women on a pedestal, linked to the adoration of the Virgin Mary, corresponds with little that we know about the status of most women in medieval society. Indeed, it may be that the development of courtly love tells us less about women than men. Women's voices are increasingly absent from the poetry, and women figure essentially as objects of male passion. Courtly love was an arena in which new versions of masculinity – chivalrous, courageous, gentlemanly – could be constructed.

Juggler troubadours, eleventh century. At first, the troubadour was a warrior like other courtly figures.

pose in the Two Sicilies (the state comprising Sicily and the southernmost tip of the Italian peninsula) from the eleventh to the fifteenth century, and throughout the lives of the Frankish kingdoms in the Holy Land. By the thirteenth century, when its use in official documents highlighted its association with the dynasty, a French literature was beginning to appear. This included chronicles, such as the crusading yarns of Geoffroi de Villehardouin and Joinville's life of Saint Louis, and sundry religious works, but most famous of all was the tradition of romances in both poetry and prose. The famous "Song of Roland" (*c.*1100–25), with its Carolingian paladins, crusading heroics and chivalric ethos, was the most celebrated of the *chansons de geste*. More ambitious were the writings in the courtly love genre, whose most brilliant exponents were Guillaume

de Lorris and Jean de Meung, authors of the hugely popular mid-thirteenth-century *Roman de la Rose* ("Romance of the Rose"). French, cleric Nicolas Oresme proudly noted in the fourteenth century, had become "the noblest language in the world".

The language of the Paris region, then, was emerging as the language of French elites, if not yet the French community as a whole, which was still faithful to its distinctive languages and dialects. Paris' own intellectual prestige in the twelfth and thirteenth century played a part in this too. The largest city in western Christendom by 1300, the booming city was, in Pope Gregory IX's words, "wisdom's special workshop". Here, as in a number of other cities north of the Alps (Orléans, Chartres, Tours and so on), loose associations of individuals had, in the twelfth century, formed around teachers who were often linked with cathedral schools. These informal groupings gradually acquired the right to teach and, recognized by both pope and king, the Paris teaching community assumed corporative status as a "university". In the thirteenth century, it was divided into faculties of law, medicine and theology. Universities posed an alternative to the education conducted within monasteries. They were as good as their teachers – and Paris had the best of them, not least the brilliant and charismatic philosopher Peter Abelard, whose bold approach to theology brought to the city a cosmopolitan and boisterous student body attracted to working at what seemed to be the leading edge of knowledge.

The universities were the most brilliant product of the "Twelfth-Century Renaissance", which encompassed art, architecture, religious revival and vernacular literature as well as learning. Like its Carolingian forebear in the ninth century, the movement exemplified a revival of interest in the literature and culture of the Ancients, and in particular a fascination with the lay learning of the ancient world, which contact with Eastern and Arabic cultures had promoted. The Capetian dynasty buttressed the university movement: the development of the state bureaucracy and the opening up of law and royal service as alternative careers to the Church were important preconditions for their expansion. The Paris university's European reputation was strongest in the fields of theology and philosophy. Teachers attempted to reconcile the beliefs of Christianity with the learning of the ancient world. The Italian Thomas Aquinas, who taught here in the mid thirteenth century, provided a merger of Aristotelianism and Christian dogma that ultimately became Church orthodoxy down to the Scientific Revolution of the seventeenth century.

Gothic architecture constituted another medium in which Capetian power was expressed. Like the French tongue, it had originated as a model within the Île-de-France, and was closely associated with the dynasty. At the root of its emergence was, characteristically, royal propagandist Abbot Suger of Saint-Denis. In rebuilding the abbey church in the 1130s, he merged the pointed arch which had been in use in some Burgundian buildings with the ribbed vault derived from Anglo-Norman models. The style was used on the west front at Chartres cathedral in the 1140s, and the teams of builders employed there then moved on to Sens which, completed by the 1170s, was the first cathedral built in the Gothic style.

Opposite A folio from the *Breviari d'amor* of the Béziers monk Matfre Ermengaut (c. 1288). The text attempts to merge the eroticism of the courtly love tradition with the more spiritual love of orthodox Christianity. Demons stalk lovers (from the top downwards) in feasts, jousts, battle, dancing and courtship, and at the end (bottom right) a demon carries off the soul of the dying lover.

By then, the style was being used in a host of cathedrals – Noyon (1140–86), Senlis (1167–91), Laon (1150–1233), Chartres (in its entirety, following a fire, from the 1190s) and, from the 1160s, Notre-Dame in Paris. By the turn of the thirteenth century, the style was ranging more widely outside the Île-de-France: Amiens, Beauvais, Le Mans, Rouen, Sées, Coutances, Angers, Troyes, Reims, Strasbourg, Bourges and so on. Saint Louis' project of building the Sainte-Chapelle on the Île de la Cité in Paris to house Christ's crown of thorns gave the style a new prestige. Constructed in the 1240s the chapel exemplified the mix of architecture, sculpture and stained glass which had become the essence of the Gothic. The style also flourished in the wake of Capetian expansion in the Midi, appearing for example in Clermont, Rodez, Albi and Carcassonne, before spreading throughout Europe, from Uppsala to Famagusta.

The Capetians gained much prestige by association with the triumph of the Gothic in Europe, the growing pre-eminence of the French language, the acknowledged brilliance of Paris University, and the city's wealth and cultural élan. Yet to concentrate attention solely on Paris and the cultural developments associated with the dynasty would be to miss the economic diversity and cultural pluralism of medieval France.

France's strong economic performance in the Middle Ages can certainly not be reduced to the dynasty's achievements alone. France drew economic succour from sources of mercantile power outside its border, notably Flanders and north Italy, but also Catalonia and northern Germany, home of the powerful trading corporation, the Hanseatic League. French commerce was geared into wider European networks and trade did not follow the fleur-de-lis. The Rhine and the Rhône rivers – the one entirely outside France, the other on its margins – were key arteries of exchange for the French, as for the European economy. One of the most prosperous trading regions in France was Champagne, which from the 1130s became the junction-box connecting trading currents from Flanders and from northern Italy, the two power-houses of the medieval economy. The fairs held in succession over six weeks in the Champagne cities of Troyes, Lagny, Bar-sur-Aube and Provins developed into major international occasions of cultural as well as economic exchange. The cloth of the prime Italian and Flemish producers was present in abundance, as were goods from the Levant (spices, silks), the far North (Scandinavian timber goods, furs) and the South (Spanish leathers). In addition, exchange took place in services, notably the banking skills of Genoa, Florence and Lucca.

Many other parts of France still looked outwards to beyond national frontiers. The booming cities of French Flanders straddled the frontier with the Empire, and also linked up with the English economy: Dunkirk, for example, developed into a major port for Anglo-Flemish trade. In the south, the economic development of the Guyenne was inextricably connected to links with England through Bordeaux – the wine and salt trades were particular beneficiaries. In Lower Languedoc and Roussillon, the economy boomed under the kings of Aragon, with Perpignan emerging as a major cloth producer. The cities of the parts of eastern France under the power of the emperors also enjoyed economic prosperity. Haguenau was for a time an imperial residence, while

Opposite Poitou and the Dordogne contain a particularly fine range of Romanesque art. Notre-Dame-la-Grande in Poitiers, constructed between 1130 and 1145, has the most richly decorated façade in France. Romanesque architecture exemplified a wide range of cultural influences, and was often linked to the movements of religious revival in the tenth and eleventh centuries.

Gottfried of Strasbourg (d. 1230), here reading poetry before a princely court, was an important influence in transmitting the romance traditions of chivalric literature into Germany. The twenty thousand verses he wrote in his romance, *Tristan and Isolde*, formed the model for subsequent poetry.

Strasbourg, through trading links with central Germany and Switzerland, became a major international centre.

Diversity was the keynote in cultural development too. The French language, which prevailed in the long term, lagged behind as a form of purely literary expression. During the twelfth century more literary works were produced in France in languages and dialects other than Francian. Occitanian, the language most in evidence in the so-called *langue d'oc* in the Midi, was the medium in which an important troubadour literature developed. Languedoc and Provence witnessed the first flowering of the courtly love traditions. Although the movement did not survive the dogmatic intolerance introduced by the Albigensian crusade, it proved a strong influence on northern romance authors.

The French language had competition from inside the *langue d'oïl* as well as from the *langue d'oc*. Picard, a close relative of French, was still an important literary language, and the chronicler Froissart, for example, wrote in it. Chrétien de Troyes composed in a modified form of Champenois. In the west, Breton lays told tales of Arthur, Tristan and Isolde and the Holy Grail. In the east, Alsace enjoyed something of a cultural renaissance in the eleventh and twelfth centuries in the medium of German.

If the Capetian court stimulated the growth of culture, the same could be said of the courts of many great provincial magnates, who engaged in lively patronage of the arts.

Before the Champagne dynasty acceded to the kingdom of Navarre in 1234, the court of the counts of Champagne was a sterling patron of chivalric literature. It was here that Marie de Champagne, daughter of Eleanor of Aquitaine, commissioned the romance *Lancelot* from Chrétien de Troyes, for example – and Villehardouin and Joinville were active here too. Meanwhile the presence of the Cistercian headquarters at nearby Clairvaux stimulated a strong current of religious art and writing. Normandy was another culturally dynamic area. It had helped to proliferate the Romanesque architectural style, whose most outstanding buildings were far from the Île-de-France (notably in Burgundy and Auvergne, but also in Poitou, Périgord and Provence) and went on to play a key role in the spread of Gothic architecture. In the Midi the court of the counts of Toulouse was a centre for troubadour poetry – before it became a home for the Albigensian heresy. If Paris University retained its prime status as a centre for philosophy, other universities were active too. The medical faculty at Montpellier benefited from links with Arabic, Jewish and Greek scholarship, and developed into one of Europe's foremost centres of medical science and teaching. Universities at Toulouse (from 1229) and Avignon (1303) were also worthy of note.

There were, then, strong countervailing cultural and economic forces resisting the apparent dominance of northern, Capetian France. It was an important marker of cultural change, therefore, when, in 1328, following the death of the last Capetian, Charles IV, the succession was debated within the political elite. The claims of Edward III, king of England, to the French throne were generally resisted on the grounds that, as one writer put it, "the French did not admit without emotion the idea of being subject to England". The Capetian dynasty had constructed a notion of French identity within the political elite which benefited the French claimant to the throne, Philip, the Valois duke. Claims for the cultural unity of France were, however, to be sorely tested in the following century.

CHAPTER 5

Valois France: The Later Middle Ages and the Renaissance

The Capetian dynasty had helped to make France one of the foremost states in medieval Europe. However, all its achievements seemed in jeopardy in the centuries which followed. A great cycle of disease, famine and warfare unleashed countless problems on to the French state. In the darkest days of the Hundred Years War against England (1337–1453), the country's very viability seemed in question, and fragmentation, similar to that which Germany was undergoing, seemed possible. The dynasty survived (though it passed to the collateral Valois line), and was able once more to piece together a strong political system – one which put paid to English rivalry and consolidated its hold over French society. Soon, though, the reborn state was engaged in conflict against the Spanish and Austrian Habsburg house for European domination.

An illusory moment of brilliance – associated with the cultural stirrings of the Renaissance – was followed by conflict and division. The Reformation, instigated by Martin Luther in Germany in 1517, had the effect of splitting the religious unity of French society. Its impact was amplified by a fresh wave of civil strife, the Religious Wars (1561–98), from which the French state was lucky to emerge intact. Survival was finally achieved by a change of dynasty: the last Valois, Henry III, gave way to the first of the collateral Bourbon line, Henry IV.

FROM GOOD TIMES TO BAD

By 1328 the legendary good luck of the Capetians in their marriage bed had run out. A line of eleven uncontestable sons ground to a halt after the reign of Philip the Fair. His three children – Louis X (r. 1314–16), Philip V (r. 1316–22) and Charles IV (r. 1322–8) – ruled consecutively, but none could produce a durable male heir. The succession debate was eventually decided in favour of Philip de Valois, nephew of Philip the Fair, who took the title Philip VI (r. 1328–50).

The constitutional controversy that followed Philip de Valois' elevation to the throne illuminates the underlying drift of political priorities. There had been lawyers who argued that Edward III, Plantagenet king of England, had a superior claim – he was son of a daughter of Philip the Fair; the blood of Saint Louis ran in his veins too; and conventional laws of feudal succession would have allowed the title to be passed through a female, even if they prohibited women inheriting in their own names. But opposition to the English claim was grounded partly in an Anglophobia which highlights a growing sense of French identity among the political elite. Legal experts at court also retrospectively invoked the Salic Law of Clovis and the Franks, forbidding the transmission of kingship through females. The Salic Law had till then been little more than an antiquarian curio. From this time onwards, however, it became the basis of the kingdom's constitutional laws, and ruled out the possibility either of a reigning

King Edward III of England formally pays homage to Philip VI of France for Aquitaine. The French monarch bestows the accolade to the approval of surrounding courtiers.

queen or succession through a female. So the ushering-in of the Valois dynasty showed not just a developing sense of French political identity; it also illustrated and confirmed changes which had been taking place, as we have seen, in gender relations.

The legal case for Philip VI had proved persuasive enough for Edward III to do homage to the new French ruler in 1329. But it made the king of England pause for thought. And when Philip attempted to copy the strategy of Philip Augustus towards John of England, calling Edward a felonious vassal and attempting to confiscate his lands in the Guyenne, Edward reacted forcibly. By 1340 he had declared Philip VI a usurper and added the kingship of France to his own titles. The Hundred Years War between France and England (1337–1453) was beginning.

International warfare and dynastic dispute between Valois and Plantagenet could not have come at a worse time. By the early decades of the fourteenth century the economic cycle on which medieval prosperity had been based was coming to an end. Some of the causes of economic downturn were accidental or became more serious because they coincided. The Champagne fairs, for example, went into decline after 1310 because Italian merchants preferred to use Alpine passes and the Rhine waterway to reach the Low Countries, or else took the sea route via the straits of Gibraltar. England was also emerging in Flanders and Gascony as a commercial rival to France.

Medieval population growth had been grounded in an ability to expand food production by reclaiming land and by increasing productivity through technical and economic developments. In the thirteenth century yields were apparently reaching maximum levels for existing levels of agrarian technology. Population growth had led to cultivation of marginal lands that could not sustain intensive farming for a generation or more without exhausting the soil. Land reclamation projects continued in Lorraine down to 1330, and *bastides* were still being established in the Dauphiné in the 1370s; but projects had dried up in the Paris region, more significantly, from the

The Black Death

"For in that time of death," wrote the chronicler Froissart of the years 1348–52, "there was an epidemic of plague. People died suddenly and at least a third of all the people in the world died then." Froissart's naive guess has been largely confirmed by demographers. Population losses throughout the Western world were immense. Certainly one-fifth, probably one-third and possibly one-half of Europe's population died as a result of the resurgence of bubonic plague following a half-millennium during which it had not appeared in the West.

Though we may discount the legend that the disease had initially been spread by Mongols catapulting plague-ridden corpses into the besieged Crimean city of Caffa, Genoan merchants, it seems, brought the disease back to the West from that region in late 1347. The disease killed horribly – victims suffered atrocious death agonies – and with horrible efficiency: the fatality rate of those who caught the disease was close to 100 per cent. "The plague," as the royal surgeon Ambroise Paré was later to note, "is a mad, tempestuous, monstrous, abominable, fearful, terrifying and treacherous disease. To escape its clutches is more due to God than to human agency." The best remedy endorsed by the medical professions was, on the appearance of plague, to "leave early, go far, come back late".

Extreme in its effects the disease brought extreme reactions. There were vicious pogroms aimed at Jews, who were held to be responsible for poisoning Christian wells with the disease or spreading it in some other manner. The sense of guilt it provoked produced hordes of flagellants, who wandered eastern and south-eastern France and Germany, whipping themselves and calling populations to repent for their sins. "The calamity instilled such terror in the hearts of men and women," noted the Florentine Boccaccio, "that brother abandoned brother, uncle nephew, brother sister, and often wives left their husbands ... Even fathers and mothers shunned their children."

In France, only the Béarn, parts of Picardy and the Massif Central escaped the huge loss of life of 1348–52. The chances of demographic recuperation were moreover wiped out by further visitations of the disease – notably in 1360–2, 1374 and 1382 – and there were more than a dozen particularly bad years in the fifteenth century.

The "Triumph of Death", a sixteenth-century work which recalls the enormous loss of life caused by the Black Death of 1348. Bubonic plague continued to afflict France up to 1720.

and costly commodity. Peasants and workers who survived the outbreaks of plague did well. They benefited from the drastic change in the labour market, their wages rose and their living conditions improved – meat-eating became widespread, for example. They did have to endure, however, an onslaught on their living standards by the feudal class. Some manorial lords tried to force their peasants to pay the cost of the crisis, cutting wages and increasing feudal dues. State legislation was introduced in 1351 to put a ceiling on wages. These efforts were, generally, in vain. Some seigneurs adapted by shifting out of domain farming, developing less labour-intensive pasture cultivation, converting labour service into cash payments or else offering favourable leases to peasants as a means of attracting labour. Others preferred a more atavistic approach to falling feudal profits: the extraction of plunder. The Hundred Years War might have started with the claims and counter claims of rival dynasties; but it also gained impetus as the feudal class (as well as many displaced peasants and townsmen) sought out new means of subsistence and enrichment.

Pillage was important for the English. The Black Prince, the son of Edward III, returned from a raid in the Midi in 1355, for example, bringing a thousand loot-filled wagons in his train. It was also crucial for the French. Troops from both sides carried off movable items of wealth, held individuals and communities to ransom, and frequently devastated the countryside to boot. In spells of peace too demobilized soldiers formed armed vigilante gangs – the *routiers* of the 1350s and 1360s and the *écorcheurs* of the 1420s and 1430s – which caused destruction wherever they went. Although only one year in every four or five was a year of warfare, and armies were relatively small – probably 50,000 men at the very most – the passage of troops, deserters, demobilized men and hangers-on became a barometer for the rise and fall in population. Damage was especially bad in the Massif Central, the Paris basin and Normandy. The Hundred Years constituted for Normandy a holocaust of Hiroshima proportions (Guy Bois), especially in the fifteenth century: "From Dieppe to Rouen," bemoaned one Norman city-dweller, "there is not a recognizable track left; there are no farms and, with the exception of a few bandits, no men." Throughout France roads were deserted, villages abandoned, fields and hamlets taken over by nettles and brambles, while wolves grew in numbers and in audacity.

Medieval medicine taught in the universities was essentially book medicine, based on reference to canonical texts by authors such as Galen and Hippocrates. It was utterly impotent in the face of the Black Death.

THE HUNDRED YEARS WAR

The war (1337–1453) started disastrously for the French. The French fleet was destroyed outside Bruges in 1340, and Edward III's expeditionary force meted out terrible defeats on the French at Crécy (1346) and Poitiers (1356). Troubles thickened under the impact of the Black Death, the loss of Calais to the English in 1347 and the capture of King John II "the Good" (r. 1350–64) in 1358. In the king's absence local estates in the south (*langue d'oc*) and the north (*langue d'oïl*) agitated for reforms, while in Paris Etienne Marcel led a municipal movement demanding greater autonomy. The English moreover demanded so heavy a ransom for their prize that tax pressure triggered discontent throughout France, exploding in the Jacquerie of 1358. By the Peace of Brétigny of 1360 John was obliged to agree to the loss to the English of roughly one-third of his kingdom.

The struggle was a civil war as well as a dynastic struggle. The feudal vassals of King John of France benefited from his discomfiture to extend their power. Charles "the Bad", king of Navarre, a grandson of Louis X through Louis' daughter Jeanne, who was also, as count of Evreux, a major landowner in Normandy, advanced claims to the succession and proved a constant thorn in the flesh of the Valois monarch. A war of succession to the dukedom of Brittany took place between 1341 and 1365. Charles, the pro-English pretender, emerged victorious and was soon acting as though he were independent of the kings of France. Much the same was going on in Burgundy.

The successor of John "the Good", Charles V (r. 1364–80), led a staunch recovery. The great military commander Bertrand du Guesclin relentlessly harried the English in the north and south-west, and by the late 1370s forced them back on a handful of ports. The reign of Charles VI (r. 1380–1422) was altogether more difficult. His uncles ruled selfishly and were at odds with each other during the period of his minority, and although Charles showed some signs of capacity when he acceded to full power, in 1392 he went mad and was only spasmodically rational through to the end of his reign.

The Hundred Years War. The powerful state painstakingly assembled by the Capetians (see p. 76) risked disintegration in the Hundred Years War. The Treaty of Brétigny confirmed England's role as a major rival within the kingdom. The low point of French fortunes was reached in the late 1420s, when the English king and the duke of Burgundy seemed to be working a partition of the kingdom. By 1461 the Valois dynasty had bounced back.

His insanity allowed faction-fighting to worsen. The main battle lines were drawn in 1407 in the middle of a truce with England, when the Burgundian duke John "the Fearless" organized the assassination of his main rival Louis, duke of Orléans, the brother of Charles VI. The Anglo-French struggle became for a moment a side-issue to the fight between Armagnacs (as the Orléanist party were called) and Burgundians. In 1415 the English came back to the fray. Henry V (king of England 1413–22) landed in France to claim the monarchy. His defeat of the French at Agincourt in 1415 was a crushing blow, while the Armagnac assassination of John the Fearless in 1419 led the Burgundians to enter into alliance with the English. They pressurized the hapless Charles VI to give his daughter in marriage to Henry V, to disinherit his own son and to make Henry V his heir. The poor dauphin, the future Charles VII (r. 1422–61), retreated southwards, leaving most of northern France in Anglo-Burgundian hands.

French fortunes took a dramatic upturn with the appearance of the peasant girl Joan of Arc (1412–31), from Domrémy in the Lorraine. Inveigling herself into the entourage of Charles, she helped him to lift the English siege of Orléans. Newly heartened, Charles advanced on Reims, where he was crowned "by the grace of God" according to time-honoured custom – a massively important step in terms of both Charles' psychological state and the dynasty's standing. His status as monarch now fortified by this homage to tradition, he found his cause going well. He made little fuss when Joan of Arc, totem of victory at Orléans, fell into the hands of the Burgundians. They duly passed her over to the English, who had her burnt as a witch. Joan had become too closely associated with the faction in the king's entourage in favour of all-out war on the English, while Charles favoured diplomatic manoeuvrings. His diplomacy paid off, for in 1432 he won over the duke of Brittany, and in 1435 wooed back into the French camp the duke of Burgundy, Philip "the Good" (duke 1419–67).

A portrait of Joan of Arc by an anonymous Franco-Flemish painter in a book of poems by Charles of Orléans, c. 1455.

It had proved difficult for the English to establish themselves outside the north of France. The French began to use scorched-earth tactics, destroying everything which lay in the path of the advancing armies, and this both undermined the quest for loot which drove English forces on and strained their supply lines. When in the 1420s the English endeavoured to shift from a war of plunder to one of occupation and colonization, they stimulated opposition. The restive feudal vassals of the kings of France wanted independence, not a change of ruler. The favouritism the English showed their allies caused much local resentment – "son of an Englishman" had become the gravest of insults in English Rouen – while the taxes they levied were even higher than those of the kings of France.

The rise in taxation owed much to the approximate doubling of the costs of warfare in the period. Major changes were taking place in the conduct of war. As the French learnt to their cost in the battles at Poitiers and Agincourt, which between them killed off a solid bloc of French chivalry, wars of knights were becoming a thing of the past. Knights adopted heavy plate armour rather than mail-coats so as to deflect missiles now propelled by gunpowder as well as bows. Hence infantrymen had the edge over cavalrymen, especially at close quarters, where knights' armour made them utterly immobile once they were knocked off their horses. But the eclipse of the knight owed as much to political as to military changes. The monarch could no longer rely on the feudal levy as a means of assembling a reliable army. The decline of the feudal tie meant that soldiers – even vassals – had to be paid, and paid in cash when booty was not forthcoming. Though expensive, mercenaries were not always reliable, especially if they disbanded at the end of the campaigning season to conduct pillaging raids. From 1439 Charles VII established a standing army paid out of a direct tax – the *taille*.

Fifteenth-century carving of the arms of the city of Bordeaux under English rule. The leopards were a heraldic device associated particularly with the kings of England.

A siege in the Hundred Years War. Cannon had been present on the battlefield at Crécy in 1346, but their effectiveness as siegecraft led to a transformation of military architecture in the fifteenth century: base walls were thickened, bastions appeared on corners, and holes were made through which defensive cannon could fire.

Charles VII's standing army formed the backbone of the force that from the 1440s drove the English out of France. It was supplemented by bowmen companies (*francs-archers*) established in 1449 and by artillery. Du Guesclin had pioneered the use of the latter in the 1370s, and by the 1440s big guns had become a key contributor to battlefield tactics and siegecraft. The French operated with no fewer than 300 cannon in what was to prove the final battle of the Hundred Years War, at Castillon in 1453. The English, who had already been driven out of Normandy, evacuated the south-west, and retained only a toehold on continental Europe at Calais.

THE REHABILITATION OF THE DYNASTY

The struggle to force the English out of France proved the laboratory in which the institutions of a strong, centralized monarchy were created. In the standing army, funded by the *taille*, the Valois dynasty had developed what was to become one of the key agents of royal absolutism. The army was financed, even more significantly, without recourse to the Estates General, and was viewed as an emanation of royal sovereignty rather than as an institution freely assented to by the nation. Taxes were about obedience, not good will.

The rudiments of the administrative system of absolutism were also fixed in place in these years, and in the decades following 1453. Under Charles VII and his wily and astute successor Louis XI (r. 1461–83) the royal council took on a less feudal, more bureaucratic complexion. The monarch relied for advice on a group of professional lawyers, not merely mighty vassals. There was a greater differentiation of royal business too. Financial and judicial functions were separated. The chancellor headed the judicial arm, which was composed of a hierarchy of royal tribunals, the Paris parlement being the most important. Finance was the responsibility of a group of "generals of finance", while specialized institutions (*chambre des comptes*, *cour des aides*) also developed to deal with financial litigation and tax affairs. Local administration also underwent reform. Four major tax areas, or *généralités*, had been created in 1390, and these were gradually added to and made more sophisticated in their operations. The courts of *baillis* and *sénéchaux*, introduced in the late twelfth century, were also increased in number, and their business expanded.

Though the formal structures of the state were increasingly bureaucratic, in fact an informal system of patronage operated in counterpoint to it. This was centred on the royal court and extended into Church as well as secular affairs. By the Pragmatic Sanction of Bourges in 1438, the king of France secured a large amount of leeway in higher Church appointments and some access to Church revenues, which he now had power to tax. He still enjoyed wide rights of appointment to offices in the court, the army and the bureaucracy – though from the early sixteenth century monarchs were also organizing the sale of office, as a means of raising revenue.

The Hundred Years War and its aftermath saw the rehabilitation of a dynasty which, in 1420, had seemed on the edge of extinction. Once the English had been disposed of, however, there remained a continuing problem with regional nobles, who were resistant to the Valois bid to centralize power. The drive against the English had allowed many feudal lords to exact a price for their support. The high nobles who led the so-called Praguerie in 1440, protesting against military reforms, for example, were bought off with land. Brittany developed a high degree of independence in the early fifteenth century, and claimed to be a separate and sovereign power. It developed centralized institutions akin to those of the Valois: a more professional administration; a complex tax system; and even its own army – indeed its militia of *francs-archers* (1425) predated the French equivalent by two decades.

Christine de Pisan presents her poems to Isabel of Bavaria, queen of France, and wife of Charles VII. In the royal bed-chamber, wall-hangings display the French fleur-de-lis alongside the Bavarian diamond motif. The comfortable private space – panelled ceilings, shuttered windows, a carpeted floor, upholstered chairs – suggests a receptive attitude towards material comfort.

Louis XII (r. 1498–1515), to separate from his own long-standing wife and marry Charles' widow, in order to hold on to the province, which was fully incorporated into France in 1532.

A woman like Anne of Brittany was an object in the game of international power relations. This was still the lot of most elite women of this period. The example of Joan of Arc made no impression on the general run of relations between the sexes. Indeed Joan's habit of dressing like a man was more disturbing to her English judges than her spiritual claims, and the French were probably more enthusiastic about her as a dead martyr than as a living question-mark against the position of women. The feminist Christine de Pisan made as little impact. Her *City of Women* (1404) was a devastating critique of male misogyny and a disturbing analysis of how much women's supposed nature had been fashioned by the male (often clerical) imagination: "The books that so sayeth" was her refrain, "women made them not." Yet she had few disciples.

Valois acquisitions of the fifteenth century utterly transformed the shape and size of France. The incorporation of the Dauphiné and Provence, plus the as yet timid steps in Lorraine, represented the first major ruptures in the frontier settlement worked out six centuries earlier at Verdun in 843. These areas were integrated into France with a good degree of pragmatism, and respect for local autonomy was shown mainly because of the need to foster loyalty. Provinces were granted their own parlements (that is, high courts of law) – Toulouse in 1443, Grenoble in 1456, Dijon in 1477, Aix in 1501,

Rouen in 1515, Rennes in 1551, and so on – and often their own *chambres des comptes* and *cours des aides* as well. In some cases these were new institutions; in others they amounted to an official endorsement of institutions which pre-existed French control. Provinces brought under the French crown were also permitted to retain their representative assemblies, or Estates. Thus Burgundy retained its estates after incorporation in 1477, as did Dauphiné, Provence and Brittany. Royal ratification of compilations of customary law in the sixteenth century had much the same rationale. "The people of each province," the legal expert Guy Coquille was to argue, "has the right to establish laws over itself which are customs." By 1789 nearly a hundred such compilations had local force of law. On such institutions was a slowly evolving sense of regional identity based.

RENAISSANCE MONARCHY, RENAISSANCE SOCIETY

Monarchical power in the late fifteenth and sixteenth centuries was still, as it had been since 987, a mixture of feudal, holy and sovereign. What had changed, however, was the relative strength of each element, the context in which they operated and the implications they now conveyed. The ruler still liked to regard himself as the "seigneur of seigneurs" and there were ritualistic efforts at feudal style – the feudal levy was invoked even as late as 1695. The royal court and the bureaucracy had become the dynamos of power, however; the Church and the great feudal lords had been pulled in on a tighter rein; and more effective instruments of control over the provinces were evolving. Significantly the Estates General, which had originated as a means of feudal consultation, was a casualty of the strengthening of the state; it was not convened after 1484 – only a succession crisis in 1560 temporarily resuscitated it. The monarch retained his sacred aura: touching for the King's Evil (scrofula) continued. But the basis of royal power now lay in sovereignty. As Louis XI put it, "the general government and administration of the kingdom … and also of our good towns … belongs to us alone."

Public authority was now held to reside in the person of the dynast, and the crown was an expression of that sovereignty. It also came to evoke the community over which the ruler presided. "How hard and painful it is," noted the councillors of Cahors following the Treaty of Brétigny in 1360, which placed them in English hands, "to abandon one's natural lord and to receive an unknown and foreign master." The dynasty adroitly manipulated that sense of identity with the crown during the Hundred Years War and stimulated a gut hatred of the English – a point which obscured the fact that a great many inhabitants were as hostile to the demands and armies of the French state as they were of any other dynasty.

Maintaining the particular forms of the regions – local estates, parlements, customs and so on – constituted one of the duties of the sovereign. "Absolute" power, a phrase increasingly used by the dynasty's propagandists, meant not just being able to legislate, but also having to respect the "fundamental laws of the kingdom" while doing so. These basic laws were held to embrace the independence of the crown from the demands of the Holy Roman Empire and even the papacy. The medieval internation-

The château of Chambord, one of the most impressive works of art associated with the Renaissance. Constructed by Francis I between 1519 and 1547, its frontage is exceptionally wide, and it boasts no fewer than 365 chimneys. Louis XIV was a particular enthusiast for the château's charms.

alism which these embodied had had its day. The French king was "emperor in his own country". He regarded the Habsburg rulers who had acquired the imperial title in hereditary possession from the mid fifteenth century as equals rather than as superiors. The papacy counted for less too: the absolutism of the king implied the relativism of the pope. Philip the Fair had brought the papacy under his wing at Avignon from 1309, and rival popes at Rome and Avignon divided Western Christendom between them from 1378 to 1417. The efforts of Pope Pius V (pope 1504–72) to mobilize a crusade against the Turks failed ignominiously.

The spectacle of over-mighty subjects aping royal splendour impelled monarchs down the road of political ostentation, propaganda and display. A policy of calculated grandeur was developed in representations of royalty. Monarchs dressed differently and they engaged in rituals which set them apart from mere mortals. The golden fleur-de-lis, symbol of royal mercy, that rulers wore on their azure coronation robe combined with the crown, the sceptre and the great sword of state as the characteristic insignia of sovereignty. Court rituals became ever more showily splendid. Orders of chivalry – the Knights of the Star (1351) and the Order of Saint Michael (1469) – were a special focus for display.

The court's ostentatious patronage of the arts made the royal palace the heir of the medieval cathedral as the site of the finest and most sophisticated art. From the late fifteenth century the chivalric art and ideas of the Italian Renaissance penetrated the French court. The impact of fourteenth- and fifteenth-century Italy's re-evaluation of the art and learning of classical antiquity had previously been limited, partly by the Hundred Years War, though the papal court at Avignon and the court of "King" René in Provence had acted as channels for Italian influence. Francis I (r. 1515–47) was an especially keen lover of Italy, importing to France artists, painters and scholars: Benvenuto Cellini was a visitor, while Leonardo da Vinci died at Amboise in 1519. Francis I established the Collège Royal (later the Collège de France) as a beacon outside the university of the humanist scholarship pioneered in Italy. Architecture was relatively slow to be touched by Italian influence, partly because the flamboyant style of the Gothic was so dynamic. Yet Italian influence began to make itself felt in the design of the palaces of the Loire valley. The châteaux at Amboise, Blois, Chambord, Azay-le-Rideau and Chenonceaux bear witness to the success with which Italian style was implanted. Later, in the palace created by Francis from the late 1520s, the "School of Fontainebleau" – mainly Italian painters brought in for the château's decoration – had a considerable influence on native styles.

If Italy brought the French court Renaissance styles and values, the French king in return exported warfare to the Italian peninsula. The Italian Wars, which were to last from 1494 to 1559, testified to the confidence of a dynasty which had mastered its internal problems. Other states at this time were expanding and colonizing in the world beyond Europe – a world opened up by the establishment of routes to the East and the discovery of the Americas in 1492. The French-backed Jacques Cartier staked a claim in Canada in 1534, but in general the French dynasty gave more attention to the Italian peninsula than to the world outside Europe.

Attack on the Iroquois fort of Onondaga led by French explorer Samuel Champlain, founder of Quebec. Champlain landed in the upper reaches of the Saint Lawrence river in 1608, and in a number of expeditions joined forces with local tribes, notably the Hurons, to establish a footing in the region.

The Italian Wars acted as a channel for the aggressive tendencies of great nobles who had plagued Charles VII and Louis XI. The cause of war was a dynastic issue – the Valois claim to the kingdom of Naples championed by the young new king Charles VIII (r. 1483–98). Although the French ruler often invoked the "nation's" interests in the conduct of the wars, the French army was a mercenary force of hardened men-at-arms from Switzerland, Germany, Italy, Spain and elsewhere, as well as from France itself. The wars confirmed the close of the era of knightly warfare: the combatants were hired professional captains, or *condottieri*, now separately equipped with portable firepower. The arquebus, then the musket, joined the pike as staple battlefield arms, while the bow became a thing of the past. The big siege artillery which Charles VIII wheeled into the peninsula in 1494 enjoyed immediate success in cracking open the walls of Italian cities. Pope Julius II (pope 1503–13), rallying local powers and hiring battle-hardened Swiss troops, led the resistance. Francis I inflicted a decisive victory over the Swiss mercenary army at Marignano in 1515, however, and secured such an upper hand that the pope was obliged to sign the Concordat of Bologna in 1516, confirming the king's rights over the French Church.

The Italian Wars were coming to be about more than Italy. The peninsula became the theatre of a more general conflict that saw France in opposition to the Habsburg power lodged in the Holy Roman Empire. When the Habsburg king of Spain, Charles V, became Holy Roman Emperor in 1519 France faced the threat of encirclement – especially as Charles' dominions included the Franche-Comté and the Low Countries. The threat seemed real enough when, after defeat and capture at Pavia in 1525, Francis I was obliged to accept humiliating peace terms in the Treaty of Madrid in 1526. The French ruler fought back from this low ebb. The "Most Christian King" did not disdain alliance with German Lutheran princes and even in 1543 – for the first time in the annals of European diplomacy – the Ottoman Turks. The Treaty of Cateau-Cambrésis which brought the wars in 1559 to a close highlighted their non-Italian aspect. The French renounced any gains on the Italian peninsula, acquired Calais from the English and secured *de facto* control over the "Three Bishoprics" of Toul, Metz and Verdun in Lorraine.

There were, Louis XII was told by one of his counsellors, three things a king required in order to fight wars: "first, money; second, money; and third, money". The French state proved able to conduct these costly wars over six decades because its new structures allowed the ruler to siphon off, by means of taxes, loans and the sale of offices, a good share of the prosperity which the French economy and society had started to enjoy. The economic recovery took root in the 1450s, after the late medieval feudal crisis, and echoed a more general revival in Europe's fortunes, which the discoveries of explorers accentuated. An accurate index of recovery was population size: at a long-term low around 1450 population grew extremely rapidly from that point on, notably in the Midi. It was approaching pre-Black Death levels by the middle of the sixteenth century. France, noted Brantôme in 1572, had grown to be "as full as an egg". It helped that mortality crises had become less severe. Plagues and famines were fewer in the first

Renaissance France

Royal Domain:
- 1461
- 1483
- 1547
- 1589

- ○ Major printing centre, early 16th century
- ○ Minor printing centre

Renaissance architecture:
- ● Under Louis XII (1498-1515)
- ● Under Francis I (1515-1525)
- ● Under Francis I (1525-1547)

Universities:
- ● Founded by 1400
- ■ Founded by 1500
- ▲ Founded by 1600

The fifteenth and sixteenth centuries saw the French monarchy consolidating its authority within the traditional heartlands of its power. It also durably extended its authority for the first time well beyond the line traced out at the Treaty of Verdun in 843. This was also a period of intellectual and cultural effervescence: the impact of print was combined with the growing influence of the Italian Renaissance. The Valois dynasty closely associated itself with the latter, notably in its château-building.

This engraving, designed for a German audience, shows Henry IV receiving mass at Saint-Denis and abjuring his Protestant faith. The picture is a kind of comic strip, with the monarch appearing in a number of places – distributing alms to the left, for example – as well as inside the church.

famously, in his own words, adjudged Paris "worth a Mass", he entered the city in 1594. Opposition was gradually unravelling and Henry spent the next four years threatening, negotiating with and buying the support of the rebels. His Edict of Nantes, issued in 1598, was a classic compromise between the two sides. Freedom of conscience and equality of rights were roundly declared, but Protestants were allowed to worship only in select locations where they had a strong community. In addition they were permitted to retain their ramparts as a guarantee of religious autonomy in 151 *places de sûreté*.

The Edict of Nantes looks far more reasonable to subsequent historians than it did to most contemporaries: the pope roundly declared it "the worst edict imaginable"; the parlements were especially concerned with the constitutional implications of the act, and the Rouen parlement only finally gave its assent as late as 1609. Even many Huguenots, whose numbers had fallen from two to less than one million, were wary. Assassination plots aimed at the king – about twenty in the course of his reign – continued unabated. The Edict was given a chance to work, however, by Henry's signing the Treaty of Vervins in 1598 with Philip II of Spain, thereby ending foreign involvement in France's civil strife. Vervins endorsed the basic positions of the 1559 Cateau-Cambrésis Treaty. France had, almost miraculously, come through forty years of civil strife without enduring significant territorial losses to greedy neighbours.

Yet if the political structures stood fast, the economy was in a lamentable state. Trade was languishing and manufacturing output was probably down by half. The wars had not been another Hundred Years War: deaths were limited and population levels overall stagnated rather than fell markedly. War, famine and disease did, however, have some impact. Population losses were severe in areas where military activity had been intense. The wars coincided too with an apparent worsening of the climate: a "Little Ice Age" set in around 1550 (and would last to the middle of the nineteenth century), characterized by cold and wet winters. This led to a string of severe harvest failures and periods of high prices (notably in 1563, 1565–6, 1573–7, 1586, 1590–2 and 1596–7). To make matters worse, there was a resurgence of plague in the 1580s and 1590s. These catastrophes, combined with continued state tax demands, triggered discontent. There was a major peasant rising – the so-called "Croquants" – in 1594/5 in the south-west, and other such disturbances in Normandy and Brittany.

The triumph of Henry IV in ending the Wars of Religion demonstrated that French society had turned away, if only temporarily, from the aim of constructing a unitary Catholic state. The price would have been enormous bloodshed and social turbulence. There was now a new political landscape grounded in hopes for social tranquillity, and French men and women must have waited nervously to see what peace and the new dynasty would bring.

CHAPTER 6

From Counter-Reformation to Enlightenment

Henry IV

The change of dynasty, from Valois to Bourbon, seemed initially to make little impression on the scale and impact of the regime's problems and on accompanying social and economic tensions. In some senses the spirit of the Wars of Religion was not wholly played out until the Fronde (1648–52), a combination of state bankruptcy, civil war and popular uprising. Yet beneath the surface major structural changes were taking place, notably through the "cardinal ministers" Richelieu and Mazarin, who dominated the king's council from 1624 through to 1661, when Louis XIV assumed full power. It was thanks largely to his predecessors that the "Sun King" was able to dominate European international relations from the 1680s through to his death in 1715. He did so, however, only by landing his successors with very considerable financial, economic and political problems.

If the period witnessed the progressive deterioration of the political climate in the run-up to the Revolution of 1789, it also contained two remarkable cultural movements: the Counter-Reformation, which had a massive effect on the social life and *mentalités* of the French people; and the Enlightenment of the eighteenth century, a diverse intellectual and cultural movement with its roots in the economic prosperity of the period. The Enlightenment would have a part to play, moreover, in changes in attitudes towards religion and government which had a major impact in 1789.

THE COUNTER-REFORMATION

France's change of dynasty, from Valois to Bourbon, marked a notable defeat for intolerant ultra-Catholicism. Religious tolerance was championed by a monarch whose tenure was still fragile. Indeed it was not until 1607 that Henry IV felt safe enough in his possession of the crown to authorize the amalgamation into France of his power-base in the Béarn. It was one of the ironies of the seventeenth century that the monarchy's growing fame as the most powerful and prestigious in Europe was accompanied by a revival of Catholicism and an intolerance of religious dissidence. Beginning with Henry's successor Louis XIII (r. 1610–43), the backlash reached its apotheosis in the Edict of Fontainebleau of 1685. By this, Louis XIV (r. 1643–1715) formally revoked the Edict of Nantes of 1598 and re-established Catholicism as the sole authorized religion.

The pathway towards Fontainebleau opened up soon after Henry IV's assassination in 1610 at the hands of a fanatical Catholic extremist. The first Bourbon's early adherence to Protestantism was a guarantee that he would resist backsliding towards an ultra-Catholicism still tarnished by unsavoury memories of the Catholic League. Louis XIII, in contrast, had been born (in 1601) a Catholic, he dedicated his reign to the Virgin Mary, and his youthful marriage to the daughter of the king of Spain, Anne of

Austria, sealed an alliance with the Habsburgs. In 1620 the decision of Louis XIII, influenced by his favourite the duke de Luynes, to enforce the precepts of the Edict of Nantes in still Protestant Béarn (where the Huguenots enjoyed a monopoly of religious worship) sparked off widespread armed opposition in the Midi. The monarch stood firm over what he took to be an attempt to set up a state within a state, and in the Peace of Montpellier in 1622 reduced Protestant garrison towns to two – Montauban and La Rochelle. Further Huguenot revolts in the 1620s climaxed in 1627, when the duke de Rohan led armed insurrection in Languedoc, while the mayor of La Rochelle made an alliance with the English, against whom Louis XIII had just declared war. La Rochelle, despite English aid, fell to a siege conducted by Louis XIII in 1628 that reduced the city by starvation from 30,000 to around 6,000 inhabitants. The Peace of Alès in 1629 reaffirmed the religious tolerance of 1598, but rights of assembly and garrison towns were withdrawn.

The decision at Alès to deal mercifully with the Huguenot rebels paid dividends for the crown, in that French Protestants now became almost more royalist than the king, and gave up dabbling in politics. The military and political threat of Protestantism had been effectively neutralized. The dynasty's decision to ally with Protestant princes

Colbert Presents Louis XIV to the Members of the Royal Academy of Sciences in 1667 by Henri Testelin. This totally fictitious scene dates from 1667, the king not actually visiting the Academy until 1682. Designed to reflect his glory, the Academy also served the role of state scientific and technological consultative agency.

Royal propaganda, showing Louis XIV hearing the petitions of the poor. The text compares him to Solomon, Charlemagne and Saint Louis. In spite of appearances, Louis presided over the erosion of the country's representative institutions – the Estates General did not meet in his reign, and many provincial estates fell into abeyance.

against Austria and Spain in the Thirty Years War (1618–48) seemed to buttress the Huguenot position. Yet the situation was far from stable. In particular Catholicism was undergoing a process of rebirth in the aftermath of the Council of Trent (1545–63). The council had crystallized Catholic doctrine around anti-Protestant positions, while also inaugurating a battle for souls. The Church was to bring orthodox piety to the masses who, it was increasingly apparent, were often ignorant of Catholic doctrine and vulnerable to conversion to Protestantism. Though its precepts were never accepted as state law by the Bourbons, the spirit of Trent infiltrated the French Church from the late sixteenth century onwards.

From the 1650s Louis XIV's personal hostility towards Protestantism also weakened the Huguenot position. After 1659 he forbade national synods from meeting, while provincial synods began to be harassed. Between 600 and 700 churches (or "temples") were demolished – probably the greatest campaign of architectural destruction before the French Revolution. Restrictions on Protestant entry into the professions and the guilds tightened. In 1676 a Conversion Fund was established which granted small sums to Protestants who renounced their faith. But where bribery failed, coercion was tried. State officials began to force Protestants to pay supplements on tax, and from 1681 soldiers in the Poitou were billeted on Protestant families. The latter practice, soon known as *dragonnades*, was introduced with some glee in the Languedoc, where the brutality of the soldiery produced tens of thousands of "conversions" – of a sincerity one can rightly doubt. The spectacle was enough to persuade Louis XIV that a full-scale attempt to crush Protestantism was in order. In 1685 the revocation of the Edict of Nantes was decreed. Protestant pastors were to leave France and Protestant worship was forbidden.

The Edict of Fontainebleau was greeted with an astonishing measure of national and international enthusiasm. Yet Louis' wager that the Protestants could be easily brought over proved disastrously wrong. Armed resistance was soon crushed, but extensive repression was required, causing mass emigration, supported by pastors whose watchword was "Leave Babylon". Perhaps 200,000 to 250,000 individuals – roughly a quarter of all French Huguenots – many of them professional people and skilled workers, left France to join the ranks of France's economic competitors England, the Netherlands and Germany. The repression provoked the War of the Camisards (1702–4) in the Cévennes, where Calvinist peasants conducted crude but effective guerrilla operations against the state.

Protestantism went underground, and the period of the *Désert* ("wilderness") began. Ironically Louis XIV was on his deathbed in 1715 when the first national synod of the survivor churches was held in the Cévennes, foreshadowing the revival of secret national organization throughout the eighteenth century. When, on the eve of the Revolution in 1788, many of the strictures of 1685 were lifted, the Protestant Church stood at some 600,000 members.

Eradication of Protestantism was only one of the objectives of the revived Catholic Church in the seventeenth century. The Counter-Reformation had its roots in a broad-based reform movement that predated Luther and Calvin. It endeavoured to remove ignorance as well as doctrinal error, and to spread principles of godliness so as to produce a Catholicization, even a Christianization, of society. Prominent in this movement were laypeople committed to these new principles who were seeking to bring about, through the quest for Christian perfection in the world, a "reformation of manners" every bit as thorough-going as that preached by puritans. Later wickedly satirized for hypocrisy in Molière's *Tartuffe* (1664), the *dévots* (the "devout"), as they were called, operated at both national and local levels, and were particularly active between the 1630s and early 1660s under the aegis of the Company of the Holy Sacrament.

Founded by the saintly duke de Ventadour in the late 1620s, the Company of the Holy Sacrament comprised a network of activist clerics and laymen, drawn from the upper reaches of the high nobility and state bureaucracy in Paris and the cream of local society in the provinces. Operating under a cloak of secrecy, the company numbered over fifty branches, co-ordinated from Paris. Activists were in the vanguard of the campaign to reduce Protestant rights at local level prior to the Revocation of the Edict of Nantes. But they were also engaged in an enormously varied range of charitable tasks – assisting the poor, visiting prisoners, redeeming prostitutes, reforming hospitals, educating the children of the poor, clamping down on profanity during religious holi-

The Camisards

I had several inspirations by which I was told to prepare to take up arms to fight with my brothers against our persecutors, that I would bring iron and fire against the priests of the Roman Church and that I would burn their altars ... At dusk ... we set out for Saint-André-de-Lancize to carry out another order uttered by my mouth, which was to put to death the priest of the locality, to burn his house, to topple the altar and to set fire to the church ...

This account given by Abraham Mazel, one of the earliest leaders of the Protestant Camisard rebels who resisted Louis XIV's imposition of Catholicism in 1685, goes on to recount how the church was indeed burned down and the priest murdered. Such atrocities were common currency in this period of civil and religious strife, which took the form of open insurrection in the Cévennes – the southern foothills of the Massif Central – between 1702 and 1704. The *dragonnades* of royal troops in the 1680s had forced Protestant pastors out of France, leaving their flocks demoralized and leaderless. An epidemic of prophesying and speaking with tongues by (largely peasant) children and adults had pushed the movement in a millenarian direction: the end of the world seemed nigh.

The decision of the local intendant to meet resistance with stern repression escalated the conflict. The Camisards – so named because they made *camisades* (night attacks) or else because they fought in peasant shirts, or camisoles – followed their leaders' inspirations blindly. They went into conflict against battle-hardened troops singing psalms (a form of psychological warfare which could be effective). The success of the operations owed much, however, to the mountainous and moorland terrain in the Cévennes, which regular troops found difficult to negotiate. The Camisards might have been an even greater threat had they managed, as was planned on several occasions, to link up militarily with their fellow Protestants from England. The open insurrection was unravelled by a mixture of toughness and conciliation and ended in 1704, but guerrilla operations rumbled on spasmodically for a decade. The Cévennes would be one of the strongholds of the clandestine Protestant Church that re-emerged after the death of Louis XIV in 1715.

A Huguenot is forced to sign his conversion to Catholicism.

days and festivals, repressing folkloric practices more pagan than Christian and so on. A whole spate of new charitable foundations – hospitals, foundlings' homes, prostitutes' reformatories, charity schools and the like – was their enduring monument.

Though the national organization of the Company of the Holy Sacrament was broken up by Mazarin in 1661, local activists continued their moralizing and charitable works long afterwards. The *dévots* aimed to make universal a notion of piety in tune with society's alleged moral and spiritual needs. This line was also characteristic of the post-Trent work of the new orders and a revitalized secular (or non-monastic) clergy. A new model of pious activism was evident in the religious orders which emerged after Trent. Pastoral care rather than mysticism was the key. Imaginative and dynamic organizers stepped forwards, such as Cardinal Pierre de Bérulle, founder of the Oratorian teaching order in France; Saint François de Sales, co-founder of the Order of the Visitation and author of the *Introduction à la vie dévote* (1608), one of the best-sellers of post-Trent godliness; and Saint Vincent de Paul, founder of the Lazarist missionary order and the nursing community the Daughters of Charity. These French bodies worked in co-operation with international organizations such as the Jesuits, whose schools educated the children of the elite. The pastoral urge was exemplified in the mission. It was directed at the heathen, but it also embraced the poor within French society, whose needs the Church felt it was failing to meet. The Lazarists and the Eudistes of Saint Jean Eudes, for example, specialized in rural missions.

A notable feature of the Counter-Reformation missionary endeavour was the activities of numerous women of a similarly pragmatic and pastoral bent – like Saint Jeanne de Chantal, co-founder of the Visitandines, or Saint Louise de Marillac, co-founder of the Daughters of Charity. Female education was a particular concern: the Ursulines took in middle- and upper-class boarders, while hosts of new female teaching orders catered for poor children. Similar female orders were also engaged in poor relief. The prototype here was the Daughters of Charity of Saints Vincent de Paul and Louise de Marillac (founded 1633), who pioneered the practice of engaging religious women in the affairs of the world. This move created high levels of patient care in hospitals and charitable institutions, which became, at the same time, enveloped in an evangelical aura. Many similar communities followed in their train, and achieved a silent takeover of the institutions of poor relief. Court figures and other wealthy women patronized such bodies and supplied the financial backing for the various teaching and charitable enterprises of the period.

Louis XIV was charitable too – albeit in a more pragmatic way. The veterans' hospital, the Invalides, which he founded in 1670, was designed to prevent ex-soldiers causing havoc in civil society as much as it was to reward them for good service. It formed part of a more general campaign to confine the poor and other social groups perceived as dangerous. Louis helped to establish the national network of *hôpitaux généraux* ("general hospitals"), initially with the support of the Company of the Holy Sacrament. They not only confined the poor, providing shelter for the needy, but also meted out correction for the dissident and work-shy. A host of repressive royal edicts, notably in the 1680s, when the anti-Protestant campaign was reaching its peak, targeted for confinement gypsies, vagrants, lunatics, alleged witches, prostitutes, delinquent children and other supposedly deviant groups. Nearly two hundred such institutions were created from the 1650s onwards. The 100,000 individuals they confined were, however, only a small proportion of the targeted groups.

The objectives which the monarch set for the revitalized secular clergy emerging in this age of religious reform were double-edged. As the "great confinement of the poor" (M. Foucault) suggests, the king required them to instil social discipline as well as spiritual orthodoxy. The Council of Trent had urged the creation of seminaries to produce more worthy priests, and from the 1620s and 1630s French bishops began to establish diocesan seminaries for ecclesiastical training. These became efficient at mass-

The "Great Confinement" extended to prostitutes and paupers, and in their case often resulted in transportation to the French colony of Louisiana. Here, in 1687, Paris prostitutes and brothel-keepers – several of whom are named – embark for New Orleans from the Paris Hôpital Général. Tender farewells to their lovers are contrasted with the more bitter remarks reserved for surgeon and apothecary (shown bearing leech and enema-syringe), presumably for their attentions during treatment for venereal disease.

producing a properly educated, well-tested, zealous and pastorally concerned parish priest. Rates of formal illiteracy, ecclesiastical absenteeism, pluralism and ignorance plummeted. The *bons curés*, or good parish priests, passed on an orthodox set of beliefs. Their task was to produce at parish level a good, God-fearing Christian – and for the state, a docile and obedient subject.

There is moreover a great deal of evidence to suggest that these Counter-Reformation shock-troops did have an impact on their flocks. In particular the astonishing fall in illegitimacy and pre-bridal conceptions – fewer than five children in a hundred were born out of wedlock in most rural areas by the turn of the eighteenth century – suggests that the preaching of godliness did not take place in a void, but that the hoped-for Christianization of social *mores* was fairly effective. The late seventeenth-century decline in provincial rioting and social turbulence commonplace a century earlier may also be linked to the wider diffusion of a more effective and zealous secular clergy, able to police political as well as religious opinions.

The Catholic Church paid a price, however, for such close links with the state. In particular it risked losing its autonomy and having its agenda set by state concerns. When ecclesiastical opinion threatened too much independence, the monarch did not hold back from acting against it. The king had the archbishop of Paris arrested and thrown in prison in 1652 (admittedly it was the arch-intriguer, the Cardinal de Retz). Throughout his reign he also proved the scourge of Jansenism, a puritanical form of

Catholicism which, he felt, inclined its practitioners towards political dissidence. Nor did he refrain from taking on the pope as well as the French Church in his determination to establish his prerogatives. Indeed at one moment in the 1680s he looked close to leading the French Church into secession from Rome.

THE MAKING OF ABSOLUTISM

"Royal authority is sacred … God established kings as his ministers and reigns through them over the nation … The royal throne is not the throne of a man but the throne of God himself." The words of Bishop Bossuet underline the organic links now connecting Church and an increasingly absolutist state. The language of absolutism was not of course new, linking with Roman law conceptions of sovereignty that had been revived in the thirteenth century. It had gained currency in the Wars of Religion, when a strong monarchy could be presented as the only viable alternative to anarchy. Political discourse then became more emphatic about the need for unquestioning obedience to the king's wishes and suspicious of checks on his power. For the humanist Jean Bodin, writing in the aftermath of the Saint Bartholomew's Eve Massacre, "a king is responsible only to God and his conscience". The bluff, no-nonsense Henry IV had followed the dictates of his conscience, converting to Catholicism in order to benefit his people. He fought hard to establish an atmosphere of tolerance in the face of doubting parlements and established authorities – and finally he was able to deliver a version of royalty from which Louis XIV (via Louis XIII) could benefit. However, the latter refurbished it with a sacred aura. This Louis, notwithstanding Divine Right theory, might not be a saint nor think himself divine. Yet as his cousin, the Grande Mademoiselle, sardonically remarked of him, "he is God".

The new form of absolutism embodied by Louis XIV was not achieved without difficulty. The assassination of Henry IV in 1610 produced a period of regency, under Marie de Medici. Monarchy was always weak in a regency, a point highlighted by the calling of an Estates General in 1614 to enlist community support. Marie de Medici seemed, however, to squander the confidence she enjoyed as Henry IV's widow, entrusting power to an unpopular Italian *arriviste* Concino Concini and his wife Leonora Galigaï, whose influence triggered a spate of noble revolts. Louis XIII marked his coming-of-age in 1617 by having Concini brutally murdered, executing his wife and dispatching Marie de Medici into exile.

From the early 1620s a new figure emerged in the king's councils: Armand Jean du Plessis, bishop of Luçon, who became Cardinal de Richelieu in 1622. Richelieu was not only effective principal minister for two decades (from 1624 to 1642), but also bequeathed to Louis XIII and the young Louis XIV a successor, Giulio Mazarini. Originally a papal diplomat, from the early 1630s Mazarini came into the service of Richelieu, who made him cardinal. Cardinal Jules Mazarin would serve as principal minister until his death in 1661. The political predominance of the two "cardinal ministers" from 1624 down to 1661 was immensely important in the establishment of the absolute monarchy. Building on the legacy of Henry IV, they first came to terms with

the turbulent legacy of the Religious Wars, crushing, as we have seen, the pretensions of Protestantism to rank as a state within a state, and also muzzling the turbulent high nobility; but secondly they also reduced the influence of representative bodies and established the institutional framework of centralized monarchy.

Richelieu is sometimes credited with almost superhuman powers of foresight in the creation of absolutism. Nothing could be further from the truth. The absolutist model emerged piecemeal and fortuitously from a welter of complex and contradictory circumstances. At the heart of change moreover was the unpredictability of war. Richelieu feared that a strong Habsburg power would use the Thirty Years War (1618–48) as a means of encircling France and establishing a grip over Europe. He therefore made an anti-Austrian and anti-Spanish position the basis of his foreign policy, even though this entailed allying with, and granting financial aid to, Protestant powers.

In 1635 Richelieu entered the war. It went badly almost at once. In 1636 when Corbie in Picardy fell, with imperial cavalry outriders skirting Paris, there seemed a real threat of massive Spanish invasion from the Low Countries. The military threat was contained with some difficulty, and by 1639/40 the war started going the French way. The brilliant victory achieved by the prince de Condé over the Spanish at Rocroi in 1643 was followed by further victories and gradual French advance on the northern front, as well as occupation of Roussillon and Catalonia in the south. These efforts were crowned with success in the Treaty of Westphalia of 1648: the *de facto* French annexation of the "Three Bishoprics" (Metz, Toul, Verdun) since 1552 was confirmed in international law; the French also acquired a good part of Alsace. War with the Spanish Habsburgs continued after 1648 and was only concluded by the Treaty of the Pyrenees in 1659. By this, Roussillon and part of the Cerdagne in the south were acquired, while France also gained a string of land advancing the frontier northwards between Gravelines on the English Channel to Thionville on the Moselle, and including most of Artois and Picardy.

These victories had only been achieved by the transformation of the French army and major shifts in the character of government and administration. The French army, though occasionally reaching a force of 50,000, had rarely surpassed 20,000 to 30,000 in the sixteenth century, and in the early 1630s stood at around 20,000. Defeat at Corbie galvanized the state into desperate measures. By the late 1630s by dint of press-ganging, call-ups and the purchase of foreign mercenary forces, nearly 100,000 men were in the field. Numbers continued to grow, with army strength reaching a quarter of a million men after the 1650s.

This "military revolution" in army size (M. Roberts) entailed a massive shift towards centralized and bureaucratic government. The cardinal ministers performed a coup on the royal council, removing feudal dignitaries who felt they had a place as of right and replacing them with their own *créatures* – loyal, dependable and administratively effective men, willing to subordinate their own opinions to the will of their master. The personnel of the council was increasingly bureaucratized. Business was handled by secretaries of state and subordinate *maîtres des requêtes* ("masters of requests"). The

Opposite Besides his role in central government Richelieu, here portrayed by Philippe de Champaigne, also played an important role as a Counter-Reformation prelate. Bishop of Luçon from 1606 and cardinal from 1622, he conducted intensive missionary work within his diocese against Huguenots.

was placed under close surveillance. Provincial estates which showed signs of dissidence were not reconvened (Dauphiné after 1628, Normandy after 1655 and so on). After the Fronde, the parlements had their rights to pose constitutional arguments against royal edicts severely reduced, to prevent them from becoming a lightning-rod for opposition.

Opinion was not only repressed, it was also shaped and manipulated. Richelieu's censorship drove out of France the greatest thinker of the age, René Descartes, whose *Discourse on Method* was published in 1637. Richelieu used paid hacks as government propagandists and hired a bevy of polemical pamphleteers. He permitted the colourful Montpellier physician and impresario, Théophraste Renaudot, to establish in 1631 the first national newspaper, the *Gazette*, which specialized in propaganda quite as much as official news. Richelieu's patronage of literary men was marked by the foundation of the *Académie française* in 1635, to uphold the purity of the French language. He and Mazarin also encouraged and patronized dramatists, painters and architects who flattered their, and the dynasty's, glory. Louis XIV would take the political uses of artistic patronage to new heights.

LOUIS XIV'S ABSOLUTISM

On the death of Mazarin in 1661, Louis XIV decided not to appoint a principal minister, but to govern by himself. This was to put the final icing on a cake whose ingredients had been so painstakingly blended by the cardinal ministers. It represented the high point of centralized government: the king's ministers reported separately to the king. For those with ambitions above their station the imprisonment and ruin he meted out in 1661 to his over-confident finance minister Nicolas Fouquet served as a deterrent. He prized loyalty and efficiency in his ministers, making use of a body of able bureaucrats left him by Mazarin, not least Jean-Baptiste Colbert. The council of state was further streamlined. In the provinces intendants were made fixtures – the last *généralité* to receive a permanent appointment was Brittany in 1689 – and they were flanked by *sub-délégués* (sub-delegates) acting under their orders. Efforts were made under Colbert to produce national criminal, civil and commercial codes. Municipal authorities were more closely supervised from above. Paris, whose turbulence during the Fronde Louis XIV had felt at first hand, was in 1667 put under a lieutenant-general of police, a minister-ranking appointment, whose job was to reduce crime and engage in urban development, while in the provinces a mounted national police constabulary, the *maréchaussée*, was organized. The spread of a network of poorhouses-*cum*-workhouses throughout the kingdom marked an important gesture towards a national poor-relief policy, and also formed an effective agency of social control.

By acting as his own principal minister, Louis XIV cut the ground from under the feet of all but the tamest political opposition. Opponents of royal policy from 1624 to 1661 had been able to adopt the polite fiction that they were "rescuing" the king from his ministers; this was no longer plausible. The brutal repression of peasant revolt in the Boulonnais in 1670, or the punishments meted out to rebels by the historical d'Artagnan (1611–73) in Languedoc in 1670, highlighted the equation between opposition and treason. For arch-ideologist of absolutism Bishop Bossuet, "However bad a prince might be, the revolt of his subjects is always more criminal."

The absolute nature of royal power was closely linked with the development of patriarchal authority within the family. The way the state developed had a direct impact on the everyday lives of men and women. Both Protestants and the Catholic "godly" emphasized the time-honoured place of the family in women's lives. The old adage *aut maritus aut murus* – "either a husband or a cloister" – could no longer apply to Protestant women, for whom no nunneries existed. The Council of Trent had stressed the importance of cloistering female religious communities and groupings – or at least of giving those who operated in the world, such as the Daughters of Charity, a spiritual armour-plating against the desires of the flesh. In the name of female sexual purity both Protestants and Catholics directed campaigns against organized prostitution and any form of sexual deviance.

The state supported these campaigns, amplifying the role of the family head in controlling and policing the behaviour of female members. Just as the poor and deviants were to be confined in state poorhouses, so women and children would be confined within the power of the family. Between around 1550 and 1700 a whole range of measures was introduced to strengthen the legal powers of the paterfamilias, often justified using the same language of absolute sovereignty that Bourbon propagandists used about the monarch. "Marriages," an edict of 1666 stated, "are the fecund sources from which the strength and grandeur of states are derived." The father's power was upheld in civil rather than church courts and concerned all aspects of relations between the sexes (choice of partner, rights over property and inheritance, marital separation and so on). The state pushed the courts to act in favour of greater male control over subordinate females. In 1684 fathers were permitted to use *lettres de cachet* (royal warrants bypassing the courts) to put away in prisons or convents those they adjudged guilty of infringing conventional sexual morality or family honour. This "Family–State Compact" (Sarah Hanley) led to the sovereign himself being conceptualized in more paternal terms: "The king," one lawyer stated, "is the husband and political spouse of the public interest."

If the family was restructured to bolster the power of the state, governments also proved adept at using arts and letters to the same effect. The aim was for the king to be "dazzling and magnificent", as Bossuet put it, so as "to make the peoples respect him". Urbanization was one area of concern. Henry IV had used building projects in Paris to attract attention to his power. For example, he completed the Pont-Neuf, the first bridge in Paris to span the whole of the Seine – an equestrian statue of him was later placed in the middle – and started the Place Royale (now the Place des Vosges). As Louis XIV's faithful minister Colbert reminded him, "Your Majesty knows that, in the absence of striking actions of war, nothing more marks the greatness and the spirit of princes than buildings." Louis XIV rose to the occasion: the Louvre was brilliantly revamped; the Place Louis-le-Grand (now Place Vendôme) and Place des Victoires

A young Louis XIV, costumed as Apollo for the ballet *Fêtes de Bacchus*, performed in 1651.

were created; boulevards were developed on the lines of the old fortress walls; and the Invalides, the Observatory and much else besides were constructed. Under pressure of these urban initiatives the city grew beyond half a million individuals. Even this, however, was eclipsed by Louis' development of the palace of Versailles, where he moved his court in 1682.

Versailles would be widely copied by aspiring absolutist monarchs throughout Europe, from Potsdam to Hampton Court and from Scandinavia to Naples. Yet bricks and mortar were only one aspect of the way the palace operated as an ideological mechanism of absolute power. It was the centre of a kind of "theatre state" in which the main actor, the monarch himself, performed a range of power rituals. The way of life in the palace – an ostentatiously large household, the ritualization of public space, the theatre of daily life, down to the mundanities of getting up, eating meals and going to bed – were emulated by nobles and rival monarchs as statements about power. The metaphor of the sun – an ever-present motif in the art at Versailles – was used in order to make the "Sun King" the point from which all power and vision radiated. The rectilinear angles of classicism converged on the eye of the ruler. So much wealth and prestige now clustered around the court that even the highest nobility felt obliged to reside there. Louis XIV had built a gilded cage in which the turbulent warriors of the Wars of Religion became the foppish courtiers of the Sun King.

Just as classical symmetries had converted unpromising swampland into the might-

"Carrousel" – a courtly and chivalric entertainment – held in Paris to celebrate the engagement of Louis XIII with the Habsburg princess, Anne of Austria in 1612. The event was staged in the fashionable Place Royale, now the Place des Vosges. This building development had been started by Henry IV in 1604.

iest palace in Europe, so the court aimed to domesticate and "classicize" culture. The early decades of Louis XIV's reign mark two of the most fertile periods of French literary history, and most of its major figures – Corneille, Racine, Molière, La Rochefoucauld, La Bruyère and La Fontaine – received state pensions, which Colbert had systematized. Symptomatically Louis took both painters and historians on his military campaigns with him, for he wished to control representations of his power. A whole range of media were used to glorify monarchy – portraits, histories, medals and coins, court ballets (Louis was his own *premier danseur* down to 1679), equestrian statues, triumphal arches, formal entries, ceremonies of touching for the "King's Evil", all added to the lustre of Louis XIV. The Comédie française, the French national theatre, was established in 1680. Louis XIV took Richelieu's idea of the academy, and applied it to specific branches of learning and culture: an Academy of Dance was established

Madame de Sévigné, patient

"After salvation," Madame de Sévigné confided to a cousin, "I count health as of primordial importance." However, how could health be guaranteed in an age whose doctors were satirized so ruthlessly by the dramatist Molière and when, it was generally reckoned, doctors killed off as many patients as they cured?

The correspondence of arch-letter-writer and court aristocrat Marie de Rabutin-Chantal, marquise de Sévigné (1626–96), provides us with a particularly full account of one woman's response to this fateful question. The importance she attached to sickness is underlined by her tendency to be most prodigal in health advice to those she loved most, notably her adored daughter, Madame de Grignan.

Madame de Sévigné displayed a fashionable disdain for medical men, grounded in a good knowledge of Molière's classics. The favoured remedy for a multitude of ills among Parisian physicians was bleedings – yet because of her small veins, which were difficult of access, Madame de Sévigné was a poor bleeder. The most highly

A surgeon prepares a lady's arm for a phlebotomy (bleeding).

regarded practitioners of the court and the capital passed under her consideration. So did high-flown surgeons such as Félix, who had made his name and his fortune for successfully operating upon Louis XIV for an anal fistula; fashionable male midwives like Joubert; and a host of apothecaries, recommending everything from powdered snake to shrimps' eyes or essence of human urine. She was an endless consumer of "waters" of every kind: emerald, chicken, Queen of Hungary's water, gunpowder, and so on. She was also a denizen of spa towns such as Vichy and Alise Sainte-Reine.

Like many at court Madame de Sévigné also displayed a liberal attitude towards irregular practitioners. Some of these had hit upon remedies of lasting value – like the Englishman "Chevalier" Talbot, famous for his support of quinine. But outright quacks also received her custom, including sundry Capuchin monks praising the virtues of different panaceas. Remedies from folklore – like those preached by Madame de Fouquet, mother of Louis XIV's notorious finance minister – also provided her with advice she generally regarded as sage.

Versailles

"Versailles: the most wretched of places, without view, without woods, without water, without soil; for all there is shifting sands and marshes, consequently without air, which cannot be good there."

The acidulous comment of the duc de Saint-Simon, the most disdainful of the chroniclers of Louis XIV's court at Versailles, was not without foundation. The site was poor – its marshiness fostered malaria, which between 1661 and 1682 caused huge numbers of deaths among workers attached to the building works. During this time what had been little more than a cosy hunting lodge for Louis XIV's father, Louis XIII, was transformed into one of the most massive architectural statements of political power in French history.

Louis himself was particularly attached to the site. He hated Paris since the dark days of the Fronde (1648–52), when as a boy he had been kept prisoner by rumbustious Parisian subjects in the Tuileries palace. He attracted the foremost practitioners of the day to make the new palace the site of artistic superlatives: the garden designer Le Nôtre, the painter Charles Le Brun, the architects Le Vau and Mansart, the water engineers the Francine brothers. The king diverted over 5 per cent of state income in the 1670s and 1680s to pay for the constructions. On military campaigns he fretted about the state of his orange groves and tapestries. And he even wrote a kind of guidebook to the palace gardens.

"I entrust to you the most precious thing in the world, my renown." Louis' comment to members of his academy of fine arts highlights the political issue at stake. Versailles was to be about dynastic self-glorification, not just private pleasures. By making his high nobles and ministers reside there as courtiers, moreover, Louis gave himself a perpetual audience. Ambassadors were received there, festivals and pageants held, paupers were touched for the "King's Evil" – the palace served as a visual amplifier for Louis' personal glory.

Above Louis XIV in the gardens of Versailles, 1713–14, by Jean-Baptiste Martin. The king is foregrounded, with his courtiers, against the Apollo fountain – the sun god in the service of the Sun King – and the grand canal.

Left The Hall of Mirrors at Versailles.

in 1661, followed by Academies of Inscriptions (1662), Sciences (1666), Architecture (1671) and Music (1672). The academies set standards of taste, as if under direction from the king, and organized learning from above.

The state's action was important in bringing major scientific changes into the public sphere. Western learning was undergoing what historians have called a Scientific Revolution in the seventeenth century. Advances in astronomy, associated with Kepler and Galileo, led to a new conception of the universe as centred round the sun rather than the earth. William Harvey's work on circulation of the blood challenged the most hallowed presuppositions of medical science. There were important advances in physics, chemistry, biology and so on. Inductive, scientific reasoning threw down a challenge to a theory of knowledge based essentially on divine revelation and Church authority. Yet such work was often the product only of small international cliques of scientists, who also had to contend with the occasional opposition of the authorities – Galileo was harassed by the Church for his views. The French state, by creating a network of academies under which science could be practised in relative freedom, with moderate levels of funding and with government backing, gave a considerable boost to the practice of science. The Scientific Revolution served the monarchy well – the heliocentric universe reflected the glories of the Sun King.

The promotion of grandeur at home was part of a more general quest for glory – *la gloire* – on the battlefield. The focus of French expansionism shifted away from the Italian peninsula, where Habsburg rivalry had been countered in the fifteenth and sixteenth centuries, notably towards the northern and eastern frontiers. A string of major wars – the War of Devolution (1667–8), the Dutch War (1672–8), the War of the League of Augsburg (1689–97) and the War of Spanish Succession (1701–13) – were conducted to execute royal aims.

Had Louis XIV died in the 1680s, his reputation would have stood extremely high. In addition to the gains made in 1648 and 1659 he had by then expanded on the northern front, notably by acquiring Flanders (1678) and, in the east, taking Franche-Comté (1678) and Strasbourg (1681). These gains were part of an on-going process of "reunion", whereby the ruler endeavoured to annex the dependent territories of cities and seigneuries brought under French power in the previous generation. He was also engaged in colonial expansion. Unfortunately, perhaps, Louis survived to carry his ambitions further, and met with almost complete failure beyond this point: his "reunion" policy broke down in 1697; his support for the Stuart dynasty in England came to nothing; his attempt to link the Spanish and French monarchies after 1702 was a flop; and at the Treaty of Utrecht in 1713 he also had to accept colonial losses in North America.

This fruitless cycle of warfare after the 1680s was, moreover, enormously expensive. By the turn of the eighteenth century France was fighting on several land fronts in Europe as well as in the colonies and at sea. Colbert had expanded the French navy from some 18 ships to 276 in 1683, and their maintenance was extremely costly. Under war ministers Le Tellier and his son Louvois the army grew to over 400,000

The *ancien régime*

Brest
Lorient
Nantes
Le Havre
Rouen
Caen
Alençon
Tours
Poitiers
La Rochelle
Rochefort
Bordeaux
Bayonne
Pau
Auch
Toulouse
Montauban
Perpignan
Limoges
Bourges
Orléans
Paris
Versailles
Amiens
Soissons
Châlons-sur-Marne
Lille
Valenciennes
Metz
Strasbourg
Nancy
Besançon
Dijon
Moulins
Riom
Trévoux
Lyon
Grenoble
Montpellier
Sète
Aix-en-Provence
Bastia

Acquisitions by:

Brought by Henry IV, 1589	Valois France
Pays d'etat and pays d'imposition	

| 1624 | 1714 |
| 1661 | 1789 |

Annexed in Louis XIV's *réunions*, 1680-84
Boundary of généralité
● Capital of généralité

Defensive fortifications:
♜ Town fortified by Vauban
♜ New town constructed by Vauban
● Major port development

The "Grand Siècle" saw the significant extension of French territory on the north and north-eastern frontiers. Fortified by Louis XIV's engineer Vauban, this represented a permanent addition to French power. The period also saw the extension of key royal officials, the *intendants*, throughout the provinces, and the *généralité* became the base unit of administration. France was still divided between a central core and peripheral areas that were less firmly controlled from the centre.

before he was cold in his grave. He had aimed to annihilate the power of the nobility: yet the regency government saw the parlement of Paris given back its powers to remonstrate against royal edicts, and aristocrats were soon competing for a place on the royal council in a way that recalled the days of the Fronde.

The monarchy was eventually able to bring its high nobles under some degree of control. Yet neither Louis XV (r. 1715–74) nor Louis XVI (r. 1774–92) was able to recapture the dynastic glories of Louis XIV. They ran the formidable administrative machine instituted by Richelieu and Mazarin and perfected by Louis XIV, making marginal improvements here and there. But they no way affected its basic structure or its social basis in the aristocracy. Bureaucratic standards were improved. State aid to trade and industry continued, and from the 1760s government policy reflected the writings of the "physiocrats" (Quesnay, Mirabeau *père*, Turgot, and others), who urged state support for the rural interest. The intendancy system was streamlined, and intendants now launched a wide range of social and economic improvements. The police forces operated smoothly – deceptively smoothly perhaps, in the light of the events of 1789. Despite sporadic problems with Jansenists, the state was still able to use the clergy as administrative and moralizing agents at grassroots level. Science policy was also developed. The Academy of Sciences was now supplemented by a wide range of other state-supported institutions. The royal botanical gardens in Paris began to operate as a scientific institution, and was headed from 1739 by the great naturalist Buffon. The *Ponts et Chaussées* department, founded in 1726, concentrated on civil engineering.

This detail from Antoine Watteau's *Gersaint's Shopsign* (1721) shows a portrait of Louis XIV being packed away at the end of his reign, while the owner invites customers to examine a painting in Watteau's rococo style. The image of the Sun King was finally in eclipse.

Madame Geoffrin was fully at her ease ... she had the good sense to talk only on those matters about which she knew something and, for everything else, to give their head to people who knew more than she ... The brightest, most animated and most amusing man within this society was d'Alembert. Having spent his morning deciphering algebra or solving problems in dynamics or astronomy, he left his study like a schoolboy leaves the classroom, asking only to enjoy himself ... Whether it was Madame Geoffrin's intention, or whether it was the natural effect of the pleasantness and brilliance that the meetings of these writers gave her home, there was not a prince, a minister nor a man or woman of renown who did not have the ambition of being invited for one of these dinners ...

The salon of Madame Geoffrin (1699–1777), on the fashionable rue Saint-Honoré in Paris, was from the 1730s one of the most brilliant and renowned of literary salons. Here artists and literati mingled with court nobles,

A soirée *chez* Madame Geoffrin

high state officials, wealthy bourgeois and visiting dignitaries to discuss, to debate and to engage in polite social intercourse.

Merit rather than birth was the key to admission to these gatherings: Madame Geoffrin famously turned down the marshal de Richelieu on the grounds of lack of distinction. Wit, urbanity, artistic ability and *politesse* ensured entrée, not genealogy. Madame Geoffrin's visitors were indeed highly distinguished: d'Alembert, Fontenelle, Montesquieu, Voltaire, Helvétius and Marmontel among the *philosophes* and, among the socially distinguished, Gustavus III of Sweden, the future Catherine the Great of Russia and Stanislas Poniatowski, former king of Poland.

The salon became an instrument of intellectual, and thereby political, power. It was said that to enter the Académie française, for example, one had first to receive the approval of the

salon of Madame de Lambert. Salons also had a powerful impact over public taste: Madame Geoffrin's salon was said to be important in winning critical acclaim for new artistic and literary works. The "Czarina of Paris", as she was called, was thus an important disseminator of Enlightenment values and shaper of public opinion.

The influence of the salons was probably declining from the 1770s as new organs of sociability and opinion-forming developed (masonic lodges, clubs and so on). The dominance of women became a target of criticism. The salonnières were seen as aristocratic bluestockings, who rendered politics and politicians effeminate. This misogynist attack was launched from within the Enlightenment. Writer and political theorist Jean-Jacques Rousseau's view, that women should be excluded from politics and should stay at home and bring up children, was influential right across the political spectrum. The ideology of "separate spheres" would be taken further in the Revolutionary and Napoleonic periods.

*Une Soirée chez Madame Geoffrin,*1812. A. G. Lemonnier's painting depicts the first reading of Voltaire's play, *The Orphan from China* (1753–4).

attacking a political establishment wedded to the established Church. It also found an audience among a population increasingly indifferent to religion. The zealous piety of the seventeenth century was giving way among the literate classes to a more materialistic, urbane set of attitudes. Religious enthusiasm was increasingly seen as poor form.

What was important about the *philosophes* was not simply that they said what they did, but that they were listened to – and listened to by ever increasing numbers. Economic growth and widening social mobility were accompanied by broader and more varied cultural activity. The literacy rate doubled over the century, and though the national figures were still only roughly 50 per cent for men and 25 per cent for women, these averages disguised much higher rates in the major cities. The scientists of the previous century had spoken to hundreds of fellow scientists; the "light" spread by the *philosophes* reached a much wider audience. The folio volumes of the *Encyclopedia* or Buffon's *Natural History* reached thousands of readers, while Voltaire's *contes* or the moralizing novels of Jean-Jacques Rousseau were read by hundreds of thousands. Publishing was indeed one of the most dynamic sectors of the economy, and the traditional book trade diversified into periodicals, journals and ephemera of all sorts.

If the press led the way as a place of cultural and intellectual exchange, other institutions followed. Scientific discussion took place in the numerous provincial academies which developed over the century. At a more mundane level coffee-houses, reading rooms and masonic lodges became centres of sociability in which ideas of all sorts could be tested and exchanged. Salons, often presided over by witty and intelligent women, were also a forum for polite intellectual exchange.

A new public sphere was opening up for the discussion of ideas. Under Louis XIV the court regarded itself as the sole generator of sane ideas and public taste. Politics was to take place, it has been said, only in the head of the absolute ruler (K. Baker), and public affairs were generally seen as the preserve of the courtier, the minister and the diplomat. But economic and cultural change transformed the limits and the elitist character of public space. The literate and polite elites could now engage in discussion and debate. Contemporaries began to perceive public opinion as a political force that was impossible to ignore. For the Swiss Jacques Necker, Louis XVI's finance minister in the late 1770s, public opinion constituted "an invisible power that, without treasury, guard or army, gives its laws to the city, the court and even the palaces of kings …"

To hear the monarch talk, one would think that the rules of absolutism had been carved in bronze: "The entire public order emanates from me," Louis XV icily informed the Paris parlement in 1766. "The rights and interests of the nation whom you dare to make a separate body from the monarch rest solely in my hands." Or again Louis XVI, when questioned in the parlement on whether an edict was constitutional: "It is legal, because I wish it." Yet things had changed. By the eve of the French Revolution, for all the absolutist bluster, even the French king was in thrall to public opinion. The court, whether it liked it or not, was having to give ground to the coffee-house as the arbitrator in public issues. Economic growth and the Enlightenment paved the way for the political Revolution of 1789.

Combat de Baune

Louis Mandrin (*c.* 1725–55), smuggler *extraordinaire*, deserted from the army before taking to a life of crime. His exploits before his capture and execution – bringing in untaxed tobacco, and cheap textiles, and fighting pitched battles against soldiers and excise men to do so – could be represented as a struggle to bring consumer goods to an increasingly consumerist audience. Voltaire and others tended to overlook his gratuitous brutality and to amplify his posthumous reputation as a "social bandit" who took from the rich to give to the poor.

flatly contradicted Necker's widely believed *Compte Rendu*. In addition Calonne's plan was widely seen as a measure aimed at increasing the power of the monarchy and the clique of parasitic aristocrats who were kept immune from economic difficulties by the oxygen of court sinecures, favours and pensions.

The government's problems were as much about credibility as about credit. Public opinion – now, as we have seen, a force to be reckoned with – was skilfully mobilized on everything relating to taxation by the parlement, which claimed to defend the interests of the "nation". Although court extravagance actually accounted for a tiny proportion of state expenditure, it was widely blamed for all difficulties. The secrecy and favouritism of court life were seen as running counter to interests of the "nation". This seemed all the more scandalous because the king was increasingly dependent on the

The theories of Austrian scientist/charlatan Franz-Anton Mesmer on "animal magnetism" were highly popular in fashionable society in the 1780s. Mesmerist sessions, in which hypnotist techniques were practised, were widely satirized for the way they took sexual advantage of gullible women.

"nation" for the loans he needed to keep the ship of state afloat. The monarchy's financial needs were too extensive to be met by the social elite alone; they required the aid of international money markets and the pocket-books of the middling as well as the upper classes. Yet just at the moment when the needs of the state seemed to demand a broadening of its social base, the monarchy was increasingly identified with aristocratic parasites. High nobles selfishly profited from the growing weakness of the monarchy. Reforming ministers found themselves victimized by court intrigue. Nobles acted to strengthen their hold on Church, army and state administration. The Ségur Ordinance of 1781, for example, restricted high rank in the army to the oldest "Sword" nobility.

In 1788 the government accepted that there was no way out of its financial dilemma except to consult the nation, in the form of the Estates General, last convened in 1614.

In the Tennis Court Oath of 20 June 1789 deputies of the Third Estate, sensing a royal attack, met informally in a tennis court in Versailles to swear not to disband until the basis of a new constitution had been established. This famous depiction of the scene, from the School of Jacques-Louis David, highlights the solemn drama of the occasion.

Most of the nobility, including the parlements, which had hitherto led opposition to "ministerial despotism", assumed that this body would meet according to the forms of 1614, when it had been manipulated by the nobility and the high clergy. They reckoned without the deep change in political mentality wrought by the Enlightenment, and the social and economic changes that had benefited groups outside charmed aristocratic circles. The assembly of the Estates General released the pent-up energies of "public opinion". Just to meet separately, as would normally be the case, as three separate "orders" or "estates" (clergy, nobility, and Third Estate) seemed an archaic relic out of tune with the times – all the more so because it threatened to allow delegations of the clergy and nobility the chance to squander this peerless opportunity for reform. "What is the Third Estate?" asked the Abbé Siéyès in a famous pamphlet of the same name in early 1789; only to answer, "EVERYTHING. What has it been in the political order until now? NOTHING. What is it asking to become? SOMETHING."

The financial crisis of the state was, then, generating a new political discourse. That

Rights of Man, rights of women

The Declaration of the Rights of Man of 26 August 1789 has proved an enormously influential political text. Its mixture of civil and political rights – individual freedom of speech, assembly and religious opinions, but also freedom from arbitrary government – has provided the blueprint for modern liberal culture. The Declaration is a key source of the United Nations' Universal Declaration on Human Rights.

Since 1789 the scope of the freedoms covered by the Rights of Man has varied. In the 1790s, for example, domestic servants, who were seen as lacking the necessary economic independence, were never fully enfranchised. The 1789 Declaration also coexisted quite happily with the institution of slavery – though to its credit the National Convention in 1794 would abolish slavery and the slave trade outright (temporarily at least). Women too were outside the parameters of the Rights of Man. The playwright Olympe de Gouges produced a pamphlet, *The Rights of Woman* (1791), demanding the extension of rights across the gender divide: "A woman has the right to mount the scaffold: she must also have the right to mount the tribune." Such views failed to make an impression on a revolutionary culture increasingly wedded to an ideology of separate spheres for the sexes. Law, politics and the economy were the male domain, whereas women were confined to a private sphere of sexual virtue, obedience and maternity.

Ironically de Gouges went before the Revolutionary Tribunal for treason in 1793 and mounted the scaffold herself. Women would get the vote in France only after World War II. For more than a century and a half after 1789 the political Rights of Man were confined in France to Men of the masculine sex.

Men rather than women dominated new Revolutionary rituals. In this gouache by Lesueur, women look on decorously and decoratively as their menfolk raise the liberty tree.

discourse – critical of the so-called "privileged orders" and demanding consultation with the "nation" – was, moreover, being heard throughout the land. When censorship was relaxed from July 1788 a flood of political pamphlets and newspapers was unleashed throughout France. The process of election to the Estates General, moreover, involved parish meetings and the drawing-up of *cahiers des doléances* ("books of grievances"). In these, under the influence of the spiralling cost of bread, the new political language fused with the hunger and anger of the poorer classes to produce an early revolutionary fervor. By the time the Estates met in May 1789, it was apparent that this was not going to be a replay of the Fronde, restricted to the political agendas of the high aristocracy, but a much broader and more challenging phenomenon.

It was Louis XVI's frightened attempt to turn back the clock that triggered revolution. Although he eventually agreed to convert the Estates General into a National Assembly charged with framing a new constitution for France, from late June 1789 he began to organize a *coup d'état* aimed at dismissing the Estates General. The next step would be to assume control in conjunction with a now compliant nobility. The city of Paris erupted into insurrection, with the storming of the Bastille. "It is a revolt, then?"

Peasants attacking and pillaging châteaux, in the great agrarian revolution of late July and August 1789. One of the most characteristic peasant actions was the burning of their seigneurs' records, thereby prompting the new National Assembly to abolish feudalism outright.

commented the king on hearing the news from Paris, only to be told coolly, "No, Sire, it is a revolution." The king backed down, and the new Assembly set about building a new constitution.

The entire constitutional landscape had changed. The king now ruled by the will of the people, not by the grace of God. Sovereignty no longer resided in the body of the dynast, but in the people. The "fundamental laws of the kingdom" were clearly insufficient to contain the implications of popular sovereignty. The nation was now made up of citizens with rights, not privately sanctioned groups with privileges. Ironically privilege had once been viewed as a bulwark against royal tyranny and as synonymous with freedom. Now it was a dirty word. It contrasted with the "rights" which all men – not just a select few – were adjudged to have, and which were enshrined in the Declaration of the Rights of Man.

The political crisis of the late summer sent shockwaves throughout the countryside. A (totally unfounded) "Great Fear" that the nobility had hired gangs of brigands who were touring the countryside destroying the harvest and frustrating any hopes of reform mobilized the peasantry into direct action against their seigneurs. Châteaux were attacked, estate managers harassed, seigneurial and feudal records burned. The new National Assembly, on 4 August 1789, not only endorsed peasant revolution by formally abolishing "feudalism". Led by enthusiastic liberal nobles like Lafayette, the assembly also extended the latter term to a wide range of *ancien régime* practices (the Church tithe, venality of office, and so on). These were added to the funeral pyre of what was already being called the "*ancien régime*" – "the former regime". The foundations of a new political culture were being laid.

FROM MONARCHY TO REPUBLIC

The Revolution was about words. Old hate-words ("privilege", "feudalism", and so on) contrasted with terms newly infused with Revolutionary meanings – "citizen", for example, and "nation", to say nothing of the Revolutionary triad "liberty", "equality" and "fraternity", which formed the building blocks of the newly emergent political culture. Terms destined for a long future were either forged, or received a markedly modern twist: "Left" and "Right", for example, "Terror", "terrorist", "bureaucrat", "conscription", "vandalism", "to revolutionize" and "to centralize".

If the Revolution was about words, it was also about symbols. From the earliest days politics saturated daily life. The Bastille, symbol of royal despotism, was transformed into a symbol of the people in arms, and found its way on to flags, wallpaper, shop-signs, pocket-knives, fans, buttons, book covers and all the bric-à-brac of everyday life. The tricolour flag was created when Louis XVI visited Paris following the fall of the Bastille, and Parisians added the Bourbon white to the city's heraldic colours of red and blue as a symbol of unity. The motif was, within hours, being worn in cockades as an emblem of patriotic virtue. The red cap too – mimicking the Phrygian bonnet, which in antiquity emancipated slaves had worn – became another Revolutionary passe-partout. To wear a white cockade, or to dress in overly elaborate aristocratic dress, was viewed as making a counter-revolutionary political statement. A subtle symbolic reper-toire evolved as the Revolution unfolded, often involving collective activities. The

The Demolition of the Bastille by Pierre-Antoine Demachy. As soon as the Bastille was captured, the order was given to demolish it. The erasure of a symbol of royal despotism created welcome jobs for the unemployed and hungry workers of the Faubourg Saint-Antoine, the eastern neighbourhood in Paris in which the Bastille was situated.

Eugène Delacroix's *The 28th July: Liberty Leading the People* (1830), commemorating one of the "Trois Glorieuses", showed that Romanticism had moved from the Right to the Left. A mixture of allegorical and realistic elements this painting was shown in the 1831 Salon.

Charles X, a converted libertine who had found piety late in life, played his cards spectacularly badly. Impervious to how much religious gestures had lost their power to enchant, he organized a traditionalist coronation at Reims, including a ceremony of touching for the King's Evil. Such symbolism looked embarrassingly fake and outmoded, as did the sacrilege law of 1825 introducing the death penalty for blasphemy. Even a cowed and surprisingly quiet opposition found these attempts to resurrect the divine right of kings too much to stomach. But it was not until 1829/30, in the context of bad harvests, high prices and business failures, that their protests began to arouse greater support. Charles X's attempt to bridle the press and to rule as if by the grace of God rather than the wish of the people assumed the shape of a royalist *coup d'état*. The regime found it had few friends when three days of insurrection in Paris – "*Les Trois Glorieuses*" (27–29 July 1830) – forced the monarch to abdicate.

While radicals and conservative governments throughout Europe felt there was a real possibility of the days of 1794 being replayed, political operators among the Bourbons' liberal opponents moved swiftly to circumvent the possibility of a reign of terror or a Bonapartist autocracy. The monarchy was allowed to continue – but in fresh hands. To cheering Parisian crowds the ageing Lafayette, "Hero of the Two Worlds", bestowed the throne on the duke of Orléans, Louis-Philippe, descendant of a branch of the Bourbon dynasty. During the Terror his father had been unable to escape the guillotine, despite dubbing himself "Philip Equality" and voting for the death of Louis XVI. The new king had served in the Revolutionary armies of the 1790s and embraced a moderate and liberal version of the Revolutionary heritage.

The "citizen king" would preside over a "bourgeois monarchy". Louis-Philippe prided himself on being able to balance the "excesses of popular power" with the "abuses of royal power". Charles X had tried to heal the sick like a saint; Louis-Philippe carried an umbrella. Charles X had sought to subvert liberal freedoms; Louis-Philippe vigorously endorsed them. So censorship was reduced, the property franchise lightened and the elected assembly allowed to initiate laws. This was no social revolution, however. The electorate was expanded – but hardly spectacularly: still only a quarter of a million landowners had the vote. Rather, the boundaries of the ruling class had been broadened to include a greater influx of lawyers, businessmen, middling landowners and financiers. The bourgeois monarchy encouraged an interchange between the financial, manufacturing, professional, agrarian and political branches of the bourgeoisie. The flavour of the new regime was redolent not of the aristocratic salon or the elegant country house, but rather the stock-exchange, the business premises and the wealthy bourgeois private residence.

The Revolutionary and Napoleonic periods had equipped France with an unmatched array of legal and administrative structures adapted to capitalist development – abolition of feudalism, a unified home market, national legal codes, uniform weights and measures, equality before the law, a national bank and so on. Yet while the Industrial Revolution steamed ahead in neighbouring Britain, France lagged some way behind. This was partly because of France's poor natural supply of coal and iron ore, but crucial too was the major realignment required of the French economy after the events between 1789 to 1815. In those years colonial trade, the most dynamic sector of the *ancien régime* economy, had been crippled. The colonial empire that France had struggled to develop in the eighteenth century was effectively wiped out. There were attempts to build a new world empire after 1815. The conquest of Algeria was begun in 1830, while there were further gains under Louis-Philippe in West Africa, Madagascar and the South Seas (Tahiti, for example, was colonized). Yet France after 1800 had a far more continental, land-based economy than prior to 1789. Indeed the

Slave revolts

Saint-Domingue (present-day Haiti) had been the most significant element in France's booming colonial trade in the eighteenth century. The success of the West Indian colony stemmed from sugar plantations that were worked by black slaves. But in the 1790s it became the site of a black liberation movement. This owed little to France itself: the first slave protests in 1790 and 1791 were put down in a pool of black blood. The National Assembly's abolition of slavery in early 1794 was, moreover, the acceptance of a *fait accompli*: since 1793 slave armies led by Toussaint l'Ouverture had taken control of the colony along with the neighbouring ex-Spanish colony of Santo Domingo.

Toussaint was the dominant leader on the island in the mid and late 1790s. A slave himself, who had been emancipated in his thirties in 1777, he was both idolized by the blacks and respected by the whites. He attempted to work har-

moniously with the white community in order to restore the island's prosperity, but the situation was far from stable. A complex game unravelled that included the French, black radicals, and British troops in the Caribbean. Toussaint's insistence that he was French and by 1800 a loyal Bonapartist was not enough to prevent his capture, deportation to mainland France and imprisonment. Napoleon sought to re-establish slavery as the basis for the island's economic recovery: "A white myself," he is alleged to have said, "I am on the side of the whites."

"By overthrowing me," Toussaint wrote to Napoleon, "you have only cut down the trunk of the tree of liberty of Saint-Domingue. Its roots will grow back, for they are many and deep." He was vindicated. Though he died in a French gaol, his black opponents in the colony were able – with the help of yellow fever – to put paid to French armed forces and in 1804 to establish Saint-Domingue as an independent black state.

Toussaint l'Ouverture. He owed his second name to the ferocity with which he made an opening ("ouverture") in the ranks of the enemy in battle.

Revolutionary and Napoleonic Wars had caused the centre of gravity of the economy to shift from the Atlantic seaboard to the eastern and northern frontier. The big ports which had benefited from France's colonial dominion and trade in the eighteenth century – Bordeaux, Rouen, La Rochelle, Saint-Malo, Le Havre and others – declined in influence and wealth, while such eastern cities as Strasbourg and Lyon saw their prosperity grow. In the north, cities close to the coal belt also started to expand.

The Revolutionary land settlement also had a major impact on the pattern of economic growth after 1800. Most peasants now prioritized self-sufficiency above all else. The long-term drop in agricultural prices after 1817 and the damage done to foreign trade by colonial losses gave them a disincentive to sell their produce on the open market. The "traditionalism" and "archaism" for which their urban contemporaries condemned peasants were thus a rational response to a difficult economic environment. Temporary or seasonal migration was another strategy for survival. The most backward areas – the Massif Central, the Alps and Pyrenees – provided the most mobile of populations, sending out hordes of harvesters, ditch-diggers, servants, pedlars, schoolteachers and entertainers (the prize possession in the inventories of many Pyrenean peasants was a fairground bear), whose earnings helped prop up family budgets.

Ironically this peasantry, which contemporaries saw as archaic and backward-looking, was adopting that most "modern" of forms of behaviour: systematic birth control. Before the nineteenth century France, like every other European society, had had high birth- and death-rates. The death-rate started to fall, as we have seen, in the eighteenth century, and would continue to do so throughout the nineteenth century. Improved nutrition was the key here, though medical advances such as smallpox vaccination (after 1798) also had an impact. From 1800, however, while France's European rivals continued to be marked by high fertility, its birth-rates plummeted: from nearly 40 live births per thousand population before 1750, the rate fell to 32 per thousand in the early Restoration, and then to 26 per thousand by mid century. The causes of this silent sexual revolution taking place in peasant beds may relate to the growth of religious indifference which distanced peasants from the precepts of the Church. More significant, however, was the introduction of partible inheritance by the Napoleonic Code, which provided motivation for peasants to limit family size. Peasants, then, adopted birth control – largely *coitus interruptus*, it would appear – so as to prevent having to split up their lands among numerous heirs, and so that their land could stay large enough to ensure continuing self-sufficiency for the next generation.

France was still overwhelmingly an agricultural and small-town society. A far higher proportion of its population lived on the land than any of its competitors. In Britain

The railway became a satisfying social metaphor. An admiring family of prosperous bourgeois watch a locomotive, representing engineering feats (tunnel, bridge), social mixing (the passengers), speed and scientific progress. In the background loom the symbols of France which need to be changed: a château, a windmill, a church, and a peasant driving a mule.

From the mid eighteenth century, a dynasty of Koechlins had pioneered light cotton manufacturing in the independent imperial city of Mulhouse. Incorporated into France in 1798, the city became one of France's leading textiles centres in the nineteenth century.

the moment when urban population outstripped country-dwellers came in the 1830s. In Italy it was in the 1870s; in Germany around 1900; in the United States of America in the 1920s. Yet in France this moment occurred as late as the 1930s. For most of the nineteenth century between two-thirds and three-quarters of the population still lived on the land. Indeed nearly half of France's departments experienced an all-time maximum of rural population between the 1830s and the 1870s. With some exceptions, moreover, the towns cut only a modest figure. Paris grew fast, doubling between 1800 and 1850, and there was impressive growth in industrial cities like Lyon, Lille and Mulhouse. More characteristic, however, was the town of around 10,000 inhabitants, whose stuffy atmosphere was captured in the novels of Stendhal and Balzac. The social mood of the early nineteenth century was set by the notables who dominated these centres: landowners (including many nobles, whose influence at local level outweighed their prominence on the national stage), *rentiers* and the professional classes.

Hence the social and demographic setting predisposed France, even with its framework of rational institutions, to an industrialization process which would be protracted, steady and solid rather than sudden or spectacular. Mechanization was slower in France than in Britain – with its large pools of out-workers France had fewer labour bottlenecks acting as an incentive to mechanize. However, France was still far ahead of the pack among Britain's economic rivals in continental Europe, and remained the second biggest exporter of manufactured goods through to 1870. Whereas Britain's exports were mass-produced middle-quality items, France specialized in the luxury and skilled finished goods (silk, gloves, porcelain, and so on) in which it traditionally had a reputation.

There were important moves in the 1830s and 1840s, moreover, to improve the infrastructure of the economy, laying down the bases of future growth. Road and canal building was accompanied by the beginnings of investment in railways. An important law in 1842 provided a partnership between the state and business for railway development. A dense rail network, centred on Paris, was already emerging by the fall of the July Monarchy in 1848. Despite France's somewhat sleepy appearance, there was a good deal of exchange and communications. The country had 7,000 fairs a year, on top of 3,000 weekly markets. The emergence of a body of commercial travellers from the 1820s, and the development of advertising in the press, also highlighted communication and exchange.

This balanced economic development muffled the growing pains of industrialization. The latter imposed strains on the working classes which did not, however, approach the appalling levels characteristic in Victorian Britain. The fact that most peasants stayed on the land cushioned cities from the emergence of a massive urban under-class. Yet conditions were still grim. The Romantic painter Delacroix portrayed workers and bourgeois in arms together on the barricades of "*Les Trois Glorieuses*" of 1830; but the bourgeoisie soon distanced themselves from their former allies, both in politics and in social policy. Calls for a radical republic were silenced. A rising of impoverished silk-workers in Lyon in 1831 was pitilessly repressed. Social concern for the condition of the poor was rejected in favour of a *laissez-faire* attitude. Supporters of the regime attacked any talk of industrial legislation, calling factories "sanctuaries as sacred as a father's house". "Whatever the lot of the workers is," a trade minister opined in 1833, "it is not the manufacturer's responsibility to improve it." Nor apparently was it the government's. In the cities inadequate provision of decent housing, water, sanitation and job opportunities produced desperately unhealthy conditions. In Mulhouse the new-born baby of a bourgeois had a life expectancy of over thirty years; that of a weaver, of four. Cholera reared its head after 1832, causing havoc among city populations; some 143,000 people died in the 1853/4 outbreak alone, which seemed a dreadful warning of the perils of urbanization.

Grim conditions among the poor produced some response from the Right. The priest Felicité-Robert Lamennais preached a "social Catholicism" in tune with the times, while Charles Ozanam created a network of Societies of Saint-Vincent-de-Paul, which practised imaginative forms of philanthropy. Though the Right remained alert to the political potential of charity as a means of winning mass support, most fellow-Catholics in the elite dreamed primarily of a return to the *ancien régime* rather than adapting to industrial society. Yet even though industrial workers found the call from the Right unappealing, the Revolutionary traditions of 1789 seemed to have been

Paris is the heart of France. Let us put all our efforts into embellishing this great city. Let us open new roads, make populous neighbourhoods which lack light and air more healthy, and let benevolent light penetrate everywhere within our walls.

Napoleon III's call for the modernization of the city of Paris was implemented by Baron Haussmann, prefect of the Seine department from 1853 to 1869. Balzac's Paris – crumbling with age, slum-ridden, insanitary, prone to cholera epidemics, over-crowded – was to be brought up to date. Some rejected the changes on aesthetic grounds; the anarchist activist Proudhon denounced "the new, monotonous and tiring city of M. Haussmann". There were also many on the Left who felt that there was a hidden political agenda involved in the change – namely, the destruction of the old workers' neigh-

The Haussmannization of Paris

Napoleon III and Empress Eugénie lay the foundation stone for the new opera house, in the company of Prefect Haussmann.

Cholera, embodied as a rag-picker, protests to Hausmann that the modernization of Paris is costing him his home.

bourhoods that had fostered the radicals and *sans-culottes* of the Parisian revolutionary tradition. Barricades and boulevards could not coexist.

Modernization was part of a more general process of making the city the showcase of the imperial regime. Prestige building integrated into the new street plan included the Opéra, the Bibliothèque Nationale, extensions to the Louvre palace, the iron buildings of Les Halles (the city market), plus the development of open leisure spaces (Bois de Vincennes, Bois de Boulogne, and so on). Such changes also had the power of example: right up to World War I a great many major cities followed in the tracks of "Haussmannization" and "boulevardization".

Modernization also involved making Paris the economic motor of the country as a whole. The fact that Paris was the hub of a new railway network under-

lined Napoleon's commitment. Just as railways acted to unify the national market and energize the national economy, so the new boulevards and broad avenues, driven through the jungle of narrow medieval streets, were to connect up and produce a more integrated urban society and economy. In practice the changes also had the effect of introducing greater social distance between the classes. Classes had traditionally been integrated vertically in the city: first- and second-floor rooms were occupied by the bourgeoisie, the top floor and garret by the poor. Haussmannization brought about a new differentiation, between richer and poorer areas. The inner city became more middle-class, while workers were pushed outwards to a proletarian "red belt" encompassing the city. Haussmann had not solved social and political problems, merely displaced them.

"The Empire means peace," Napoleon had proclaimed in 1852. Yet although it never rivalled the systematic aggressiveness of the First Empire, the Second Empire did have a strongly militaristic strain, which Napoleon fitfully disguised behind a pacifistic rhetoric. The emperor dispensed with the timidity which had marked French foreign policy in preceding decades, establishing a worldwide presence. He doubled French colonial holdings most notably in Indo-China, central and West Africa and the Pacific, and prepared France for the scramble for colonies which would take place after 1880. The new banking institutions also stimulated foreign investment worldwide. The Suez Canal, opened in 1869 by Napoleon's wife, Empress Eugénie, was the achievement of a French man, Ferdinand de Lesseps, and had been largely financed from the savings of the nation's bourgeoisie. Yet Napoleon was unable to wrest the initiative in world trade and colonization from Britain. And his ill-conceived plan to establish an empire in Mexico in the 1860s resulted in a humiliating fiasco.

Manet's depiction of the slaughter meted out in the Paris Commune of 1871.

He did little better in Europe. Though his acquisition of Nice and Savoy (from neigh-bouring Piedmont-Sardinia) in 1859 marked the only major extension of French fron-tiers between Waterloo and the present day, he received little credit for an achievement that was overshadowed by his failures. The biggest of these proved to be his inability to master the rising tide of nationalism in Europe, notably in Italy and Germany. His acquisition of Nice and Savoy was achieved in exchange for giving military assistance to Piedmont in forcing through Italian unification against Austria. He got the worst of both worlds, though, upsetting Catholics by allowing the forcible incorporation of the papal states into the new Italy, yet alienating liberals by later sending French troops to defend the pope in the Vatican. On the European stage he was also easily outplayed by Prussia's Bismarck, and an attempt to trade French neutrality in the Austro-Prussian War of 1866 rebounded disastrously on him. He had hoped to be rewarded by the acquisition of Luxembourg for his neutrality at a moment when Prussia was establish-ing primacy in central Europe, and creating a German national state. He was humiliat-ingly snubbed, and found himself threatened by two new nation states.

And humiliation did now count; for public opinion was re-emerging as a political force in the 1860s. The authoritarian days of the 1850s had given way to a period of experimentation with liberal reform. Press censorship was relaxed; the circulation of Parisian newspapers, which had stood at 50,000 in 1830, reached 700,000 by 1868. Laws on public meetings were progressively weakened, too, and in 1864 the right to strike (though not yet to organize or to picket) was authorized. Radicalism grew steadily in the workplace – in the 1860s French workers were to form the largest national delegation to the First International. A republican opposition also began to coalesce – its adherents were mostly those who rejected socialism but planned liberal reforms, spiced with the doctrinaire anti-clericalism which was becoming a conven-tional attribute of French republicanism. Napoleon permitted ministers to have greater responsibility for their decrees to parliament and also introduced a number of mea-sures which allowed the Chamber of Deputies to assume greater autonomy.

As a result discontent with the regime grew quickly, especially as the economy was experiencing a rather bumpier ride in the 1860s than in the golden days of the 1850s. Meanwhile Napoleon's increasingly fraught and reckless foreign policy was also attracting criticism. The opposition parties won 40 per cent of the popular vote in elec-tions in 1869. When plans to become a fully parliamentary regime were put to the voters in a referendum in May 1870, they won a massive five-to-one majority. These changes could have proved a significant test of the democratic credentials of what had begun as an essentially authoritarian regime. The constitutional experiment was, how-ever, still-born; by the end of the year the Second Empire had ignominiously fallen.

The collapse was military and diplomatic. Army reforms in the 1860s had not pro-duced the looked-for improvements in military organization and morale, with the result that once Napoleon took to the field, he found his troops outmanoeuvred by the superbly effective Prussian fighting machine that Bismarck had assembled. Holed up in Sedan with nearly 100,000 troops Napoleon surrendered, and was sent to prison in

Germany. He never returned to France. The scale of the defeat led politicians in Paris to declare the end of the regime and to install a provisional government. They would be obliged to sign a humiliating peace, by which France surrendered the provinces of Alsace and Lorraine to the new German state. Hence the regime which had gained Nice and Savoy would be associated with a territorial loss greater than France had experienced since the Hundred Years War. The incoming regime would have to cope with continued political division, as well as the humiliation and economic damage caused by the loss of two strong and prosperous northern provinces.

THE COMMUNE AND THE POLITICS OF THE THIRD REPUBLIC

The Third Republic was born with France in trauma. The omens, when set against the volatility and brevity of regimes since 1789, were not good. Even the regime's midwife – Adolphe Thiers, who headed the provisional government, and was the first president – gave the infant republic little chance of survival. In the event the Third Republic was to last until 1940, making it the most enduring regime in modern French history. And indeed, although its history between the two world wars was to be troubled, the regime's prestige up to the peace treaties at the end of the World War I was extremely high. By then it had achieved its main foreign policy objective – the reconquest of Alsace and Lorraine. It had presided over extensive colonial expansion. It had maintained enviable financial stability. It had brought considerable material progress to the majority of French people. And it had been associated with a cultural life as rich and varied as that of any other period in French history: Cézanne, Monet and Matisse in painting; Auguste Rodin in sculpture; Zola and Proust in literature; Verlaine, Rimbaud and Mallarmé in poetry; Debussy in music; Pasteur in medical science; the Curies in physics; Poincaré in mathematics; Bergson in philosophy; Charcot in neurology; and Durkheim in sociology, to name only some of the most outstanding figures.

There was little in 1870 and 1871 to suggest the achievements to come. War continued after the overthrow of Napoleon III, with Paris endeavouring to hold out against a Prussian siege. The charismatic young politician Léon Gambetta escaped by balloon from a city whose inhabitants were reduced to eating rats; but his attempts to raise an army in the south were in vain. In January 1871 the provisional government capitulated, signing a peace treaty which ratified the loss of Alsace-Lorraine and imposed a war indemnity of 5 million francs, obliging France to suffer the humiliation of a German occupying army until the sum was forthcoming. Paris smarted under the blow, and elected a municipal government, which, in the spirit of national defence of 1792, took on the title of "the Commune". This time, however, there was to be no replay of history. Thiers established himself in Versailles, his position buttressed by a newly elected monarchist majority in parliament, and undertook a new siege of Paris, in which the Commune was introducing radical social legislation and calling for the prosecution of the war. With German occupying troops watching with grim fascination, a bloody dance of death ensued. Thiers' troops penetrated the city towards the end of May and began a ferociously brutal conquest of the city. The Revolutionary Tribunal

Madame Curie

Marie Curie, née Sklodowska (1867–1934), was among the most outstanding of a wave of French scientists with worldwide reputations, whose careers illuminated the intellectual history of the Third Republic. Born in Poland, and entering France in 1891, she pursued a brilliant student career before working in the scientific team of the physicist Pierre Curie, whom she came to marry in 1895. Röntgen had just discovered X-rays, and Madame Curie worked to find compounds of substances besides uranium which produced them. By 1898 she had discovered the element radium, which she and her husband succeeded in isolating in 1902. They were jointly awarded the Nobel Prize for physics in 1903.

Madame Curie continued to work in the same field after the death of her husband in 1906, and was awarded a second Nobel Prize in 1911. She was particularly interested in the use of radium in medicine. In World War I she personally supervised the provision of portable X-ray equipment for French troops. Though she had been refused admission to the Academy of Sciences in 1908 – presumably because of her gender – she received a full measure of state support after the war. After her death her work was carried forward by her daughter Irène Joliot-Curie.

The popular press played an important role in publicizing the "patriotic" science of the Curies. In 1994 President Mitterrand announced the transfer of her remains into the Pantheon.

between 1792 and 1794 had accounted for fewer than 3,000 deaths; in a single week anti-Commune justice meted out on the streets of Paris accounted for between 25,000 and 30,000 deaths by summary execution, with over 40,000 Parisians taken prisoner. Hostages taken by the Commune, including the archbishop of Paris, were shot. Fires swept through the city, burning down the Tuileries palace, the Hôtel de Ville and other public buildings.

The searing memory of the Commune affected both Left and Right. It formed a myth whose heroic resonance the Marxist Left would long exploit. The Right constructed a different myth, of Paris as hotbed of sedition, home of red revolutionaries, wild anarchists and crazed women (the *pétroleuses* – female petrol-bomb throwers alleged to have started the city's fires – had a particularly blood-curdling impact on the bourgeois psyche). Even though the Haussmann reforms were already transforming the social composition of the city, forcing workers into the "red suburbs", and producing a conservative inner city, the Commune served as justification for outright reaction. Paris was kept under siege conditions until 1876. In contrast with France's other 38,000 communes, it was denied the right to have a mayor – a refusal that lasted until 1976. Only in 1879 did amnesties begin to be given to those Communards imprisoned in 1871.

With the Commune utterly discrediting and dividing the Left, the Right enjoyed a political field day. The monarchist majority in the new assembly triumphantly assumed that they constituted a kind of antechamber to a revived monarchy. This

The industrial transformation of France

	Industry c. 1880			Number of steam engines, 1878				
Territory acquired in 1860–61	⬛ Coalfields	▢ Cottons		Less than 100		251–500		1001–1100
Territory lost in 1871	△ Metallurgy	○ Woollens		101–250		501–1000		Over 4000

While the political geography of France changed little after 1815 the country's industrial geography was transformed, highlighting the importance of local supplies of coal and the acceptance of steam power. While new industrial heartlands evolved in the far north, the east and the Lyonnais, many areas of traditional manufacturing – such as the woollen industries in Languedoc – failed to adapt. A contrast was opening up between a "modern" north and east and an "archaic" south and west.

Prototype postage stamps (not released) of the opportunistic General Boulanger – a form of publicity to which few could aspire. Stamps had been introduced, and their sale in tobacconists' authorized, in 1849.

anti-republican attachment to the Church and the far Right. Elsewhere traditionalist "white" areas turned "red" under social and economic pressures, so that radical peasants could now link up with urban workers against the political centre.

The Opportunists held essentially liberal views; laws in the 1880s ensured freedom of speech and assembly, for example. But even they bowed to peasant pressure when they reintroduced a degree of agrarian protectionism – notably in the Méline laws of 1892 – to mollify rural areas. They were less prepared to pacify the proletariat. Although they legalized trade unions in 1884, they tended to deny the existence of a "social question". Measures of social security were lamentably slow to develop in France, especially in comparison with Great Britain and with Bismarck's Germany. By 1914 achievement in social reform was slight: a ten-hour day for women and children from 1900; eight-hour shifts in the mines from 1905; a mandatory one day of rest in seven from 1906; optional (and under-used) social insurance measures from 1910. As a consequence, mutual aid societies were highly developed, containing over two million workers by 1914.

Disregarding social reform, Opportunist politicians prized a unifying republican ideology. Significantly, in 1879, "The Marseillaise" became the national anthem, while in 1880 Bastille Day (14 July) was agreed as a national holiday. The town-halls of France were equipped with busts of Marianne, a symbol of the republic since the 1790s which emphasized unity rather than division, and which was often modelled on the statue unveiled in the Place de la République in Paris in 1883. Opportunist politicians also drew on republican mythology in a heightened emphasis on anti-clerical policies. Gambetta's cry, "Le cléricalisme, voilà l'ennemi!" was sufficiently rooted in the republican tradition to find allies on the Left without the need to accommodate radical social reform. Education became the battlefield on which the struggle was fought: the children of Marianne had to be rescued from the divisive and vengeful clutches of a backward-looking, anti-republican Church. In legislation between 1881 and 1886, sponsored by Jules Ferry, free public primary education was introduced for children between six and thirteen years old; all children between those ages were to attend either a lay or a religious school; public secondary education for girls was put on a proper footing for the first time; and generous provision was made for teacher training and school building. These important laws were supplemented by more specifically anti-clerical measures: the major changes to the Falloux Laws of 1850, which had given religious teaching communities greater freedom to operate; the removal of churchmen from the councils of universities (which were also reformed and expanded); a ban on Church institutions offering university degrees; and so on.

Ferry's "schools without God" were bitterly opposed by churchmen, who too easily saw them as the work of Protestants and freemasons, both of which groups were strong supporters of the republic. Yet despite their contested beginnings the schools proved one of the most enduring cultural achievements of the early Third Republic. Village schoolhouses still stand as monuments to the republican values of the late nineteenth century. Schoolteachers came to represent an alternative cultural focus to the parish priest, and proved the republic's most ardent supporters: the death-rate among school-teacher volunteers in the trenches of World War I (roughly one-fifth) was higher than in any other social group.

Lay schooling was seen as a means of removing children from the Church, but also from the noxious influence of women. Anti-clericalism was very much a male province – orthodox conformity was far more widespread among women. As a result they came to be seen as handmaidens of the Church's mission to turn young minds to God. The lay schools aimed to instil metropolitan and masculine values. Petty bourgeois virtues

Third Republic history school textbook. Strong hints of hostility towards German "barbarian" pillagers in the guise of Clovis' Franks blend uneasily with an awareness of the role of the Franks in the development of the French nation.

of hard work, reward for merit, reliability, thrift and respect for property were preached. The loss of Alsace and Lorraine, moreover, stimulated a kind of muscular nationalism. Physical training and sport could ensure that the fight for the integrity of France might yet be won on the playing-fields of, say, Palavas-les-Flots. History teaching preached a cult of the fatherland and its defence. In textbooks "patriotic" figures such as du Guesclin, Joan of Arc, Philip Augustus and even Robespierre enjoyed prominence, while scorn was reserved for the Merovingians, who had proved constitutionally incapable of maintaining their kingdom's integrity – and who were kings to boot.

To many who attended them, however, these schools must have appeared as colonial as well as republican institutions. The metropolitan bourgeois values they promoted were foreign to many peasants, workers and women. Despite the universalist and meritocratic assumptions behind the Ferry legislation these three groups did markedly worse in the classroom, and this made the school a means of social control as much as of career mobility. This was truer the further southwards and westwards one went from the capital city. Social commentators were already remarking on the existence of "two Frances" on either side of a line joining Saint-Malo and Geneva. To the south and west of this line populations were shorter in stature, less well-fed, less highly educated, more prone to violent crime and more likely to evade taxes and desert from the army. Research in the 1860s suggested that in roughly one-quarter of French communes – most of these in this south-western bloc – French was still not spoken. Law-courts in Provence, Brittany and the Limousin were still having to use interpreters in order to deal with the testimony of peasant "natives". On the eve of the 1789 Revolution half of men and three-quarters of women had been unable to sign their names. In the early years of the Third Republic, the comparable figures were one-quarter and one-third.

The "two Frances". Economic and industrial change (p. 219) was highlighting the profile of "two Frances". The division between north and east on the one hand and south and west on the other was cultural as well as economic. The north and east had far more impressive levels of literacy (centre) – a fact that owed something to the enduring presence of non-French languages in the south and west (left). The divergence was attitudinal as well as linguistic: the north and east found it easier to accept that emblem of modern life and personal freedom, the bicycle (right).

French-speaking communes, 1863

Literacy, 1885

Number of bicycles and tricycles, 1899

■ Patois indicated	Significantly non-French speaking
⧄ Some non-French speaking	Predominantly non-French speaking

■ 90–100%	70–80%
80–90%	50–70%

Over 3500	1000 or fewer
⧄ 1001–3500	

One of the avowed aims of lay schooling was to remedy these defects, and to acculturate those parts of France resistant to bourgeois metropolitan culture. A prominent tactic here was the emphasis on the French language as the sole means of communication within the school. Though this approach infuriated the regionalist intelligentsias, the latter failed to find mass support. Illiteracy was equated with inability to speak French, ignorance with anti-republicanism. The Opportunists linked up with the rhetoric of the 1790s revolutionaries, for whom French had been "the language of liberty", while "the mass of corrupted dialects" represented "the vestiges of feudalism". Speech, like the republic, had to become "one and indivisible" if brutalized peasants were to be brought back within the pale of civilization. Children who broke into their native idioms within school walls were humiliated and punished. National conscription, introduced from 1872, proved an important supplementary means of linguistic control. The marked reduction in levels of illiteracy – by the early 1900s less than 10 per cent of conscripts were unable to sign their names – demonstrates the success of this programme of cultural assimilation.

The "civilizing mission" of the politicians of the Third Republic also found fertile terrain in the colonies. Though some opposed colonial ventures as a diversion from the essential task of winning back Alsace-Lorraine from the Germans, the years down to 1914 saw France increase its overseas holdings tenfold – the empire extended to three million square miles and contained fifty million inhabitants. France participated in the "scramble for Africa", building up spheres of interest in East and central Africa and strengthening its hold on the north. Indo-China was effectively colonized and gains were made in the Pacific and Indian Oceans. Significantly it was the arch-educationalist Jules Ferry who was the crucial figure in acquiring control of these regions. Ferry once commented that the only aspect of the empire to arouse French passions was the belly-dance. However, though he bemoaned his fellow-citizens' lack of enthusiasm for these new arenas of domination, he helped establish France as the world's second imperial power, behind Britain.

THE NEW MATERIALISM OF THE *BELLE EPOQUE*

In 1889 an International Exhibition was held in Paris, the crowning glory of which was the iron tower erected by the Burgundian engineer Gustave Eiffel. Standing at over 300 metres, the tallest metal structure in the world, and illuminated at its inauguration by over 20,000 gas lights, the Eiffel tower symbolized the Third Republic's attachment to its revolutionary heritage. Opened in the centenary year of the Revolution of 1789 by Eiffel planting a tricolour flag on its summit, it was a secular riposte to the building of the basilica of the Sacré-Coeur, which ardent clericalists had erected at Montmartre to atone for the death of the archbishop of Paris in the Commune of 1871. With its modernistic design and electric elevators the tower illustrated the Third Republic's respect for science and technology. And it also exemplified a new craze for mass entertainment – hundreds of thousands of visitors flocked in within months of its opening – and a flagrant, somewhat self-indulgent materialism.

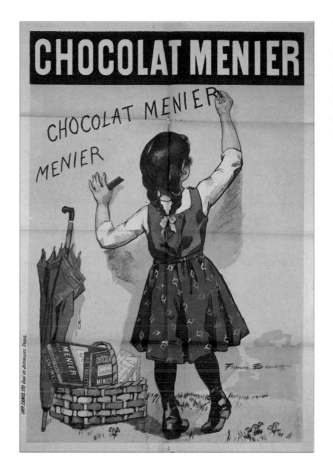

This advertisement for Menier chocolate by Firmin Bouisset (1892) pays unwitting testimony to the progress of female literacy in the *belle époque*. The period saw posters take off as a brilliant new art form.

The first half-century of the Third Republic saw massive shifts in the material culture of most French men and women. The writer Charles Péguy, commenting on the eve of World War I, estimated that France had changed more since he was at school in the 1880s than it had since the time of the Romans. Material improvement was grounded in the continuing progress of industrialization. France's economy continued its slow and steady expansion. Overall France was slipping from second to, by 1914, fourth greatest industrial world power, yet this still represented considerable growth. On top of the already impressive increases seen during the Second Empire, industrial output tripled and national income doubled. Growth was fastest in the period after 1896 and in particular in the decade before the outbreak of war. Steam-power increased sevenfold in industry from the 1880s, and this was used in the progressive iron, chemistry and automobile industries, which were the key sectors of this second phase of the industrialization process. The electricity industry also developed, including hydro-electric power. Peugeot, which had originally made its money in textiles, switched to bicycles, then to automobiles by 1914. Along with Renault, Citroën and others the automobile industry was second only to that of the United States, and produced twice as many cars as Great Britain. Already Michelin was making its name in the rubber industry, servicing motor cars, while Blériot's famous

Opposite Poster for the 1889 Universal Exhibition held in Paris. The Eiffel tower, an engineering triumph, and here bedecked by a tricolour pennant, was the star attraction. Most of the other exhibition buildings were subsequently demolished.

flight over the Channel in 1909 also signalled France's pioneering role in the aeroplane industry.

As the latter examples suggest, improvements were especially marked in the communications sector of the economy. The so-called "Freycinet Plan", launched in 1878, set about improving communications in all parts of France. The plan broke with the custom of having the rail network centred on Paris, for example, and the increase in rail kilometrage from 24,000 to over 64,000 between 1881 and 1914 included a great many branch lines extending into formerly quite untouched areas. Canal building and improvement doubled the volume of goods carried by water over the same period, while massive road construction also helped to integrate and extend the national market. From the 1890s trams came into wide use in cities, while in Paris the metro system was introduced in 1900. Personal mobility was also increased by the spread of bicycles, which numbered 375,000 in 1898 and 3.5 million in 1914. These changes in the distribution and communications sectors of the economy caused a major shift in employment patterns: one-fifth of workers had been employed in this sector in 1850, but by World War I the figure had risen to nearly one-third.

This reflected changes in other forms of communication, too. The electric telegraph was being used from the 1850s and was able to convey intercontinental messages from the 1860s. The telephone made large strides too: public booths were introduced in the 1880s. The total number of telephones rose from some 12,000 in 1889 to over 300,000 by 1913. In 1878 the telegraph services were combined with the postal services and in 1889 the PTT (*Postes, Télégraphes et Téléphones*) was formed to combine the three services. The village postman became a standard figure – his daily round would take him the equivalent of seven times round the globe in his career! In 1911 it was a French man who initiated the world's first air-mail service.

The output of the printing presses was also revolutionized, helped by the growth of literacy and the rise of larger middle- and lower-class readerships. As newspapers entered the mass age, costs continued to fall because of the growth of advertising and technological improvements (the advent of the rotary press from the 1860s, the linotype from 1880s and so on). The number of Parisian daily newspapers had doubled in the July Monarchy and quintupled under the Second Empire; it rose fivefold again up to 1914, which still marks the high-point in French newspaper-readership. The provincial dailies followed this upward trend. Circulation had rarely exceeded 10,000 to 20,000 before the middle of the nineteenth century. *Le Petit Journal* in the 1860s was the first to aim for a mass audience, cramming its pages with crime stories, serialized novels and human-interest items, and soon managed one-third of a million copies – over one million by the 1890s. The advertisement was another form of communication to develop fast. The liberal bill-sticking law of 1881 allowed the wall-poster to come of age as an art form as well as a means of communication and persuasion: wines, liqueurs, patent medicines and all forms of entertainment were among the most widely peddled items.

These changes in patterns of communications marked the rise of the mass consumer. This was evident in diet, where there were changes, especially from the 1890s,

Au Bon Marché

The vestibule [was] changed into an Oriental salon. From the doorway it was a marvel, a surprise that ravished them all ... From the ceiling were suspended rugs from Smyrna with complicated patterns that stood out from the red background. Then, from the four sides, curtains were hung: curtains of Karamanie and Syria, zebra-striped in green, yellow and vermilion; curtains from Diarbekir, more common, rough to the touch, like shepherds' tunics; and still more rugs ... strange flowerings of peonies and palms, fantasy released in a garden of dreams.

This description of a Parisian department store in Emile Zola's novel *Au Bonheur des Dames* (1883) captures well how exotica were used to sell goods in this new mode of retailing. Art and reality sustained fruitful interactions: Zola based his description on Paris' first great department store, Au Bon Marché, founded in 1852. But within a couple of decades department stores and displays were being deliberately modelled on Zola's inspired imaginings. However, even the largest and grandest of newcomers – notably La Samaritaine (1869) and Galeries Lafayette (1895) – were far behind the annual turnover of Au Bon Marché, which until World War I was the biggest department store in the world.

The roots of the department stores' popularity were economic: they offered a wider selection of products at lower prices, and their practice of setting fixed prices made a pleasing break from the need to haggle. Their emergence also testified to a new prosperity among a mass clientele. Yet it was the novelty and wonder of shopping within these cathedrals of consumption that completed the allure. Browsing, mingling anonymously with crowds of like-minded consumers, window-shopping, impulse buying – all created a quite new experience of commodity consumption, to which entrepreneurs responded with ever more fantasy and flamboyance.

The grand staircase of the Paris Bon Marché.

in both the quantity and the quality of food consumed by the average person. From the middle of the nineteenth century down to World War I consumption of those great staples, bread and wine, increased by 50 per cent. More marked, however, were rises in other constituents of popular diet: meat, beer and cider consumption doubled; other alcohol tripled; and sugar and coffee quadrupled. The diversification of national tastes even helped to check the rural exodus by allowing farmers to specialize – the fruit and vegetables grown on the lower Rhône, for example, revitalized the region. More scientific farming techniques – mechanical harvesters, for example, or chemical fertilizers, which vastly increased productivity – also allowed farmers who had emerged from the pre-1896 agrarian depression to adapt successfully to new patterns of consumption.

French men and women had more money in their pockets. Real wages rose 50 per cent for urban workers in the last two decades before 1914. To meet the demand for consumers' ready money, the number of bank branches quintupled. New forms of retailing made clear how much lifestyles were being transformed. Most notable, perhaps, were the big department stores springing up in the major cities, supplemented

Poster (*c.* 1900) celebrating the virtues of Papillon cycles. Children catch butterflies ("papillons"), while a young woman celebrates the new-found independence a bicycle affords by leaving her groom at the altar.

by catalogue buying through the post. Universal exhibitions – held in Paris in 1855, 1867, 1878 and 1900 as well as in 1889 – helped to stimulate a concern for novelty and fashion. Women's fashion became a matter of popular, not just elite, concern, and was helped by the rise of the sewing machine from the mid century onwards. Six million women's corsets were in circulation in the 1870s. Bourgeois comforts spread downwards in society: running water, decent sanitation, gas and electricity transformed the character of home life for the comfortably-off.

The *belle époque*, as this period came to be called, is particularly associated with the rise of new forms of mass entertainment. The music hall had its heyday. The Moulin Rouge, haunt of Toulouse-Lautrec and a fashionable *demi-monde*, opened in Montmartre in 1889 – and soon gave the world the can-can. Other enduring entertainment centres (the Folies Bergères, Olympia, the Casino de Paris) were also established at this time. Tourism developed as a leisure industry: Deauville became Parisians' weekend jaunt, while the Côte d'Azur became a fashionable resort in the Midi. Cheap swift transportation revived the medieval pilgrimage as a form of mass leisure. Half a million visitors passed through Lourdes each year, with over 1.5 million coming in 1908, the fiftieth anniversary of Saint Bernadette's visions. Sport too developed as a form of mass leisure and entertainment: soccer, rugby, gymnastics and rowing developed national organizations, while in cycling the famous Tour de France started in 1903. Sport won approval for toning up the nation for forthcoming anti-German conflict. Nationalism was so rife in sport that even the idealistically internationalist aims of Pierre de Courbertin, who convened the first Olympic Games of the modern era in 1896, ended up as part of a chauvinistic desire "to show the Boches".

France's economic growth may not have matched that of its trade rivals, then, but the experience was still extremely positive. Wealth was filtering through to the general populace – not least because demographic growth was still very slow. The population grew from 36.1 to 39.6 million between 1871 and 1911 – a rise of less than 10 per cent – while Germany's population mushroomed by 50 per cent from 41.1 to 64.9 million over the same period. The death-rate had continued to fall – the development of bacteriological theory by Louis Pasteur helped here, as did improvements in public health

Scientific lecture on the evils of alcoholism in the Fresnes Prison in 1903. The "disciplinary society" (M. Foucault) exemplified in penitentiary institutions stressed surveillance, bodily control and the training of individual consciences. Alcoholism was seen as the seedbed of vice and crime.

early 1890s. A bomb was lobbed into the Chamber of Deputies in 1893, and President Sadi Carnot (grandson of the famous "Organizer of Victory" in 1793/4) was assassinated in 1894. Although these incidents won little mass support, they were symptomatic of a more general suspicion concerning the parliamentary pathway towards socialism. The sphere of worker activity had been widened by the legalization of strikes in 1864 and trade unions in 1884. Union activity divorced from the political sphere attracted many workers. At local level the emergence of the *Bourses du Travail* – local trades councils and labour exchanges – provided the focus for militancy. Many militants gave preference to direct action and the doctrines of revolutionary syndicalism, arguing for a general strike which would lead to a collapse of government and the installation of a workers' state. The national trades congress the CGT (*Confédération Générale du Travail*), which met for the first time in 1896, was generally antagonistic to parliamentary manoeuvrings. It seemed confirmed in its views by the toughness, even viciousness, with which Radical ministries treated mass strikes, especially from 1906 to 1910. Radical minister Clemenceau gloried in the title of *le premier flic de France* ("France's top cop") and brutally put down strike action.

Militant workers were in demand from many organizations. The CGT, which represented only one worker in six, found itself vying with an overtly political socialist Left which was also fundamentally split. There were five main socialist groupings by the 1880s. The most authentically Marxist of these – Jules Guesde's Workers Party, or POF (*Parti ouvrier français*) – scorned electoral politics as feeble reformism. They were, at best, "schools for socialism", which could educate workers in the futility of parliamentarism. Guesde also disdained as "gas and water socialism" the call to implement socialist policies at local level – a policy advocated by rival Paul Brousse's French Socialist Party (*Parti socialiste français*).

It was difficult for socialism to make headway at national level. Socialists won a few seats in the 1880s and around forty in the 1893 elections. But it was the southern deputy Jean Jaurès who helped to mould these socialist factions into a respectable political force. An Opportunist deputy in 1885, he evolved towards socialism in the 1890s, and in 1905 brought the various strands together into the "French Section of the Worker's International" or SFIO (*Section française de l'Internationale ouvrière*). In 1906 the Socialists polled nearly a million votes and had fifty-one deputies elected, and these figures rose to 1.5 million votes and about a hundred deputies in 1914.

As international tensions mounted, this Socialist advance was made doubly problematic given the proudly proclaimed internationalism of the French Left. While the extra-parliamentary Right was draping itself in the tricolour, the Left had developed strong strains of anti-nationalism, anti-militarism and pacifism. They had strongly criticized the decision in 1913 to extend the period of conscription from two years to three, and in the same year the CGT specifically resolved that its members should not fight if war broke out. Jaurès too distrusted the apparent rush towards war – though his influence was removed at the crucial moment in 1914 when he was assassinated by a right-wing fanatic. Yet though the future of the republic in 1914 seemed to hang

The Winegrowing Crisis from Le Petit Journal, 9 June 1907. A crooked (that is, teetotal) businessman comes under attack, as protesting peasants march under the tricolour.

uncertainly on the resolution of this political tension, it was not the Jaurès murder but another assassination which gripped the minds of the French public in 1914. News of the worsening international crisis was driven off the front pages of the national newspapers by a sensational murder trial. The editor of Le Figaro, Gaston Calmette, had allegedly been shot and killed by the wife of prominent Radical politician Joseph Caillaux, after the newspaper's character assassination of her husband.

In this fateful summer of 1914 the trial of Madame Caillaux brought to the front of the reading public's mind another source of tension during the belle époque – namely, the "woman question". The "woman question" was to a large extent a "man question". A cult of masculinity had emerged under the Third Republic, linked with a sense of national shame after the loss of Alsace-Lorraine. Muscular – especially sporting – chauvinism was accompanied by an almost pathological penchant for private violence in the form of the duel. The duel allowed individual male honour to be settled by violence pending collective resort to the battlefield in the settlement of national honour. So the Rhineland for a short time in 1923 in an attempt to force Germany to step up its reparations schedule. This pressure led to the 1924 Dawes Plan for repayments, but difficulties continued. Even the Locarno Treaties of 1925, by which France, Germany and other powers committed themselves to mutual respect of existing frontiers failed to convince the French that its eastern frontier was secure – especially given the growing influence of right-wing parties, *revanchiste* in their turn, in the Weimar Republic. It was in this charged atmosphere that the decision was made in 1929 to build the Maginot Line – a highly modern, supposedly impregnable defensive structure on the eastern frontier, from Switzerland to Montmédy, near Verdun.

The work of economic reconstruction depended on recovering war costs from Germany. Yet, though the reparations slowed to a trickle, the French economy did extremely well in the decade following the Versailles Treaties. The switch from war to peace production was far from straightforward – in 1918 war industries were employing 1.7 million workers, who did not adapt easily to peacetime production. In addition German occupation of the north had disrupted the economic life in this traditional homeland of heavy industry. Recovery was helped by the modernization of much French industry under wartime conditions. New principles of "scientific" management, such as Taylorism, had made important industries leaner and stronger than they had been in 1914. Iron and steel did particularly well – but so, too, did the key secondary industries of rubber, automobiles, aeroplanes, petro-chemicals and electrical equipment. The French aircraft industry was a world leader during the war, though it slipped behind the United States soon afterwards. By 1924 overall industrial production had reached 1914 levels. The growth of consumer demand after the hardships of war helped in this, as did the lowered value of the franc.

The French economy was growing faster in the early 1920s than that of any of its

Populationist postcard message aimed at the troops and their families, and sent from Verdun in 1917. Such propaganda failed to stir the demobilized footsloggers into action: the birth rate stayed low throughout the inter-war period. The issuing of condoms within the army probably aggravated matters.

competitors. By 1929 industrial production was up 40 per cent and foreign trade up 66 per cent on 1913 figures. France's population, in contrast, was far less dynamic. With much of the adult male population of marriageable age in their graves the basis for demographic recovery was poor. The government responded to labour shortage by attracting immigrants, especially from Italy, Spain and Poland – with a smattering of White Russians, Belgians and other groups. There were roughly a million foreigners resident in France before World War I, but half a million entered during the war, and the inflow continued apace over the 1920s. France became (after the United States) Europe's melting-pot, containing some 2.5 million foreigners by the mid 1930s – nearly 10 per cent of the adult population.

Governments, then, tried to deal with the country's demographic problems partly by mobilizing immigrants into the workforce. Conversely they also acted to *de*mobilize women and to return them from the workplace to the hearth, and hopefully to encourage them into procreation. The war had provided a powerful stimulus to female labour, notably in war industries, but also in white-collar jobs. The wartime press had habituated the public to the idea of women bus-drivers, munitions workers, blast-furnace workers and riveters. Though their wages were still only a fraction of male workers', women probably enjoyed a higher living standard than ever before. This caused male resentment, even among the politically progressive.

A French lesson in Alsace, now reincorporated into France. The postcard, dispatched in 1918, bears the message, "France is our fatherland." Smiling children seem to go together with the tricolour.

The Surrealist Manifesto

SURREALISM (noun) Psychic automatism by which it is proposed to express, whether verbally, or in writing, or in any other manner, the real functioning of mind. Dictation of thought, in the absence of any control by reason, beyond aesthetic or moral considerations.

(Philos.) Surrealism is based on a belief in the superior reality of certain associations, neglected hitherto, on the all-powerfulness of dream, and of the disinterested play of thought.

These somewhat opaque definitions were offered by the poet André Breton, proclaimed leader of the new surrealist movement, in the Surrealist Manifesto of 1924. They highlight the importance in poetry and art of dreams and forms of action which bypass normal rational procedures. Breton, exposed to nervous disorders when working as a medical orderly in World War I, had been influenced by the writings of Freud, but wished to tap into the subconscious for reasons other than to seek out symptoms of psychic malaise. Rather, he wished to discover the basis of new forms of artistic expression – notably in the form of "automatic writing", or spontaneous, dream-based compositions.

Through the manifesto Breton was setting out a programme for the artistic development of the poets associated with him – Paul Eluard, Louis Aragon, Robert Desnos, Philippe Soupault – as well as a number of artists, including Picasso, André Masson, Man Ray and Max Ernst. But also the surrealists came to prominence as their original inspiration, the Dada movement, was running out of steam. A nihilistic movement, led originally by Romanian-born Tristan Tzara, Dadaism had its roots in a sense of rejection of the bourgeois values which seemed to accept the slaughter of World War I. Having developed in Zurich, then Paris, Dada aimed to subvert conventional values by systematic provocation on all fronts. One of its famous moments, for example, was the presentation by Marcel Duchamp of a urinal (with the title, *Fountain*) as an artwork for exhibition, which caused a tremendous scandal.

Breton wanted to go beyond wild playfulness to form a movement which, while retaining Dada's iconoclasm, could have a positive impact on the parameters of human imagination and experience. The wish to bring about change led the surrealists to form alliances with, first, the Communist Party and then, from the mid 1930s, with Trotskyists.

Although surrealism's political projects ran into the sand in World War II, by then it had had a major impact on French poetry as well as on artistic expression. The surrealist vision has been one of the most profound influences on twentieth-century art and – not least through its adoption by advertising agencies from the 1960s – on everyday life.

Photograph of leading Surrealists, their portraits grouped around a painting by Magritte, published in *La Révolution Surréaliste*, no. 12, in 1929, as the group was issuing a Second Surrealist Manifesto. Besides poets (Breton, Aragon, Eluard, Peret), the group includes artists (Dali, Tanguy, Arp, Ernst, Magritte) as well as film-maker Luis Buñuel.

Politicians were viewed as being in the pockets of businessmen. Though popular perceptions were rather jaundiced about "hard-faced men who had done well out of the war", employers emerged with their morale and ambitions high. A Lyon chemical manufacturer had noted with satisfaction during the war that "It is for the industrialist that people fight. It is he who will later gain the economic victory", and something of this spirit was detectable after 1918. Employers became better organized than before; a national confederation of industrialists was founded in 1919, and industrial associations were common. These groups acted as powerful pressure-groups and lobbies in the political arena.

French society was riven with social tensions. Radical change of any kind seemed fraught with difficulties and the cards remained heavily stacked in the favour of the social elite and the business classes. In these circumstances it is hardly surprising that the political establishment came increasingly under attack. Indeed it is remarkable that the regime was able to absorb so much criticism and to continue to function effectively. A lingering sense of despair was partly attributable to the impact of mass warfare. Henri Barbusse's anti-war *Le Feu* (1916) was a best-seller, and pacifism grew deep roots, especially through the veterans' associations which developed after 1918. Movements of political provocation and subversive rejection of bourgeois values also prospered in intellectual circles. In the art world notable examples were the Dada movement, which began during the war, and the surrealist movement, which developed out of it in the 1920s. Jean-Paul Sartre's novel *La Nausée* (1938) was a late-flowering bloom of much the same anti-bourgeois disgust. The yearning for a new kind of society took many participants in these movements towards left wing politics. Others drifted into the ranks of the extreme Right. Maurras' still influential *Action française* gave house-room to many young disenchanted right-wing authors. The novelists Drieu la Rochelle and the rabidly anti-Semitic Céline were among others drawn to a critique of contemporary society from the far Right.

Where artistic movements of revolt and rejection did not embrace left- or right-wing politics, they often led their participants towards individualistic hedonism. Victor Margueritte's much condemned (and therefore much read) novel, *La Garçonne* ("Bachelor Girl"), in 1922 described a bohemian female existence laced with free love and lesbianism. The book created a moral panic among the strait-laced. The sexual overtones of short hair, short skirts and flat chests were endlessly (often pruriently) debated. Though there was much about such works which was in the (bourgeois) tradition of shocking the bourgeoisie, they also reflected ideological changes and conflicts within society. Male wartime mortality had spurred an increase in the numbers of independent women, with unmarried and widowed middle-class women now entering the labour force in large numbers. Three years after the war, 42 per cent of adult women were still in gainful employment, and they comprised two-fifths of the total labour-force. The fuzziness in the boundaries between the sexes – highlighted in the debate on shell-shock (it seemed contradictory to talk of male hysterical illness) – had not therefore been erased by the return to peacetime "normality". Evidently women with

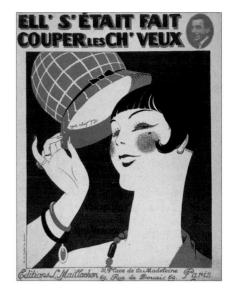

Having one's hair cut short was to the 1920s what bra-burning would be to the 1960s. It was held to proclaim a new spirit of independence among women, though critics feared the advent of a "civilization without sexes" (M. L. Roberts). Cloche hats – sometimes likened to soldiers' helmets – bold cosmetics and costume jewellery completed the effect.

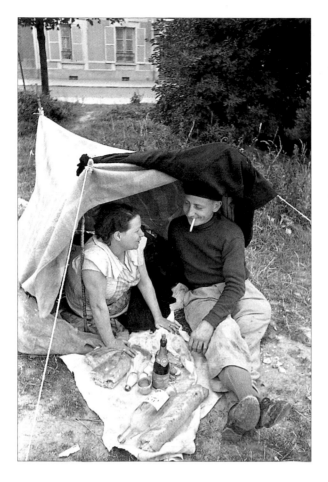

The Spirit of 1936 by Henri Cartier-Bresson. The provision of two weeks' paid holiday per year was, along with the reduction of the working week to forty hours, an integral part of the Popular Front's economic strategy of soaking up unemployment. It was perceived as making a significant improvement to the working classes' quality of life.

classes – Blum claimed he had "injected a little beauty and sunshine into lives of hardship". Yet his government found it impossible to keep together both its parliamentary following and its mass support in what were clearly difficult times. The Spanish Civil War (1936–9) posed a real dilemma: to support the Republicans, as he wished, would lose Blum his Radical allies. In the end he opted for a studied neutrality which, however, disenchanted the Communists and many Socialists too. The poor state of the economy, moreover, negated the effects of his social reforms. The strategy of limiting the working week as a means of reducing unemployment was a spectacular failure: unemployment stubbornly refused to come down. Wage increases were offset by price rises. Industry was disrupted – production was lower when Blum left power in mid 1937 than at the time of the 1936 elections. A flight of capital put pressure on the currency, yet, by delaying a devaluation, Blum denied his government the chance of benefiting from a lower franc in export markets.

Beset from all sides Blum abandoned his post as prime minister in June 1937. There were several governments based on the Popular Front – including another led by Blum in early 1938 – that attempted to keep the political strategy intact. But social reform had been put on hold, and the popular enthusiasm which had greeted the elections of

Opposite Miners in their workclothes, following a political rally at a sports stadium in Montrouge outside Paris on 14 June 1936 to celebrate the end of their strike. The Popular Front was enormously effective in mobilizing militancy in the workplace, but less successful in rewarding it.

actively promoting France as part of the "New Order" in a Nazi-dominated Europe. Nowhere was this more evident than in the regime's enthusiastic anti-Semitism. Though it drew strongly from a vigorous native tradition, it was no less shocking for that, especially in a state which, since 1789, had been a world pioneer of Jewish emancipation. The special status given Jews by Vichy in 1940 was freely volunteered by the regime, without German pressure. Foreign Jews – many of whom had come to France specifically to flee Hitlerian persecution – were targeted first for rounding up. In June 1942 over 12,000 Parisian Jews, including young children, were rounded up in one swoop and held in a sports stadium, converted into a temporary concentration camp, prior to deportation. The wearing of a yellow star was made compulsory. In all, besides homosexuals and gypsies, who also felt the anti-Semite's wrath, over 75,000 Jews (about a third of them native French Jews) were deported. Only about 3 per cent ever returned – and none of the children.

The repressive arm of Vichy was increasingly turned against non-Jewish citizens from 1942 onwards, under Nazi prompting. The *Milice*, organized under Joseph Darnand in 1943 as a kind of home-grown political police, worked hard to root out opposition. It used torture systematically for the first time in France since before the Revolution of 1789. It had no shortage of victims, for hostility towards the regime was by 1942 and 1943 growing fast. Life had had to go on after the catastrophe of 1940, and this involved for most people, certainly in the north, some degree of compromise with the occupying forces – though whether one calls this collaboration is a moot point. There were enthusiastic collaborators: Breton, Flemish and Occitanian "nationalists", who saw a role for themselves in a more regionalist "New Order", were cases in

Procession of the Black Virgin at Moulins, 15 August 1941. The upper clergy was generally highly in favour of the Vichyite regime, which accorded the Church better treatment than it had received under the Third Republic. Here the bishop of Moulins leads a procession which combines two other Vichyite specialities: youth organizations and local folkloric groups.

point. Yet the total number of active collaborators was probably quite small – perhaps only about 150,000 individuals.

The stakes of association with the Nazi regime grew higher, moreover, as time passed, and as the French economy was subjected to a kind of rape at German hands. Pétain's "shield" was quite powerless to prevent this happening. By 1943 Germany was creaming off 40 per cent of France's industrial production and 15 per cent of its agricultural product. A quarter of all French meat was shipped out to the Third Reich and over half of the country's new aircraft, automobiles and machinery. France had become Germany's biggest supplier of war materials and it also became the third largest (after Russia and Poland) supplier of manpower. The system of forced labour service (*Service du travail obligatoire*, or STO) from early 1943 intensified a demand for labour which had been perceptible from the earliest days. Over a million French workers migrated to Germany during the war, to add to the 1.6 million soldiers also kept there.

These demands, on an already weakened economy, were highly damaging. Industrial and agricultural output dropped. As imports were few and costly, systems of rationing and wage-control had to be introduced. Even so, inflation was rife, with prices doubling between 1940 and 1944. A flourishing black market was unable to prevent serious damage to the population's health. Nutritional levels were lower in France than anywhere else in occupied Europe, with the exception of Italy. Rationing allowed for only 1,200 calories per day by 1943 – a recipe for malnutrition. It was little wonder that life expectancy dropped by some eight years in the Vichy period.

By associating itself so closely with an occupying force which imposed this level of privation on a developed nation, Vichy was effectively writing its own death-warrant. The handshake which Pétain gave to Hitler at Montoire in October 1940 had a high symbolic price. Vichy went beyond passive, defensive collaboration, placing France's military, police, communications and judicial apparatus very much at the disposal of the German occupiers. Its repressive policies, however, ensured it a broad and growing opposition. It created its own undertakers. To victimized Jewish, masonic and Communist opponents were added a good handful of republican refugees from the Spanish Civil War and, after 1943, huge numbers of young men wishing to evade compulsory labour service in Germany – not to mention all those increasingly disgusted by the damage being wreaked on French society by Vichyite policies.

Draft evaders from the STO swelled the ranks of a Resistance movement which had been slow to develop. In the early years of the regime opposition to Vichy had been sporadic, small-scale and highly personalized. Its amorphousness owed much to the originality of the situation in which resisters found themselves. Those in the Cévennes were following in the now faint footsteps of their Camisard ancestors under Louis XIV; but this was the exception. Broadly speaking, there was no script for resistance such as the Parisian *sans-culottes* and their descendants from 1789 to 1871 had had for revolutionary opposition. Resisters were obliged to improvise, then, to learn by trial and error. It was also new to have a movement of resistance involving the full range of the

Jewish yellow star, as worn in Paris from 1942. The regime's knee-jerk acceptance of anti-Semitism was to have a long-term effect in alienating some Jews from their adopted homeland.

The "scientific" Institute for Jewish Studies was established in Paris to research the nefarious impact of Jews on French society. In this poster the Jew is viewed as a cancer, rotting the fabric of every aspect of national life.

political spectrum. Though in the southern, Vichyite zone the traditional elites rallied to the regime, so that resisters were normally left-wing, resistance in the north had a much more politically ecumenical feel to it. Unity had, as ever, a strong symbolic element. "The evening the first arms arrived," a Burgundian peasant-farmer later reminisced, "we came to this cellar. I remember we sang the Internationale. We weren't Communists though. It was just that Pétain sang the Marseillaise, so we had to sing the Internationale."

The return of Communist militants to the fold after Hitler's attack on Russia in 1941 had brought into the Resistance some of the most zealous and committed of working-class militants. After the war Communists would claim to be the party of the "*75,000 fusillés*" ("75,000 firing-squad victims"). Though most Resistance networks tended to be localist in outlook, and confined to one or other of the two zones, the Communist-based "National Front" network straddled the border and came closest to being a national network. The forces of Resistance grew stronger by 1942 and 1943, as Germany tightened its political and economic grip on France. Sabotage, sheltering of and organizing escape lines for Allied airmen and agents and intelligence-gathering intensified. Armed action also began to be more common and the *maquis* – Resistance militants, refugees and draft-dodgers who established camps in the upland heaths of the Massif Central and the Alps – were increasingly important in this respect. Perhaps 20,000 strong in 1943 they had grown to 40,000 by early 1944, and had soared into six figures by the late summer.

The Resistance was never a mass movement in Vichy France: at the most, 1 per cent of the population was probably actively involved. The circulation of the Resistance press – prominent among which were the newspapers *Combat* and *Libération* – was about two million, though readership was probably far larger. Listening to BBC radio broadcasts was also an increasingly common clandestine act, which involved even greater numbers of "armchair resisters" (R. Kedward). Yet to be effective a movement like this required active, reflex support from the population as a whole; the Resistance agents had to move unrestricted, like fish in water. Just seeing and keeping your mouth shut was in this sense an act of supportive resistance. Continuing high levels of denunciations for underground activity showed that France was still split, and that the struggle continued to have some of the features of a civil war. Yet as the war progressed, it became increasingly apparent that the balance of tacit support was swinging in the Resistance's favour.

What these numerous and increasingly well-supported Resistance networks lacked, however, was overall organization. In the event this came from outside, through the agency of ex-junior war minister Charles de Gaulle. He had escaped to Britain in the rout of May–June 1940, and on 18 June launched his famous message on BBC radio, calling for the continuation of the struggle. He may have occupied the high moral ground, but at this stage he had precious little else in his favour. Though Churchill recognized him as the leader of French forces carrying on the armed struggle against

Opposite In a secluded farmhouse in the Haute-Loire department a budding group of the *maquis* receive firearms training, using rifles parachuted in by the Allies.

Vichy, he was largely ignored within France, and very few expatriate Frenchmen rallied to his cause. Early attempts by his "Free French" to win over French troops in the colonies failed. The United States, which came into the war in 1941, seemed to prefer to support internal critics of Vichy rather than this imperious and notoriously difficult outsider, in whom they claimed to detect dictatorial ambitions. Winston Churchill famously remarked that the "cross of Lorraine" – the insignia which de Gaulle had adopted for the Free French – was the heaviest of all the crosses he had to bear during the war. When in 1942 the Allies invaded North Africa – French colonial territory – they neglected even to inform de Gaulle.

De Gaulle was able to make himself useful to the Allies. He had, first of all, military advantages to exploit. Despite the failure of attempts to win over Vichyite Senegal to the Gaullist camp, by 1942 just about all the rest of France's colonial empire (with the notable exception of Algeria) had come over to him. When the Vichyite governor of Algeria turned coat and came over to the Allies' side, de Gaulle was able to work the situation to his advantage: the French armed forces and the Gaullist Free French were combined into the French Committee of National Liberation. De Gaulle took care to co-opt to it a smattering of Third Republic politicians like Pierre Mendès-France and Vincent Auriol. Three days before D-Day, when the Allies launched their cross-Channel offensive against Germany, the Committee declared itself the provisional government of France.

If de Gaulle and the Free French finally proved useful military allies for the British and Americans, they also had the considerable advantage of close contact with the internal Resistance forces. In January 1942 an agent of de Gaulle, the former Prefect Jean Moulin, had been parachuted into France with the specific task of co-ordinating Resistance networks. He was able to overcome geographical and political divisions within the movements, creating by May 1943 an umbrella organization. Moulin presided over this National Council of the Resistance, which incorporated all the major networks. He was soon afterwards captured and died under torture at the hands of Klaus Barbie, the so-called "Butcher of Lyon". His successor, Georges Bidault, continued Moulin's work, making the Resistance Council not just a military committee, but the basis for organizing a transition of power; trade unions and political parties were all represented within it. Political co-ordination was a delicate task. De Gaulle himself was something of an old-style patrician, far distant from the political views of much of the Resistance network, and many in his entourage were drawn from the pre-war Right. The Resistance Council's call for "real economic democracy" after the overthrow of Vichy, however, set down a marker which de Gaulle came to accept.

De Gaulle had by 1944 made himself a force which could not easily be ignored. He was bitterly resentful that the Free French did not figure in the Allied landings of D-Day, 6 June 1944 – though there were French troops involved in the campaign. He and the internal Resistance forced themselves into the scheme of things. In Paris the Resistance opened an insurrection on 19/20 August to put the German defensive forces on the back foot. Allied commanders eventually gave way to pressure and agreed to include French military forces under General Leclerc in the liberation of Paris on 25 August. By that time a Franco-American force, with a large French component under de Lattre de Tassigny, had landed in Provence and was already advancing up the Rhône valley, liberating cities as it went. Meanwhile Resistance forces were co-ordinating with the Allies in mopping-up operations behind the advancing front.

On 26 August 1944 de Gaulle could make a triumphant procession up the Champs-Elysées in Paris. This traditional gesture was immensely important for a nation which seemed to have lost sight of the repertoire of political symbols inscribed in its republican past. De Gaulle went on to evoke a city "liberated by its population, with the help of the armies of France's allies". It would be churlish to suggest that others might have given the two factors a rather different weighting – irrelevant, too, for by lodging the French people and French armies at the heart of the overthrow of the Vichy regime and establishing a new myth of foundation for the new, Fourth, Republic, he allowed French society to approach the *après-guerre* in a mood of renewal – a mood soon, however, to be sorely tested.

American photographer Robert Capa captures the jubilation on the faces of Parisians as their city is liberated by de Gaulle and the Allies on 25 August 1944.

CHAPTER 10

Post-war France: Expansion and Beyond

"There was nothing else to do but work seriously and devotedly, struggle for food, see friends quietly, and look forward to freedom." The comments of the painter Pablo Picasso, who spent the war years in Paris, are probably more representative of the bulk of the French population than those militant minorities involved in either open collaboration or paramilitary Resistance activity.

The hopeful edge to the future which the involvement of the French in their own liberation had brought was, however, soon lost. Freedom carried a heavier price than had been anticipated. The process of establishing a new, Fourth, Republic was bitter and divisive, and formed part of the broader backdrop of the Cold War between the main victors, the Soviet Union and the United States. The prize of ultimate victory was scarcely glittering: the Fourth Republic soon settled into a round of parliamentary wranglings which recalled the stalemates and compromises of the Third. Politics was also increasingly poisoned by bitter colonial conflicts, at first in Indo-China (to 1954), and then in Algeria (to 1962). Deadlock over Algeria in 1958 led to a constitutional crisis, with the Fourth Republic giving way to the Fifth, supervised by a reinvigorated de Gaulle, its first president.

Some argued that the Fifth Republic had been tailored so exactly for the requirements of de Gaulle that it would not survive his removal. This has proved not to be the case. Despite the alarms set off by the politically unclassifiable May Events of 1968, which seemed to come close to overthrowing it, the regime survived his retirement from politics (in 1969). However, the presidency (from 1974) of the Centre-Right Valéry Giscard d'Estaing owed little to the Gaullist inheritance. This stabilization of the regime owed much to the unparalleled period of economic growth which France enjoyed from the late 1940s down to the mid 1970s – growth which brought major changes in styles of life and outlook among the French population.

RECRIMINATION AND STABILIZATION

"No serenity was possible," wrote Simone de Beauvoir, long-time friend of existentialist writer Jean-Paul Sartre, of the post-war period. "The war was over: it remained on our hands like a great unwanted corpse, and there was no place on earth to bury it." The events of autumn 1944 and spring 1945 had been uplifting indeed: the liberation of Paris and successive provincial cities; the incorporation of the internal Resistance forces into the regular army; the penetration of the German heartlands by the forces of de Lattre de Tassigny; and celebrations for victory in Europe. But the buoyant spirit of the times was undercut by more sombre events. News of the concentration camps was confirmed by the Russian arrival in Auschwitz in January 1945 and the return of French deportees in May. Accounts of Nazi atrocities brought home the enormity of the

The existentialist cafés of Saint-Germain-des-Prés

"The Saint-Germain-des-Près quarter has become a campus for the American collegiate set," noted American resident Janet Flanner sniffily in the summer of 1948.

The Café de Flore serves as a drugstore for pretty upstate girls in unbecoming blue denim pants and their Middle Western dates, most of whom are growing Beaux-Arts beards. Members of the tourist intelligentsia patronize the Rue de Bac's Pont-Royal bar, which used to be full of French existentialists and is now full only of themselves, often arguing about existentialism.

The arrival of American hordes in the aftermath of the Liberation and the Marshall Plan converted into a tourist attraction a number of Left Bank cafés which had a long history of supporting networks of artistic and intellectual social life. The Deux Magots had been an important centre for surrealist groups in the 1930s, while the Brasserie Lipp was a hangout for the more politically oriented. Communist groups had other locales, painters and sculptors others, and so on. To this café society was linked a warm hotchpotch of night-clubs, jazz spots, restaurants, art galleries and small theatres, which formed at once the means of expression and relaxation of this diverse intelligentsia. Before 1944 these public locations offered warmth as well as companionship. "Towards the end

The Deux Magots, in the heart of Saint-Germain.

of the Occupation, in the winter of 1943/4, everyone came there to keep warm," one writer later remembered of the Café de Flore. "One had the impression that the first-floor room was a classroom. Sartre was installed at a little table, writing *Paths of Freedom*, Simone de Beauvoir, at another table, was writing *All Men Are Mortal* ... close by, Arthur Adamov was writing, too, doubtless one of his plays ..."

Jean-Paul Sartre came to be the star of the show, and American students would ask waiters if they could sit in his usual chair. The existentialist philosophy which he developed, in association with founding feminist Simone de Beauvoir, his life-long companion, derived from the German philosophers Husserl and Heidegger. The existentialists sought to base principles of human responsibility and action on the raw materials of human existence rather than on abstract, metaphysical ideas. Tinged with a strong pessimism, and a resistance to easy answers, the movement of ideas responded to the mood of the period.

The café scene helped to make the existentialists famous: Sartre was more widely known than any philosopher since Voltaire. Popular success also compromised their sociability. Early on, Sartre and de Beauvoir had moved to the basement bar of the Hôtel du Pont-Royal, where they had to write on barrels. "Sartre?" the owner of the Flore later commented, "He was my worst client. Hours scribbling on a piece of paper, sitting in front of a single drink, which he didn't renew from morning to night."

Cartoon by Jacques Sennep. While Simone de Beauvoir writes at a table, Jean-Paul Sartre approaches the bar at the Pont-Royal for an existential cocktail, and is offered a choice between Plato-flip, Nietzsche-fizz and Spinoza-gin.

Woman collaborator paraded shaven-headed through the streets of Chartres in late summer 1944. The happy crowds who had cheered the passage of General de Gaulle soon turned to resentment and spite, now under the tricolour flag. Fortunately, such attacks on women who had consorted with German troops did not last long.

Holocaust, and provided a kind of anti-fascist vaccination which would last decades. The explosion of the atom bombs at Hiroshima and Nagasaki to end the war with Japan in August 1945 also put a question-mark against the humane values for which most had thought they were fighting in the war years. Many would have their disillusionment completed by reports, from 1949, that the Soviet Union too had had its labour and concentration camps, and had indulged in its fair share of atrocities.

No one seemed to have clean hands. Waves of vicious recrimination against alleged Vichy collaborators and black-marketeers were able to gather momentum in the power vacuum caused by the overthrow of the Vichy regime and the retreat of the Germans. Even a moderate like Edouard Herriot had few qualms in envisaging "a blood-bath" to purge the country of its noxious elements. In the event, things were not as bad as at one stage looked likely. Talk of 100,000 summary executions now seems exaggerated; there appear to have been fewer than 10,000. Trials of leading figures such as Laval (sentenced to death) and Pétain (imprisoned for life) were the tip of only a moderately large iceberg. Some 30,000 to 40,000 individuals were tried and imprisoned for collaboration – and most had been released within a few years. In some barbaric vigilante action, prostitutes and other women alleged to have engaged in "horizontal collaboration" were stripped and their heads shaved.

Though such actions soured the fresh smell of freedom, the scale of violence involved was moderate compared to that experienced in France's past – from the Wars of Religion to the Paris Commune. Given the initial power vacuum – especially in the Midi – a good deal of preventive action was taken: civilians were disarmed from October 1944; and 100,000 individuals were taken into protective custody. De Gaulle's commissaries, who helped to set up the new local administrations, acted to heal rather than heighten animosities – not least because they feared a Communist takeover if passions got out of hand. There was thus a good deal of continuity between Vichy and Liberation administrative structures. The 11,000 dismissals for collaboration left most of the bureaucracy intact.

As "dictator by consent" for over a year, de Gaulle operated through a government of national unity that included all shades of opinion, plus some notable figures from the Third Republic. The call for reconstruction and radical economic and social action reflected the popular demand for a break with Vichy values, but was also a good excuse to end recrimination and encourage a fresh start. After four years' subjection to Nazi priorities under Vichy, the French economy was in dire straits. In fact it would take a long time for standards of living to improve – another cause of disillusionment among those who had expected better once the war was over. Only half the rail network was still in place, half a million buildings had been destroyed and raw materials were in desperately short supply. As a result there were numerous shortages – bread rationing continued until 1949 – and inflation was rampant. The government took advantage of the chastened mood of employers, many of whom had collaborated, to bring much of the economy (gas and electricity, many banks and insurance companies, Air France, Renault and so on) under state control. This was accompanied by radical measures of state welfare – notably the creation of an impressive social security system and, at the workplace, works councils. The vote was also extended to women for the first time.

The establishment of a new constitution proved, however, a painful process. A referendum in October 1945 revealed that 96 per cent of voters were against the continuation of the Third Republic, but it proved difficult to find something recognizably different to put in its place. Elections had revealed a quite new political landscape. The old Radical party and the Right had been decimated, and the largest party was now the Communists, who played to the hilt their wartime role as the *75,000 fusillés*. They shared the limelight with the Socialists and a new progressive Catholic grouping, the MRP (*Mouvement républicain populaire*), headed by ex-*Résistant* Georges Bidault. Above them all floated de Gaulle, whose call for a more presidential style of constitution incited the major political formations to take up contrary positions. De Gaulle resigned in January 1946 – a tactical move which was, however, to consign him to the political wilderness for more than a decade. The failure of the first constitutional project to attain a majority in the referendum of May 1946 led to the eventual passing of a revised constitutional statute, which commanded little public enthusiasm.

The constitution of the Fourth Republic ended up by strongly resembling that of the Third. In the twelve years to 1958, there would be more than a score of prime ministers. Control shuffled between different power blocs drawn from the three major parties, the Communists (the PCF – *Parti communiste français*), the Socialists and the MRP. The decision of socialist prime minister Paul Ramadier in May 1947 to eject Communists from the governmental majority ended the phase of "tripartism" and marked the political marginalization of the main working-class party – it was another thirty-four years before they would re-enter government. Under the influence of cold war attitudes, the PCF would be one of the most irreconcilable critics of the new political arrangements, which placed France solidly in the American camp. The spirit of post-Liberation solidarity and revolutionary optimism had broken irremediably.

DECOLONIZATION AND THE ADVENT OF THE FIFTH REPUBLIC

The political scene was dominated by a sense of stalemate, with party groupings clustering around the Centre because of what were perceived as threats from both Left and Right. To the Right de Gaulle seemed to be posturing in Bonapartist fashion as a critic of the parliamentary system. He campaigned against the second referendum on the constitution, then in March 1947 set up his own party, the RPF (*Rassemblement du peuple français*). He made a good deal of headway – the RPF won 40 per cent of the national vote in the 1947 municipal elections. But his mass rallies and man-of-destiny appearances were frightening to many, and he eventually backed off, retiring from politics once again in September 1952. "De Gaulle marched us at full speed to the Rubicon," the writer and faithful Gaullist André Malraux later recalled, "and then told us to get out our fishing rods."

The Communists had been critical of governmental power even when they had been in the government themselves. Eventually they had been ejected from office in 1947

Maurice Thorez at the microphone during the elections of 1947. Leader of the Communists from 1930 till his death in 1964, Thorez had spent the war in Moscow, but returned to become a government minister during the period of tripartism in 1945–7. His influence helped make the PCF one of the most hard-line of all Western Communist parties.

VOTER COMMUNISTE C'EST VOTER POUR L'OCCUPATION RUSSE

CENTRE DE DEFENSE DE LA CIVILISATION ET DE LA LIBERTE – PARIS

Poster issued by the Centre for the Defence of Freedom and Civilization during the election campaign of 1950. The end of "tripartism" and the advent of the Cold War brought a strong current of anti-communism into French politics.

for supporting Renault strikers protesting against government pay cuts. The cold war made the Communists feared as ruthless Party infiltrators, and the pro-Stalinist line followed by Maurice Thorez, the PFC leader, who had spent the war years living in Moscow, as well as by the Communist CGT trade union, seemed to give some credence to this belief. In fact, by contrast with Stalin, the Communists were far more interested in maintaining their support among the working class than in seizing power, and stayed well within the bounds of legality. However, when American President Harry S. Truman began in 1947 to preach containment of Communism throughout the world, the French political establishment was forced to make a choice between the two cold war combatants. The decision to throw in France's lot with the United States ensured unremitting PCF hostility, but had the considerable advantage of attracting Marshall Aid from America, which was crucial to France's economic recovery. France also played a part in forming the military defence league NATO (the North Atlantic Treaty Organization) in April 1949.

Although extremism was seen as threatening political stability, the voting system of proportional representation favoured the Centre parties. For electoral reasons and to emphasize their autonomy, the latter tended to accentuate differences between them-selves. Thus the Socialists retained an anti-clerical aspect which set them at odds with the Christian Democrats of the MRP. The Radicals also made a comeback, and played a crucial role as tactical prop in a number of ministerial pacts. The relative stagnation at the heart of the political system was underlined by the rabble-rousing political campaign led by Pierre Poujade in the early 1950s. Based on a small shopkeeper mentality, which attacked the government for high taxes, and which was spiced with a fashionable anti-Communism and a vestigial anti-Semitism, the Poujadist party managed fifty-three seats in the 1956 elections.

Perhaps the only time in the Fourth Republic when a new mood permeated political life was the brief premiership of Pierre Mendès-France in 1954/5. A determined effort to extricate France from its serious colonial entanglements was accompanied by a programme of economic modernization that won a good deal of support. The cult of personality which appeared to be developing around his name made him a soft target. Moreover, though aimed mainly against unlicensed moonshine producers, his campaign to reduce alcoholism and increase milk-drinking had a comic element in such a wine-producing and wine-consuming society as France, which served him ill.

This political quagmire was a poor context for the resolution of problematic colonial issues. Insurrection in Madagascar in 1947, which resulted in the death of huge numbers of rebels, highlighted the seriousness of the issues. Indo-China was also by that time proving difficult to deal with. The nationalists in Vietnam were headed by Ho Chi Minh, who, following the withdrawal of the Japanese, set up a provisional government in August 1945. The possibility of France working with the Viet-Minh, however, was frustrated as a result of colonial administrators on the spot playing fast-and-loose with the Viet-Minh and with the Japanese occupying forces. In the hostilities which followed, the French use of former Nazi German soldiers who had been smuggled out of Europe along various "rat-lines" caused something of a stir in France, as did the troops' use of torture. It was as if the French were inflicting on the Vietnamese the kind of treatment which the Nazis had visited upon the French from 1940 to 1944. It took a major military defeat at Dien-Bien-Phu in 1954 at the hands of the Vietnamese general Giap – subsequent strategist of the Vietnamese war against the United States – to make the Indo-Chinese issue more than an academic question.

Negotiations skilfully conducted by Prime Minister Mendès-France helped France disengage from Indo-China less painfully than might have been the case. Mendès also proved accommodating towards Tunisian independence, and set in motion talks with Morocco which were to lead to its independence in 1956. Algeria was, however, altogether a bigger and more difficult problem. French since 1830, it counted one million Europeans out of a total population of nine million. Since 1954 the minority had been resisting a wave of co-ordinated violence conducted by the FLN (*Front de libération nationale*). All the major political formations in Paris were internally split over the Algerian crisis, while the frequently changing ministerial line-up made it impossible to develop a consistent political strategy. Military activity and bipartisan violence came to fill the vacuum. A savagely dirty war evolved, with atrocities on both sides. Bombs were detonated in mainland France, while in Algeria the French army began to use torture as a standard weapon of counter-intelligence. Intellectuals blew the whistle on these clear violations of human rights, but many French men and women and European colonists accepted such steps because they were expedient. The army was also determined to win at all costs. Many professional soldiers had felt humiliated by Dien-Bien-Phu, and wished to set the record straight.

Attempts by government to force the colonists into conciliatory reforms were only partly successful, while negotiations with the FLN ran aground on colonist intransigence. The strike against Colonel Nasser in Egypt by a Franco-British-Israeli force had other origins, but was further justified in French eyes by the fact that Nasser was supposed to be providing material aid to FLN rebels. The strike failed dismally, but the

"Suez Crisis" only strengthened French resolve that something had to be done. The war was not only politically divisive, its expense was threatening France's financial and economic stability. Secret negotiations were halted, however, by a sudden and unanticipated colonist *coup d'état* on 13 May 1958. Right-wing colonists seized the levers of power, and the French military establishment in Algiers felt itself unable to do any more than endorse their action. General Massu presided over the colonists' Committee of Public Safety – a reference to 1793/4 that made the call to keep the republic "one and indivisible" all the more patriotic. General Salan was heard to shout "Vive de Gaulle!" in Algiers, and de Gaulle announced himself willing to re-enter politics. The

Photograph of a routine episode in the war against Indo-China. Colonial wars in Indo-China, then Algeria – dirty, badly conducted, ill-conceived, and swimming against the tide of history – were to be the death of the Fourth Republic.

In the Algerian cities a war of bomb blasts and barricades developed. A ferocious policy of repression, including widespread and systematic torture, was unable to contain the rebellion.

rebel generals sent in parachute regiments to take over Corsica, while in mainland France nervous Parisians scanned the sky fearfully for parachute drops.

In this atmosphere of imminent civil war, with the major political formations in apparent deadlock, free agents within the political establishment began to fish in troubled waters. The idea of de Gaulle as political saviour was warmly endorsed by the Algerian colonists. De Gaulle's pose as man of destiny seemed to be reaching its justification. He distanced himself from the generals, evidently not wishing to lead a *coup d'état* which would leave him beholden to the military. His Resistance past also ensured him a following on the Left as well as on the Right. So he collaborated closely with President Coty to maintain every appearance of legality. On 1 June 1958 a chastened National Assembly agreed that de Gaulle should be recalled and given emergency powers for six months. The decision to draw up a new constitution was now a formality. This effective constitutional suicide by the Fourth Republic must have gone some way to vindicate de Gaulle's twelve years in the wilderness. When he returned to his Parisian hotel on the evening of 1 June he told the hotel porter, "Albert, I have won."

Winning, however, had its responsibilities. The new constitution de Gaulle drew up was very much made to his own measure. Many on the Left doubted that under its provisions they could ever climb to power. The focus of power was shifted firmly away from the National Assembly towards the president – along lines which de Gaulle had himself advocated in 1946. The practice of referendums was widened. The underlying conceptual framework was that the president should be above the mêlée and should resist and counterbalance various interest groups – political parties, unions, and so on. The new system also gave the president a good deal of leeway for a foreign policy independent from parliament.

The solution to the Algerian crisis was, moreover, very much a personal *tour de force* by the new president. At first he seemed to go along with the European minority; on a visit to Algiers, in which he received an ecstatic welcome by the Europeans, he commented, "Je vous ai compris" – "I have understood you" – an oracular phrase whose ambiguity would only become apparent in time. He soon realized that no military solution to the insurrection was possible, while most political solutions on offer bore too high a price. To assimilate Algeria into France ultimately risked – because of the high Algerian birth-rate – the chance of a Muslim majority in the French National Assembly. On the other hand, a solution based on a wholly French Algeria, with the power of the

The *pieds-noirs*

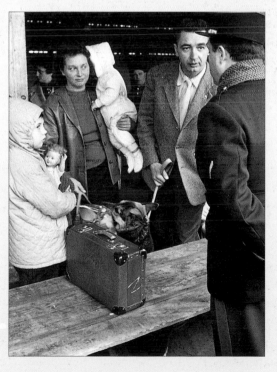

French decolonization in North Africa produced population displacements which are comparable with the more famous migrations in central and eastern Europe in World War II. From the early 1950s to early 1960s some 1.3 million Europeans were "repatriated" from Morocco, Tunisia and Algeria. Algeria provided the bulk of these, reflecting the greater duration of French occupation, and perhaps two-thirds of the "refugees" left between 1961 and 1963, as the Algerian War drew to a close.

The origin of the term *pieds-noirs* ("black-feet"), used to describe the returning colonists, is uncertain. At first they were called Algerians – Algerian Arabs were called first "natives", then "Muslims" – but this term became too loaded with ambiguity over the course of the 1950s. After 1955 they accepted the term *pieds-noirs* to describe themselves.

Though there was a *pied-noir* diaspora throughout the world, the bulk of the European population of Algeria settled in France, where they received compensation from the French government. Though they felt that this was well below what they were entitled to, the *pieds-noirs* appeared to bring little enduring bitterness into the metropolitan country with them, and set about making a new life with some gusto. The vast majority of *rapatriés* concentrated in cities south of a line between Bordeaux and Lyon. A young, fairly active population, they rejuvenated these areas, increased their birth-rates and boosted local economies. The influx of *pieds-noirs* caused little lasting hostility from the host population either, highlighting the importance of the economic environment – which was booming – in helping to integrate immigrant groups. Their Arab compatriots would prove less fortunate in the 1970s and 1980s.

European minority maintained, meant that the war might continue at unacceptably high costs. Having decided that no alternative was open to him, de Gaulle moved fast. In September 1959 he announced his readiness to accept Algerian self-determination, and entered into negotiations with the FLN. The result was the Evian agreements of 1962, which gave Algeria full independence.

The decision to grant Algerian independence led to a backlash by the European colonists. From 1961 they founded the OAS (*Organisation Armée secrète*), along with disaffected army officers (such as Salan), Rightists and disgruntled politicians in France (such as Bidault). The OAS conducted terrorist attacks in Algeria and mainland France, including a number of plots on the life of de Gaulle himself, and a further attempted *coup d'état* by senior army officers in Algeria in 1961. De Gaulle, however, prevailed. The problem of the European minority was "solved" by providing for their return to metropolitan France. Some 800,000 Europeans – *pieds-noirs* ("black-feet") as they were called – left Algeria, mainly settling in southern France. The war had caused some 20,000 French deaths, as against several hundreds of thousands of Muslim deaths.

The colonial catastrophe in Algeria pushed France further down the decolonizing road. In 1958 de Gaulle had offered the colonies of central and West Africa the option of independence without subsequent aid, or partial autonomy with continuing associ- ation with metropolitan France. Sekou Touré's Guinea took the former option, but the other states chose the latter. In 1960, however, the terms of the arrangements were altered in order to encompass full independence. France retained a number of overseas territories: the "DOMs" (*Départments d'Outre-Mer*) (notably Martinique and Guade- loupe in the Caribbean, and Réunion in the Indian Ocean), which enjoy full French nationality, including the right to elect deputies to the National Assembly; and a hand- ful of "TOMs" (*Territoires d'Outre-Mer*), which have a lesser status and fewer political rights. Yet these are merely the appendix to what had been one of the greatest colonial empires in world history. De Gaulle closed this chapter in French history – and closed it definitively. Aid from metropolitan France fell fast, while trade with the colonies dwindled away, as France found its major trading partners inside Europe rather than outside it. Where the Third World had accounted for a fifth of French trade in the late 1950s, by the late 1970s it was down to a twentieth.

Whereas Fourth Republic foreign ministers had been endlessly harassed by colonial problems and their scope for action limited by the darkest days of the cold war (and by dependence on American aid), de Gaulle in the 1960s was able to pursue policies of calculated *grandeur*. He put something of a brake on the move towards European integration, famously vetoing the entry of Britain into the European Community, for example. He also withdrew France from NATO, developed an independent nuclear deterrent and sought out ways of establishing diplomatic links without slavishly seek- ing clearance at Washington. He took some pleasure in thumbing his nose at the "Anglo-Saxons" – as with his famous cry for a "Free Quebec" during a state visit to North America in 1967. This independent line highlighted the growing self-confidence of a France whose economy was pushing up the league of great powers.

THE "THIRTY GLORIOUS YEARS"

France had a more impressive economic performance than at any other time in its history stretching back to 1945 and lasting through to 1974. Its record stood up well against any of her international competitors. It was fashionable, especially amongst Gaullists, to contrast the Fourth and Fifth Republics. The former was allegedly scarred by frequent political deadlock and lack of political will; whereas the latter, with its more presidential constitution, allowed for a greater degree of continuity – and therefore effectiveness – in policy. Certainly the political calm and ministerial continuity that developed in the 1960s – in stark contrast to the more troubled days of the previous decade – provided a more helpful framework for social and economic policies to take effect. Yet the contrast was more apparent than real. The economic achievements of the Fifth Republic owed a great deal more to the groundwork performed under the

Soldiers and civilians, Arabs and Europeans mob General de Gaulle with enthusiasm in his visit to Algiers in June 1958. The photograph is a reminder of the large numbers of allies the French had among the Arab inhabitants of Algeria.

Fourth than Gaullists liked to admit – and more to some of the state-oriented social thinking mapped out in the early days of Vichy than most French people cared to acknowledge.

Perhaps the most evident symptom of the transformed economic environment of these *trente glorieuses* – the "thirty glorious years" from the mid 1940s to the mid 1970s – was a complete turn-around in the country's demographic performance. France's population started to grow fast – for the first time since the eighteenth century. Population rose from 40.3 million in 1946 to nearly 50 million by late 1958, and to 56 million by the 1990s. Improved medicine was starting to have a more long-term impact on the death-rate: life expectancy in 1946 was 60 years for men and 65 years for women; by 1965 the figures were 67 and 75 respectively, rising further to 72 and 80 by the early 1990s. Yet the major cause of demographic vitality was a post-war baby-boom, which continued well into the 1960s. The birth-rate was 50 per cent above pre-war levels for most of this time and, moreover, above average European levels. State encouragement, in the form of welfare arrangements and generous family allowances, played a part in this boom but was not a determining cause – the boom started under Vichy, before the welfare state was in place. The major determinant of the rising birth-rate appears to have been a healthy economic environment.

Much the same was true of the other main contributor to population growth. The baby-boom slightly depressed the percentage of women in the labour force in the 1960s, and it was immigration which took up the slack in the expanding economy. The number of foreigners resident in France had fallen in the repressive Vichy years to around 1.5 million. A massive influx in the 1950s and 1960s – encouraged by employers, who needed the labour supply, especially at the lower wage-rates immigrants would accept – boosted these levels significantly. By 1975 there were roughly four million foreigners, around half of whom were from the Iberian peninsula (especially Portugal), together with half a million North Africans. Immigrants composed some 8 per cent of the labour force – and formed 17 per cent of industrial workers.

A bigger, younger population gave a powerful injection of demand which in turn helped to trigger economic growth. The state was also a major player in the post-war economic revival. Bold nationalization policies were supplemented by the decision to institute a National Plan, the brainchild of former Cognac merchant Jean Monnet, whom de Gaulle appointed in 1946 to serve as the Plan's first commissioner. Government, business and trade unions were encouraged to work together to reach approved economic targets. The technocratic edge to economic decision-making was underlined by the creation in 1946 of a national administrators' college, the *Ecole Nationale d'Administration* (ENA), and "*énarques*" came to be the missionaries of the state-led economic revival, forming a back-room technical lobby of immense importance through to the present day.

The First Plan was established to last from 1947 to 1952, and made the reconstruction of the war-damaged infrastructure and the supervision of industrial recovery the main priorities. The focus was put on production – coal, steel, cement, tractors,

Colonization and decolonization

French Canada
(lost 1763–1800)

St.-Pierre and
Miquelon

St.-Domingue (lost 1791)
Guadeloupe
Martinique
French Guyana

French
Polynesia

Mayotte

Réunion

Wallis and
Futuna

New
Caledonia

Main French colonial possessions before 1919

Acquired before 1830

1830–81

1882–1919

Area under French mandate 1920
(became independent 1941–44)

Independence gained:
● Before 1960
▫ 1960 and after

French Overseas Department
(*Département d'Outre-Mer*)

French Overseas Territory
(*Territoire d'Outre-Mer*)

transport. The consumer was as yet the last in the line. France's performance was immensely assisted by Marshall Aid from the United States, which was particularly generous to France, and which helped maintain the pace of change right through to the early 1950s. By then new structures were emerging. Of key importance here was the Coal and Steel Treaty, brainchild of Monnet and MRP deputy Robert Schumann, which was arranged in 1951 with West Germany, and which formed the first step in the creation of the European Community.

Industrial performance was impressive: the years from 1950 to 1958 witnessed an 80 per cent increase in output, as the economy as a whole continued to grow at over 5 per cent a year. Agriculture was also part of the picture of dynamism: the "tractor revolution" helped to boost productivity on farms of all shapes and sizes. The number of tractors increased tenfold from 1946 to 1958. A sign of new levels of performance was the fact that, rather than hide behind tariff barriers, France was prepared to participate in the burgeoning economic community by submitting the agrarian sector to greater foreign competition. The Treaty of Rome of 1957, which established the "Common Market" of France, Germany, the Benelux countries and Italy, extended to agriculture as well as industry. Even though their position was bolstered by the price guarantees

France had built up an impressive colonial empire in the seventeenth and eighteenth centuries, notably in Canada, the West Indies and West Africa. Losing the so-called "Second Hundred Years War" (1689–1815) against Britain necessitated starting again almost from scratch. Algeria was colonized in 1830, but most French colonization took place from the 1880s until the First World War. Decolonization following World War II proved especially painful for France, including humiliating military defeat in Indo-China and devastating wars in Algeria.

and income-support mechanisms of the Common Agricultural Policy (1962), French farmers were still under a challenge to produce more efficiently. The challenge had a tonic rather than a depressive effect, with farmers seeking to reorganize and modernize in order to remain internationally competitive. The price of modernization, however, was that a large number of the workforce shifted away from agriculture. Farmers had composed over a third of the active population in 1946; by the mid 1950s the figure was drifting below 30 per cent, and by the late 1960s had hit a mere 16 per cent – drifting downwards to 6 or 7 per cent over the next decades.

The shake-out of agricultural labour was less painful than it might have been, because the rest of the economy was doing well enough to absorb the additional manpower. The regeneration of productive capacity began to work its way through into other areas of the economy. Besides industry the service sector of the economy was also booming. Up to the mid 1950s the Plan had seen heavy industry as its main priority; now a more balanced pattern prevailed, with housing and food production included. Economic recovery was by then beginning to have a major impact upon living standards. The trade unions had had to work hard in the aftermath of war to keep wages even within shouting distance of prices. The problem of inflation was temporarily resolved by the significant devaluation of the currency which de Gaulle imposed in 1962. Among other measures of monetary restraint he introduced a "New Franc" for every 100 old ones.

In the 1960s the trappings of consumerism hit a society long resistant to commercialism. Half of all households possessed a refrigerator in 1965 (only 7.5 per cent had done so in 1959); a car in 1966 (only 30 per cent had done so as recently as 1960); a television also in 1966 (as against 26 per cent in 1962); and a washing machine in 1968 (in 1954 a third of homes did not even have running water). The number of televisions rose from 1 million to 11 million between 1958 and 1973, cars from 5 million to 15 million over much the same time-span. Other indicators of consumerism attested to the depth of the transformation. Less than a fifth of homes possessed central heating in 1962; by 1982 it was over two-thirds. The number of supermarkets rose from forty in 1960 to 1,000 by 1970. New forms of leisure were encouraged by statutory provision for three weeks of paid holidays per year in 1956 – which was raised to four weeks in 1963 (and ultimately to five weeks in 1982). New forms of holiday such as the eco-friendly Club Méditerranée began to grow, and the increasing habit of taking off for *le weekend* spurred a craze for second homes. Indeed the number of *résidences secondaires* rose from 330,000 in 1954 to 1.7 million in 1975.

The new materialism made waves within the intelligentsia. There was a strong backlash critical of this "commodification" of French culture. Much blame was pinned on American cultural influence – *franglais* (Americanized French) in particular became the subject of hot debate. Yet cultural imports made a significant impact on French high culture. The revival of theatre from the early 1950s, for example, owed an enormous amount to foreigners based in France, notably Ionesco (Romanian), Beckett (Irish), Adamov (Russian), Obaldia (Panamanian) – and, later, Peter Brook (British). The "theatre of the absurd" questioned the conventionalities of everyday life, as did, in another medium, the practitioners of the *nouveau roman* ("new novel"), such as Alain Robbe-Grillet, Michel Butor and Nathalie Sarraute. The *nouvelle vague* ("New Wave") in French cinema which emerged in the late 1950s – Truffaut, Godard, Chabrol and Rohmer all made their first serious features in 1959 – also celebrated rather than condemned overseas culture. Hollywood directors such as Alfred Hitchcock received adulation and homage from the New Wave directors.

Not everyone won prizes in the consumerist race; there were losers as well as winners. Geographically, "have-not" regions in the south and west contrasted with "have" regions to the north and east of a line running roughly from Le Havre to Grenoble. Many small businesses went to the wall when confronted with competition – textiles, leather and clothing industries were especially badly affected. Small-shopkeepers were hard hit, too, and formed the backbone of the politics of resentment preached by Pierre Poujade. Anyone on a fixed income suffered from the inflationary pressures of the 1950s and 1960s. Material life could be grim on the bottom of the pile. Much housing, badly affected in the war years and made a lower priority in the early phases of the Plan, was of poor quality. In the 1960s, for example, half of all dwellings lacked a bath or a shower, and nearly half had no inside toilet. Living conditions for immigrant workers, grouped together in veritable shanty-towns (*bidonvilles*) on the edge of cities, were worst of all. New housing for workers, notably the "HLM" (*habitations à loyer modéré*), was moreover often soulless, overcrowded and miserably maintained. The pleasures of

Two realities of working-class housing in the 1950s and 1960s: on one hand, the shanty towns ("*bidonvilles*"), lacking the most basic amenities. On the other, towering in the distance, the shabby anonymity of tower-block housing.

Two Citroëns

It was the sight of the new Citroën DS ("Déesse") in the 1950s that inspired writer Roland Barthes, semiotician of everyday life, to compare the modern automobile to a medieval cathedral. "Supreme creation of an era, conceived with passion by unknown artists and consumed in image if not in usage by a whole population that appropriates

A souped-up "Déesse" (*left*) and a "Deux-Chevaux" (*above*) in all their glory.

them as a purely magical object," he noted, before going on to describe the faithful caressing the door-handles and fondling the internal cushioning like so many holy relics.

The car was the ultimate status symbol in a society won over to the proclamation of status through consumer goods. Sitting by the kerb, "like a huge breathing oyster, about to snap off the leg of any passing pedestrian" (M. Larkin), the DS was for three decades an esteemed asset to any front drive.

It contrasted with the other main money-making car which Citroën produced in the post-war years, the 2CV

("Deux chevaux"). The 2CV, launched in 1948, had its roots in France's agrarian past. It had been modelled in 1935 as the TPV ("Toute Petite Voiture"), capable of transporting two peasants in clogs along with a 110-pound sack of potatoes, and was made saleable at considerably lower cost than most other models. The 2CV was in some senses the polar opposite of the DS in that it made a total aesthetic sacrifice for the sake of utility. Answering perfectly to the consumer demand for cheap, practical, personal travel, some seven million 2CVs had been sold when the model went out of production in the late 1980s.

the consumer society disproportionately benefited the rich: only 40 per cent of workers took a holiday away from home whereas 90 per cent of the bourgeoisie did so. The latter also dominated the elite positions within the higher education sector. When university expansion came in the 1960s, it was done on the cheap, creating resentments which would soon boil over.

THE EVENTS OF MAY 1968

With the benefit of hindsight, it is not impossible to grasp some of the origins of the Events of May 1968, which seemed to come close to overthrowing the government and indeed the whole political system. But we should not let retrospective analysis obscure the fact that what occurred in 1968 was essentially unpredicted and unpredictable.

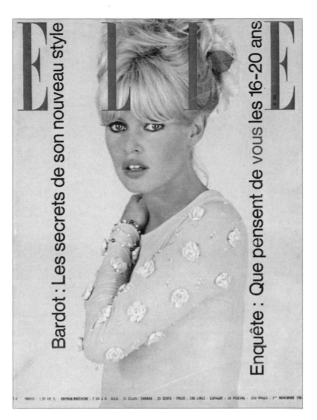

Founded in 1945, *Elle* caught the wind of post-war interest in home consumerism and fashion. In the mid 1960s it was selling three-quarters of a million copies – a figure that had halved by the mid 1990s. The film star Brigitte Bardot, here gracing the November 1963 edition, could be counted on to raise circulation.

De Gaulle spoke for much of the political establishment when he declared the Events "incomprehensible". What started as a campus protest in Nanterre, on the outskirts of Paris, burgeoned into a round of barricades on the streets of the capital and a massive, nationwide workers' movement of revolt, which was dismantled only with difficulty. The Events were moreover suffused with new cultural forms, which highlighted the inadequacies of the existing party-political scene. Those in power had failed to respond to and absorb new social energies unleashed by economic modernization.

This was all the more surprising in that politics after 1958 had seemed to take a step towards the conventional and classifiable rather than the experimental. One of the effects of de Gaulle's coming to power in 1958 was that the Right and Left became clearly polarized into two sides, unlike the ragbag of often tiny formations which had characterized the Fourth Republic. In the constitutional referendum and in national and local elections in 1958, the Gaullists – grouped together into the UNR (*Union pour la Nouvelle République*) – gained three-quarters or more of the vote. In electoral terms there was de Gaulle – and then there was the rest. Important centrist formations under the Fourth Republic, like the MRP and the Radicals, were now sucked into the government majority. In addition, the use of referendums also worked to clarify and simplify the key issues.

The *bête-noire* issues of the Third and Fourth Republics were, moreover, becoming outmoded: the constitution was now fixed, clericalism and anti-clericalism were in

A classroom in the Sorbonne, May 1968, sees the sons and daughters of the bourgeoisie call on the proletariat to unite. The Events were an engaging mix of the ludic and the ludicrous.

their death throes as religious attitudes became more relaxed and less intransigent, and the colonial question had become a thing of the past. Economic questions now seemed to be of more substance in determining political choices. It was noticeable that the electoral geography of France – which had its roots, as we have seen, in the country's response to the Civil Constitution of 1791 – began to shift into new patterns from around this time.

There were some on the Left, including Mendès-France, who held that the cards had been stacked up too high for them ever to achieve power. Certainly, if it was to make any headway at all, the Left had to become better organized, and better able to articulate the grievances of working people. The two-tier electoral system established in the 1958 constitution made a run-off between a Left and Right candidate likely, so electoral pacts became part of the currency of political life. The politics of personality also contributed after 1958 to this simplification of the political landscape. Supporters began to treat de Gaulle as a kind of deity, which had the unlooked-for effect of boosting the prestige of his chief opponents. François Mitterrand gained enormous prestige in the presidential elections of 1965 (since 1962 by universal suffrage) simply by taking de Gaulle to a second ballot. In 1967 he gathered the old SFIO and a number of other socialist groupings into the FDGS (*Fédération de la Gauche démocratique et socialiste*), which transmuted in 1969 into the PS, or *Parti socialiste* (Socialist Party).

Mitterrand was the veteran of countless Fourth Republic governments, and from 1971 became undisputed leader of the PS. More than anyone on the Left he benefited from this personalization and repatterning of party politics. With the support of the Communists and other Left formations, the Socialists had done particularly well in the 1967 elections, putting the government coalition under some strain. In particular Valéry Giscard d'Estaing, leader of the *Républicains Indépendants*, who formed part of the government coalition, openly expressed reservations about government policy. The government was also attracting criticism for its inept involvement in dirty politics. It seemed clear, for example, that the French secret services had been in cahoots with the Moroccan secret police in the assassination of their opposition leader Ben Barka in Paris in late 1965. This scandal was whipped up because of the general context of economic malaise in France in 1967.

It was from the universities, rather than the industrial sector, that the first signs of discontent manifested themselves in May 1968. Student baby-boomers entering university in the late 1960s found the system incapable of coping with the tenfold increase in the student population since World War I levels. Poor conditions in the Nanterre campus of the Paris University stimulated student radicalism – in the event, over American conduct in Vietnam. This led to protests whose impact was amplified by police brutality. The trade unions reacted by calling for a one-day general strike, coinciding with a big student and worker march in Paris. Then critically – and quite spontaneously – student protest fanned out into a nationwide revolt, and between nine and ten million workers came out on strike, many occupying their factories.

There was undeniably a copy-cat element in this worker revolt, but it was fuelled by its own grievances – low wages, poor working conditions, unemployment, poor management practices and unimaginative trade-union leadership. There was, too, an awareness that the benefits of the consumer society had been slower to come to workers than to their social betters. The union leadership was as much taken by surprise as anyone. The PCF-backed CGT followed the party lead in condemning the movement and calling for the restoration of order; but the call by young workers, in particular, for greater participation in management was heeded by the other unions. Participation was also the watchword among many professional groups who joined in the protest: doctors, for example, journalists and workers in radio and television. Many schoolchildren took over their schools, too, attacking the hierarchical rote-learning aspect of *lycée* education, and calling for a less authoritarian form of teaching, which developed all aspects of the personality. The Odéon theatre in Paris was opened to the movement by its director, Jean-Louis Barrault. Night after night this venue, as well as the nearby Sorbonne amphitheatre, witnessed a kind of perpetual teach-in and complaints forum for anyone who chose to attend.

There was a variety of elements within the movement of May 1968. Its carnival character was combined with the call, from a minority of left-wing students and workers (Trotskyist, Maoist and anarchist), for political and social revolution. Underpinning it all was the more materialistic demand of workers for more pay and more control over their lives. All these elements were magnified, moreover, by the crass over-reaction and brutality of the police forces. They beat and tear-gassed indiscriminately, harming by-standers as well as protesters.

In hindsight one can see that the major movements of cultural politics in the last twenty-five years were spawned in the May 1968 Events. The 1917 Bolshevik script, preached by the Marxist Left, was arguably less significant in the longer term than other, less traditional forms of *gauchisme* ("Leftism"). The imaginative use of slogans and publicity images, which had close affinities to the advertising world, made conventional party publicity seem old hat. Amid a veritable firework display of political extremism of every kind, a number of important developments in cultural politics fell into place. The feminist movement, the "green" movement and gay politics, for example, all drew new strength and direction from 1968. The Events were a signal that French society was changing faster, and social expectations were being transformed more radically, than the political establishment had been able to accommodate. Extinguished almost as soon as it had begun, May 1968 embodied an important long-term message.

Yet 1968 was not settled in the long term but in the short. The forces of opposition were too deeply split to have much chance of success. Of crucial importance in the stability of the regime was, ironically enough, its sternest critic, the Communist Party, which ascribed the whole movement to left-wing deviation and petty bourgeois adventurism. Communist support was more than helpful to de Gaulle, who had come close to cracking under the strain. His loyal supporter from Algerian days, General Massu, stationed on the Rhine, had bolstered his resolve. For a figure who bore the hallmarks of an early twentieth-century elite education and training, de Gaulle had always dis-

The battle-lines on the streets of Paris, as dawn breaks. Police repression of the rioting provoked a wave of indignation against the regime.

Operations room for the May Events, containing many of the posters which were spread around the walls of the city.

played a surprising knack at communications. His famous speech on BBC radio on 18 June 1940 had made his name. His performances during the 1958 crisis and the Algerian troubles had been of sterling worth. Now, just as his government's fortunes looked at their lowest, he used the media to proclaim a determination not to quit. There would be, he announced, no change of government, no resignation from himself and no change of policies. His prime minister, the tough and resilient Georges Pompidou, dismantled the oppositional movement by offering wage rises of between 7 and 10 per cent to workers and increasing the national minimum wage. De Gaulle also called for fresh elections – a move which turned out to be a master-stroke, allowing a right-wing backlash to get organized in the face of the indeterminate and divided left-wing threat. In late June, elections gave the unified Right, now renamed the UDR (*Union des démocrates pour la République*), a massive majority of 358 out of 485 deputies – the largest right-wing vote in the history of the Fifth Republic hitherto, and more than enough to take the wind out of the electoral sails of the far Left. Edgar Faure steered through some reform of higher education, establishing a good degree of decentralization for universities and allowing students increased participation in university governance. Campuses were the site of political chaos for some time to come; but there were no more insurrections.

Despite the glowing success of the 1968 elections, much of the old de Gaulle magic had disappeared in the crisis. The government's survival owed as much to Pompidou as to de Gaulle, yet the latter almost at once dismissed his prime minister – a move many interpreted as jealousy. Yet the old warhorse went on his terms rather than at the behest of the voters. In 1969 he put plans for Senate and regional reforms to a referendum, threatening to quit if he was not given proper popular support. The loss of the referendum – by 53.2 per cent to 46.7 – did not necessarily entail his removal, yet he chose to fall on his own sword. On 28 April 1969 he went on to the radio to announce tersely: "I am ceasing to exercise my functions as president of the republic. This decision will take effect from today at midday." He walked away from politics as he had done in 1946, but this time never looked back. He died in 1970.

Could there be Gaullism after de Gaulle? Indeed could there be a Fifth Republic after his departure? Georges Pompidou was the man who answered both questions in the affirmative. Though he lacked de Gaulle's penchant for self-aggrandizement, he

"The walls speak": Paris in 1968

A particular target of the rioters and *gauchistes* during the Events of May 1968 was the close control that the government kept over the media. Government domination of television was legendary – "the government in your dining-room," as the critics of television news put it – while freedom of the press was also felt to be compromised by unseemly ministerial pressures on editors. Official news was criticized not only in the content of the political activities, but also, implicitly, in their form. Tons of paper were used to make news-sheets, handouts, broadsheets and posters of every imaginable sort. More than that, walls in public spaces became a primitive canvas for critical expression, and anonymous graffiti became a political art form. Rather than defining a pragmatic programme of action, the multimedia communications of May 1968 offered a different kind of political language, one which hoped to transcend the banal and the routine, and to place, as the graffiti stated, "imagination in power".

The May Events had been sparked off in crowded and ill-equipped Nanterre campus – here staging a 1968 sit-in – which remained a hot-spot of student activism for many years afterwards.

was a tough operator and shrewd enough to draw political sustenance from the Gaullist inheritance. Thus he maintained, for example, the independent foreign policy line which de Gaulle had developed. His commitment to Europe was strong too; he permitted an enlargement of the "Six" who had pioneered the Common Market into the "Nine" of the European Community (with Britain coming in along with Ireland and Denmark in 1972).

At home the weakening of the Left in the aftermath of the May Events and the subsequent right-wing backlash made his job initially easier. So did the continuation of the

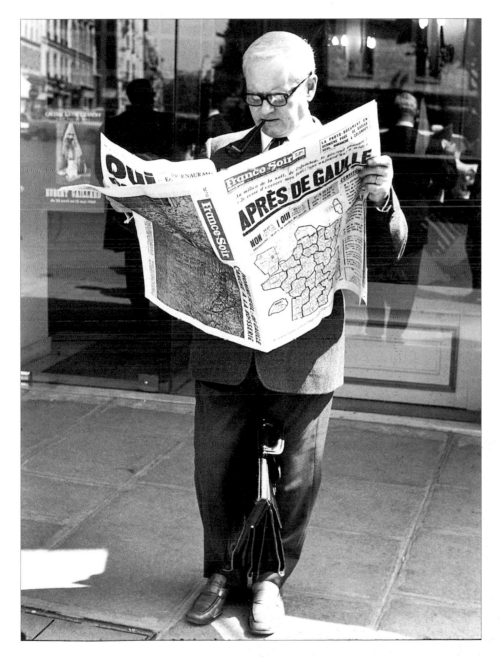

De Gaulle's departure in 1958 found the Parisian daily *France-Soir* at the top of its influence, selling 1.4 million copies (only 300,000 twenty years later). This picture was taken by the great photographer Henri Cartier-Bresson.

long-term wave of prosperity which France had managed since the late 1940s. Average income increased by 4.5 per cent per person per year between 1959 and 1973. Pompidou tinkered minimally but sagely with the system which had served France well. The grip of central government was slightly relaxed in certain areas (notably control over the nationalized industries).

Pompidou became aware of, and then reacted to, a sea change that was occurring in the political meaning of regionalism. The spirit of decolonization had spread to mainland France. In 1965 the young socialist Michel Rocard had called on government to "decolonize the provinces", a demand that proved a landmark in regional thinking. Before, it was almost unthinkable for the Left, with its strongly centralizing, Jacobin tradition, to support regional power, which was usually the watchword of the backward-looking and traditionalist Right. By his measured programme for regional development Pompidou took some of the wind from the sails of this pro-regionalist Left. For the first time since their creation in 1790 departments had certain economic tasks taken out of their hands and placed in the control of assemblies at the supra-departmental, regional level. Certain major economic programmes also had the effect of stimulating the regions. Much of the aerospace industry behind the Concorde project was based in Toulouse, for example, while the building of the massive oil refinery at Fos, near Marseille, from 1970 onwards helped the Mediterranean economy. There was also gigantic tourist development – the flagship of which was the pyramidical apartment blocks of La Grande Motte on the formerly malarial Languedoc coastline. Ridding its beautiful beaches of mosquitoes made them fully inhabitable for the first time. Massive motorway building in association with private enterprise also helped to stimulate the regional economy. Major efforts were made in another branch of communications, the telephone system. The number of lines quadrupled in a matter of years rather than decades; where only one home in seven had possessed one in 1968, three-quarters did so in 1982.

Though he lost some of the left-wing voters whom de Gaulle had personally attracted, Pompidou maintained the right-wing umbrella formation which de Gaulle had developed. Under his guidance it became a formidable political machine. His choice of the mildly liberal Chaban-Delmas (who had served under de Gaulle in London during the war) as his first prime minister was a sensible measure which made post-1968 reforms possible. Chaban's growing popularity led Pompidou to replace him in 1972 by the more rigidly uncompromising Pierre Messmer. Continuing nervousness in government ranks at a possible repetition of 1968 meant that he stayed firmly authoritarian on public-order issues. Anyone who visited Paris in the late 1960s and late 1970s will remember the extraordinary police saturation there, which was maintained at all times. Protest demonstrations and marches would as likely be interrupted by police stooges and *agents provocateurs*. Police powers were still wide – and much used.

Paris was also, however, the centrepiece of Pompidou's calculated investment in the politics of cultural grandeur. To some degree this was a continuation of the de Gaulle era. De Gaulle's minister of culture, André Malraux, had in 1962 introduced heritage legislation which led to a major clean-up of all public buildings. The grime of centuries was peeled away from such cultural monuments as Notre-Dame to reveal a novel cleanliness that only the niggardly could bemoan. Malraux also aimed to spread high culture to what were seen as the culturally under-developed regions. In 1966 he opened at Le Havre the first of a dozen or more *maisons de la culture*, or cultural centres. These Malraux identified as the cathedrals of the cultural future. He viewed them as missionary outposts, dispersing the classical cultural heritage of the educated, particularly Parisian, elite. "In ten years," he announced in 1966, "this hideous word 'provincial' will have ceased to exist."

The *maisons de la culture* were not destined for a happy future. Although they did something to bolster the regional devolution which Pompidou was urging, the cultural suppositions behind Malraux's "civilizing mission" in the regions were old-fashioned and elitist. The consumer society had pulled to pieces many of the assumptions behind high culture. Television, records, pop music radio stations and the other media of the consumerist age all highlighted culture as pluralistic rather than unitary, popular

Opened in 1977, the Pompidou Centre proved to be the most popular museum and public building in France. The hordes of visitors placed a strain on the fabric, and in 1994 the building was closed temporarily to allow essential works and redecoration to be undertaken.

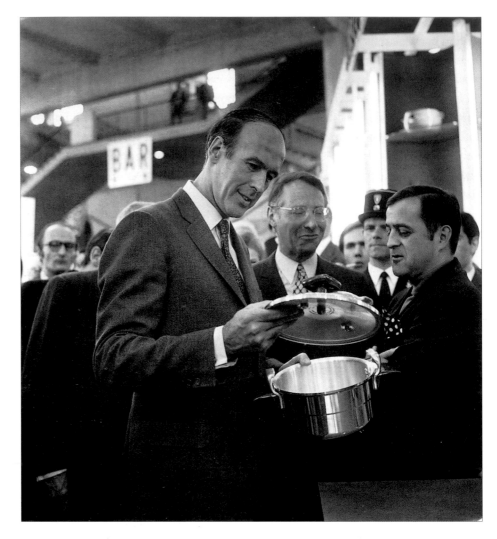

President Giscard d'Estaing examining a pressure-cooker at an ideal home exhibition. Giscard's attempts to show the common touch rarely convinced.

without the husband's consent. In 1972 equal-pay provision was introduced for women (though it would be a long battle to enforce it effectively). The "right to choose" was a key women's issue: in 1971 some 343 women, many of them from public life, signed a manifesto in the *Nouvel Observateur* weekly, calling for the legalization of abortion, themselves admitting to having had an abortion. A law of 1975, directed through parliament by Simone Veil, responded to this demand by making the operation more easily and legally available, and thereby ending the dominion of the back-street abortionist. A law in 1974 built on a measure of 1967 to make contraception more freely available, too. Divorce was also liberalized in 1975.

Giscardian liberalism, underpinned by his quest for a relaxed, loose media image, was given some chance to establish its credibility when squabbling broke out on the Left between Communists and Socialists in the late 1970s. Indeed, for a time, Giscard had far more trouble within government ranks than with the opposition. His dismissal of Chirac in 1976 boomeranged badly. Chirac banged the door shut after him, and transformed the Gaullist UDR into the RPR (*Rassemblement pour la République*). The new party's Gaullist-sounding initials obscured the fact that it was a vehicle for his own ambitions, in which the old Resistance barons had little place. The RPR far outsized Giscard's own UDF. In 1977 Chirac stood for, and won, the post of mayor of Paris, which Giscard had created as a private fief for his friend Michel d'Ornano. Chirac's influence was sufficient to frustrate a number of the liberal reforms which Giscard had in mind, and which might have won him some support from left-wing voters. Giscard was obliged to move towards the Right, as a means of ensuring that his government coalition remained intact. The revival of the Left at the end of the 1970s also made his liberal claims seem thin.

Giscard's once relaxed presidential style had by then developed into something altogether stiffer and more imperial. His habit of being served first at official banquets and his decision to slow down and make less martial "The Marseillaise" were the kind of preoccupation with petty issues which irked many. His diplomacy also became a cause of concern. His call for the "globalization" of French foreign policy seemed a liberal enough gesture. Yet in Africa, in particular, he sponsored neo-colonial moves which looked frankly dynastic: French troops crushed rebels against Mobutu in Zaire in 1978, and supported then helped to overthrow the dictatorial Bokassa in the Central African Republic. His love of hobnobbing with the great also rebounded on him. Bokassa had offered him diamonds as a personal gift, and Giscard's evasiveness over this was an unexpected but significant vote-loser for him in the presidential elections of 1981.

By then he was facing a Left reunited around the candidacy of François Mitterrand – "the eternal loser", as Giscardian supporters sneered. Yet he was obliged to go to the polls when the Western economies were still in very poor shape. Barre had done a fairly effective job at stabilizing the economy in the mid 1970s, but when further oil price rises occurred in 1979, the government opted out of the difficult and probably unpopular policies required. Instead they sat back and waited for the 1981 elections, even as the recession seemed to be getting deeper and deeper. Because of the nature of the coalition which he headed, moreover, Giscard found it difficult to present himself as the liberal he claimed to be. It had been his misfortune to come to the presidency at a time when the world economy was leaving little scope for genuine liberal policies. In the 1981 elections he paid the price, and had to give way as gracefully as he could to "the eternal loser", François Mitterrand.

CHAPTER 11

The Mitterrand Years

François Mitterrand's election as president in 1981 and 1988 for two terms of seven years ensured him an enduring place in French political history. Only de Gaulle, who was in power for thirteen years (1944–6, 1958–69), approaches this span of time at the top of the political tree in the twentieth century. As France moved towards a new *fin de siècle* – which would also be a *fin de millénium* – this personal dominance under the constitution of the Fifth Republic contrasted strikingly with the feverish volatility of governments a century earlier, in the Third Republic's *fin de siècle* as well as under the Fourth Republic, which formed the workshop where Mitterrand's political apprenticeship took place.

Mitterrand maintained his grip on power through a mastery of political compromise learnt early in his career. Though he worked under Vichy as a civil servant, he was an active member of the Resistance, for which he was subsequently decorated. When he was a minister in his twenties under the Fourth Republic, his political party had a key role in propping up governmental coalitions, and he served endlessly on the ministerial merry-go-round. Though his career surely marked him out as a man of leftish principles, it was not always apparent what those principles were – despite his enthusiam in 1981, for example, he was a late convert to socialism. Though his integrity was confirmed in his odyssey through the oppositional wilderness from 1958 onwards, his ability to accommodate and to survive seismic shifts in the political terrain served him well as president after 1981, when he had to preside over governments drawn from right across the political spectrum.

On this point, personal destiny merged with constitutional stability. Despite the "custom-built" character of the Fifth Republic at its outset the regime had proved able to accommodate a president who was neither de Gaulle (Pompidou, from 1969), nor even a Gaullist (Giscard d'Estaing, from 1974). Mitterrand threw down further challenges to the Fifth Republic's constitutional arrangements. Not only did he begin as a president from the Left, he then from 1986 to 1988 (and again after 1993) continued as a left-wing president working with a right-wing government. The new doctrines of "cohabitation" of Left and Right within the same regime, and of *alternance* ("alternation") between the two wings, proved sufficient to meet those challenges.

THE APOTHEOSIS OF THE FIFTH REPUBLIC

From the very start of his presidential term, Mitterrand showed a sensitivity to history and social memory. He affirmed the great Socialist victory celebrations on the Place de la Bastille – traditional site of left-wing demonstrations – and made an early visit to the Panthéon, where national heroes are interred. There he honoured the memorials of Victor Schoelscher, the Second Republic politician responsible for the final abolition of slavery in French domains in 1848; of Jean Jaurès, the great Socialist leader assassinated in 1914; and of Jean Moulin, the Resistance hero. He also held a special reception

Opposite The Socialist electoral victories of 1981 produced a tremendous mood of elation: most of the young had never known a left-wing government. Hopes were soon to be dashed.

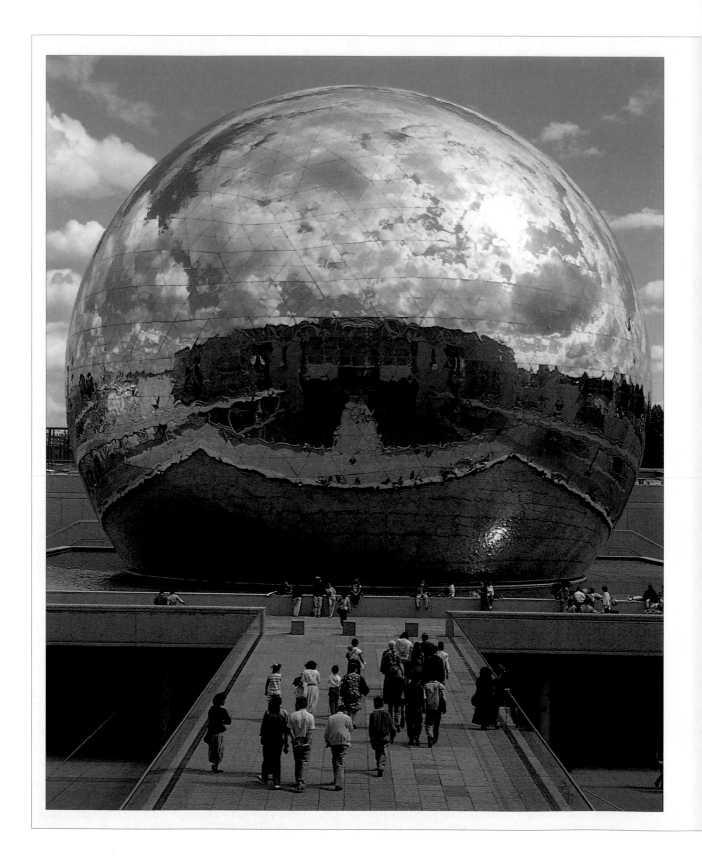

A distinctive characteristic of the presidents of the Fifth Republic has been a strong commitment to prestige projects. The Concorde, which by the 1990s was an ageing veteran of the sky, remained a questionable heirloom from the days of de Gaulle. In the 1980s the high-speed train, the TGV (*Train à grande vitesse*), after opening on the Paris–Lyon route, was expanded by government to run on other networks, involving massive investment in rail infrastructure.

The politics of cultural grandeur

projects, often planned by the international high-fliers of the architectural world, who showed lofty disdain for any criticism, were accompanied by massive publicity hype.

To the 1977 Pompidou Centre, designed by Englishman Richard Rogers and Italian Renzo Piano, were added

Pei's glass pyramid in the courtyard of the Louvre (the latter also earmarked for major redevelopment), the Opéra Bastille and the massive Arche de la Défense, opened to coincide with the 1789 bicentenary celebrations in 1989 in the La Défense development on the outskirts of Paris. Before the end of his presidential term Mitterrand also planned to open a new national library, the TGB (*Très Grande Bibliothèque*).

Presidents from de Gaulle onwards,

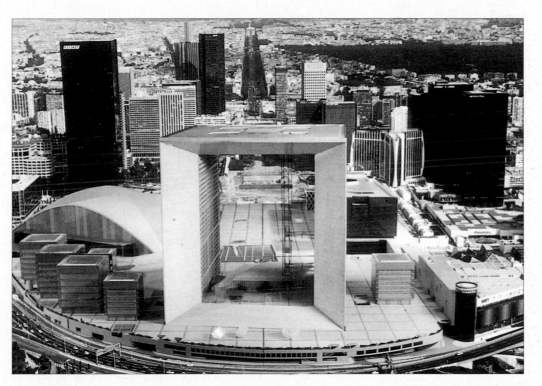

It was Georges Pompidou, however, who set the tone for prestige building projects, particularly ones located in the capital. Giscard continued this work. While freezing some of his predecessor's more over-ambitious plans, he backed the transformation of the dilapidated Orsay railway station into a museum, and approved the development of La Villette park and science museum. The tendency reached it peak under the presidency of François Mitterrand. Such

La Défense, the business and residential centre on the western fringes of Paris, developed in the 1960s and 1970s, is crowned by the Grande Arche. This commemoration of the 1989 bicentenary of the French Revolution is placed in a direct line down the Champs Elysées towards the Étoile.

to be fair, have also been associated with plans for urban renovation and heritage development that place France among the most progressive of European governments. The crumbling Marais district in Paris, for example, has been transformed into a superb showcase of the architecture and design of the seventeenth and eighteenth centuries. Mitterrand also considerably increased the share of the national budget allocated to the arts and culture.

increases were made to the state welfare programme. The minimum wage was increased by 10 per cent, but this was dwarfed in importance by 25 to 50 per cent increases in family allowances, housing subsidies and old-age pensions, along with significant changes in medical benefits. The working week was reduced from forty to thirty-nine hours, and a fifth week of paid holidays was introduced – a striking homage to both the programme of the Popular Front and Fifth Republic leisure consumerism.

Who was to pay for this unparalleled largesse? The government introduced a wealth tax on the largest fortunes and increased the tax liability of employers, but these steps had only symbolic value, given the extent of additional state welfare commitments. Mitterrand and Mauroy wagered on Keynesian-style policies triggering an expansion in the economy which would absorb the new social costs. The government tried to turn over a new leaf after Barre's austerity, and go for growth. To that end liberalism and decentralization were accompanied by an extension of state economic power unmatched since the Liberation. The state increased its control of the economy in order to channel investment rationally. In the process they hoped to control exchanges, boost exports and trigger rises in production. Legislation in 1982 saw five industrial giants nationalized, plus the main private banks. State holdings in other major businesses were increased to give a majority holding position. By the end of 1982 thirteen out of France's largest twenty companies were effectively in government control. The proportion of the labour-force directly beholden to the state doubled, rising to over 20 per cent, when supplemented by the 140,000 new jobs in the public sector which the government went on to create, many of them in prestige cultural projects.

"I was carried away with our victory; we were intoxicated. Everyone … predicted the return of growth by 1983. Honestly, I lack the necessary knowledge to say they were wrong." Mitterrand's frank confession dates from as early as July 1983. By then the high hopes of 1981 had largely evaporated, and the government was engaged in damage-limitation exercises in enforced austerity. The Socialists had wagered on state-led growth curtailing rising imports and stimulating exports. The "republic of teachers" had failed to do their maths homework. As they were later ruefully to accept, the economic environment was almost wholly inauspicious for this scenario. Extra purchasing power within the French economy tended to be spent on imports rather than home-produced goods, unsettling the balance of trade and weakening the currency. There were enforced devaluations of the franc in 1981, 1982 and 1983. The rocketing price of oil imports only made matters worse, and helped to send inflation spiralling upwards. Despite the devaluations, moreover, the franc was probably still overvalued on world markets, which made French exports uncompetitive. Ominously unemployment continued to edge upwards, passing the two million mark.

In these stormy economic waters Mitterrand, the political arch-survivor and past-master in the skills of compromise, chose not to go down strapped to the mast of unbending socialism. In classic austerity packages – notably in June 1982 and March 1983 – he and Mauroy took the deflationary path: wage and price freezes, cuts in public expenditure, increases in health service charges, imposed ceilings on pay rises, exchange controls and so on. The Right, of course, rubbed its hands in gleeful *schaden-freude*. It was given the chance to flex its muscles by the Savary law of 1984, which envisaged closer state control over private – which meant in effect Roman Catholic – schools. The opposition to this law owed little to the confessional struggles of the past. Indeed many Church leaders, long thankful for the dowsing down of the fires of anti-clericalism, were faintly embarrassed by the political capital which the Right made of the issue. It was privacy rather than Catholicism which parents valued most in Catholic private schooling. Four-fifths of them were not even practising Catholics, but such schools were favoured for their middle-class cachet, generous teacher–student ratios and reputation for academic success. A demonstration in Paris that rallied over a million persons – making it, by some counts, the largest public protest in French history – forced the government to back down and withdraw the legislation.

The growing unpopularity of the government was signalled even more clearly in the elections to the European parliament, which also took place in 1984. The Socialists slumped to a mere 21 per cent of the vote. Ominously many disgruntled voters chose to divert their votes not to the alternative left-wing party, the PCF, which did poorly, nor even to the conventional Right. A newly-emergent far Right, Jean-Marie Le Pen's frankly anti-immigrant but also clearly anti-Semitic National Front (*Front national*), became the crucible for grumbling discontent. It attracted 11 per cent of the vote – roughly the same as the Communists. In 1981 Le Pen had been unable to command the necessary support to put himself up in the presidential elections, and his party attracted less than 1 per cent of the votes in the 1981 legislative elections. A former Poujadist, Le Pen developed his organization cannily, building up strong support in regions with a large immigrant population, notably in the Mediterranean south and in some larger industrial cities. His racist opinions brought a new tone of resentment and viciousness into the political arena.

The Socialist magic lamp, it seemed, had succeeded in uniting the conventional Right and bringing forth the Le Pen genie. By 1984 it was clear that a change of direction was essential if the PS was to perform even passingly well in the 1986 legislative elections. Mitterrand consequently dropped Mauroy, bringing in as prime minister the young *énarque* (that is, graduate of the technocratic *Ecole Nationale d'Administration*), Laurent Fabius. Fabius aimed to shore up the economy by moving further and more systematically away from the social and economic programme of 1981. The Communists withdrew from the government – and many left-wing Socialists became disenchanted, too, as Fabius attempted to rehabilitate the government by stealing the clothes of the opposition. Priority was given to reducing inflation and increasing productivity. There were further public spending cuts, pay restraint and tax incentives to private industry. By the 1986 elections Fabius had performed moderately well according to his own lights. Economic growth was slow but steady, inflation was down to 5 per cent (it had topped 15 per cent in 1982) and exports were rising. Unemployment, at over 10 per cent, was still high, but early retirement and job-creation schemes had kept it within bounds.

Poster culture brings National Front leader Jean-Marie Le Pen and singer Michael Jackson, then touring France, into an uneasy juxtaposition. Le Pen's sloganizing called for "Frenchmen first", which meant defining second-generation immigrants as "ethnic", and therefore non-French.

Not only had Fabius helped to bring the economy round, he had also helped to make the idea of the social market economy acceptable within his own party and within public opinion generally. It remained to be seen, however, whether this was the basis for a successful electoral campaign. With fascistic extremism suddenly à la mode, and with the conventional Right making a strong showing in the opinion polls, the Socialists did not have left much of the optimism of 1981 to show for their five years in power. The success they enjoyed came from operating the economy in the spirit of Barre, Giscard and Chirac. This was hardly a strong endorsement in the eyes of an elec-torate which had been led to expect better in the heady days of 1981.

ADJUSTING TO POLITICAL ALTERNATION

Long before the 1986 elections the runes had been read. Could a Socialist president remain at the helm with a right-wing majority in the National Assembly? There were some who claimed that this was unthinkable – former premier Raymond Barre was among them. However, those rather better placed than he to benefit from a right-wing victory in 1986 – notably the RPR leader Jacques Chirac and former president Giscard d'Estaing – accepted the possibility of "cohabitation".

Cohabitation matured into a fundamental doctrine of republican constitutionalism under Mitterrand's term of office. After presiding over Socialist reform from 1981 to 1986, from 1986 to 1988 he was willing to take a back seat and allow premier Jacques Chirac, who led the right-wing majority in the Assembly, to call the shots. Mitterrand used his constitutional prerogative, however, following his victory in the presidential elections of 1988, to dissolve the Assembly and call for fresh legislative elections. These proved favourable to the PS and led to his appointment of Socialist premiers down to 1993. Victory for the Right in the 1993 legislative elections saw Mitterrand maintaining his hold on power, even as the government passed back into the hands of the Right.

In the stately progress of political alternation there were numerous confident predictions of Mitterrand's demise – prophecies that were given new impetus when he was diagnosed in 1992 as having a minor cancer problem. These proved ill-founded. Three factors helped his durability. First, the 1958 constitution placed so much power in the hands of the president that it proved difficult for parliamentary manoeuvrings to end a president's tenure, which had been grounded since 1962 in election by universal suffrage. Second, wherever possible Mitterrand treated foreign policy as his personal domain, using his growing stature as an international statesman to enhance his political reputation at home. At first, in 1981, he displayed a concern for human rights abroad that chimed with his principled domestic plans. The shift to "realism" in domestic economic policy was, however, matched by a move towards *Realpolitik* in international relations. His agreeing to the use of French troops in internal dissension in Chad in 1983 recalled the neo-colonial rashness of Giscard, while by 1985, he was even welcoming General Jaruzelski, the scourge of the Polish Solidarity movement, to the Elysée palace. The *Rainbow Warrior* affair of 1985 – in which French secret service agents destroyed a ship in a New Zealand harbour belonging to the Greenpeace movement, prior to its being used to protest against French nuclear testing in the South Pacific – also suggested a degree of presidential cynicism in the protection of state interests.

Such incidents failed to detract from the international stature which Mitterrand enjoyed. His apparent reversion to foreign policy positions viewed as authentically Gaullist won him support within France from traditional supporters of the Right. Though his commitment to a European future for France was well in advance of de Gaulle's conception of national sovereignty within a loosely affiliated Europe, in many other respects he proved as Gaullist as de Gaulle (and often more Gaullist than the Gaullists in the National Assembly). His role – and the participation of French troops – in the Gulf War of 1990/1 won plaudits. The timing of the crisis helped to ensure that, when in 1991 the French media drew up the balance sheet of his ten years in power, the prognoses were pretty favourable.

A further reason for Mitterrand's popularity, and the third factor explaining his political longevity, was his ability to distance himself from the hurly-burly of party infighting and to pose as being somehow above politics. While basking in any credit and popularity coming his way, Mitterrand proved particularly adept at using successive prime ministers as lightning rods for any unpopularity attracted by his governments.

The popularity of the Minitel spawned a host of services and networks making use of the system. Minitel dating has proved particularly popular and has deprived the newspapers of a traditional source of revenue.

in road and rail communications. These "neo-villagers", along with tourists, at least brought added wealth back into many rural areas. The distance which such workers were able to put between their homes and their place of employment illuminated the continuing increase in the proportion of the workforce who were salaried – managers rather than small businessmen or property-holders. Where two-thirds of the labour force had been employed in agriculture or industry in 1945, two-thirds by the early 1990s were employed in the service sector of the economy.

Population patterns changed somewhat after the 1960s. The high birth-rates detectable from the 1940s slowed down, a development which seems to have been linked to more permissive sexual attitudes arising from easier divorce and new, more accessible contraception (notably the "pill"). From the late 1970s onwards the birth-rate was below its pre-war levels. The number of children adults regarded as ideal slipped from 2–3 to 1–2. Partly this was a consequence of increased social and geographical mobility, which had removed small children from the supportive network of grandparents and other kin. This tendency was partly offset by the excellent provision for infant education (half of two- to five-year-olds attended *écoles maternelles* in the 1960s, while by the 1980s, the figure was 80 per cent and rising). On the other hand, the high participation of women in the labour force also acted to reduce aspirations for large families.

Family patterns seemed to be in flux. A dip in the marriage rate from the 1960s reflected a sharp rise in couples living together outside marriage. As a result illegitimacy rates rose, from one-twentieth in the post-war years to between a quarter and a third in the early 1990s. Divorces too became more frequent, more than doubling between

A Paris street filled with Muslims at prayer. Islam became France's second religion during the Fifth Republic, with three million adherents. Arab workers were usually, however, far worse paid and less well-treated than their native French comrades.

the 1960s and the 1980s – nearly a third of marriages ended this way. The rise in the number of abortions pointed in a similar direction – from roughly 130,000 in the mid 1970s, when terminations became legal, to over 160,000 in the late 1980s.

However, the most significant demographic fact in the 1990s was also the one with the most ominous economic consequences for state and society – namely, the ageing of the population. The baby-boomers of the 1940s and 1950s started losing their teeth. In 1946 one French person in six was over 60 years old; by 1991 the figure was one in five. The situation will be even more pronounced in following decades. Increased life expectancy, and the spread of early retirement packages aimed at soaking up unemployment, means that there will be more individuals approaching retirement age around the millennium than ever before in French history. It will be between 2006 and 2010 that the peak birth-rate group of 1946–50 reaches its sixtieth birthday.

The ageing population means that there will be increasingly large numbers of economically inactive people in the future. One likely consequence of this is the continuing, and possibly growing, role of women in the workforce. The period after the 1960s saw the resurgence of female employment. Nearly 40 per cent at the turn of this century, it fell markedly in the post-1945 period, climbing again during the recession to reach 43 per cent in the early 1990s. Women were popular with employers, because they accepted lower wages than men, thereby keeping down production costs. Although a larger proportion of girls than boys left school with their *baccalauréat*, women were consistently to be found in the least well-rewarded sectors of the economy. Their marked under-representation among the political class was mirrored in the most prestigious professions and the higher echelons of business and bureaucracy.

Opinion polls and under-registration of the female unemployed suggest that high unemployment since the 1970s had a disproportionately heavy impact on women wanting to work. Indeed unemployment seemed to punish the most defenceless: as well as women, immigrants, the unskilled and young workers (especially in areas stripped of heavy industry by the recession) were particularly badly affected. Casualization of the workforce in many industries also produced more under-employment than can easily be quantified. Want and need, in the context of an increasingly materialistic consumer society, produced a backlash of delinquence. The crime-rate rose by 250 per cent between the mid 1970s and mid 1980s. Even allowing for increased police registration, these were woefully impressive figures. Unattached single males were the biggest offenders. Half of prison entrants were less than twenty-five years old, while three-quarters were unmarried. These developments triggered a sense of insecurity among the public at large, to which politicians of all parties became increasingly alert.

This state of public insecurity was an essential component in the rise of far-Right politics, and when wilfully mixed with the issue of immigration, it composed a vicious cocktail of hate. Paradoxically immigration became a political issue when it was in a phase of slowing down (from the mid 1970s) rather than increasing. France's economy had long depended on attracting unskilled or semi-skilled cheap labour; three-quarters of population expansion in the 1920s, for example, was through immigration. Indeed it has been calculated that around one-third of the French population in the early 1990s was a first-, second- or third-generation immigrant. Yet immigrants were no more numerous proportionately in the 1990s than they had been in the 1930s. Unchecked until the 1970s numbers stabilized at around four million – roughly 8 per cent of the total population.

Immigration was therefore as French as croissants. What made it a contentious political issue was the greater cultural visibility of the immigrant population in the middle of an economic recession. Past waves of immigrants had integrated themselves relatively painlessly through their jobs. Mass unemployment from the 1970s onwards knocked away the ladder by which they could climb within French society. In addition the immigrants tended to be concentrated to the north and east of a line between Marseille and Le Havre, and were particularly strongly represented in big cities. The fact that much of the most recent immigrant wave was also not white – Arabs from North Africa, Asians and Turks – made them easy targets, too. The religious issue may have counted for some: almost unobserved, Islam became the second religion of France. Town councils began to receive applications for mosque-building. The Muslim community endeavoured to knit together a full community on their own terms, sometimes overtly rejecting integration and the secular culture which French society offered. The 1980s also saw the emergence of a "Beur" culture followed by second-generation Arab adolescents, and largely on the margins of mainstream youth culture.

The rise of extremist intolerance towards immigrant groups should perhaps be seen as part of a wider picture of political fragmentation that was becoming clear by the 1980s. The transformation of society since 1945 had produced a sea change in political allegiances. The evaporation of the peasantry lost the Socialists and Communists some of the traditional heartlands of their support. In the same way the disintegration of the big proletarian cities, notably of the north and east, meant the break-up of former Communist strongholds. The proportion of the labour-force who were members of trade unions fell from 20 to 15 per cent by the late 1980s. The startling decline in the PCF – from the largest party in 1945 down to level pegging with the far Right in the late 1980s and 1990s – had less to do with politics than sociology. Though the PCF leadership proved singularly inept at adapting its policies to the times, the fact was that social change was destroying the old working class.

The political landscape was, then, increasingly fluid as the end of the century approached. The strengthening of the presidential system under Mitterrand was accompanied by the emergence of new political groupings and new political styles. These could be quite diverse in character. The National Front traced its lineage back to the 1930s. Immigrant support groups, in contrast, had to improvise: there were no strong indigenous traditions to follow. A good many of the groups on the Left conveyed something of the values arising out of the 1960s – and of 1968 in particular. The feminist movement is a case in point. Feminists were galvanized into forming a political pressure-group by the events of 1968. The experience of the May Events was negative, in the sense that many women discovered just how sexist most male-dominated left-wing groups really were, but positive in that it encouraged solidarity and mutual support, and provided models of cultural politics – lobbying, demonstration, artful publicity and outright provocation – which could be used to forge a specific political identity. The feminist movement was characterized by rifts and an obsession with theoretical issues in the 1970s and 1980s – another legacy of 1968! It was also relatively unsuccessful in linking up with the experiences and aspirations of working-class and immigrant women. The gay movement also drew strength and inspiration from the 1968 experience, though the foundation of the *Front Homosexuel d'Action Revolutionnaire* drew as much inspiration from the US Gay Liberation Front. Though the gay movement's impact on mainstream politics was not great, the heady early liberal phase of Mitterrand's presidency saw the revoking of anti-homosexual legislation that had been on the statute books since Vichy. The anti-racist movement – notably Harlem Désir's *SOS-Racisme* – had more effect, drawing its repertoire from the American civil rights movement of the 1960s as well as from French experience.

SOS-Racisme

"*SOS-Racisme's* France is the France of 1789, the France of free contract, the France of rights respected." The comment of Harlem Désir, chair of the anti-racist organization *SOS-Racisme*, highlights one of the principal aims of immigrant groups: to get an equal chance in the home of the Rights of Man.

SOS-Racisme was founded in 1984 by Désir, himself of mixed racial descent, after young immigrant groups were spurred into action in the so-called "March of the Beurs" in 1983. This event was triggered off by the killing of a young immigrant in a Parisian suburb and took the form of an American-style civil rights march across the country. The aim was to publicize the conditions of discrimination under which young Arabs lived. The word *beur* derives, through a curious form of back-slang known as *verlan* (*à l'envers* = backwards), from *arabe*, and was assumed as a mark of identity by young, often second-generation adolescents, from

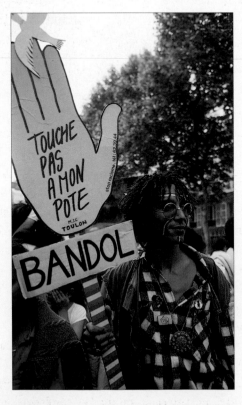

immigrant backgrounds. The movement, fuelled by clashes between immigrants and police forces in a number of major cities, endeavoured to give voice to a current of opinion on the margin of the political nation. This was in a climate, remember, when Arabs felt themselves under attack from the racist taunts of the National Front's leader, Jean-Marie Le Pen.

Marshalled with consummate skill by Désir, the movement took as its symbol a hand raised in warning, accompanied by the slogan: "Touche pas à mon pote" ("Hands off my pal"). It acted as an organization of solidarity, but also as a publicity machine, lobbying for legislation, fighting for legal assistance in discrimination cases and providing press releases to publicize the key issues and improve public relations. In the early 1990s the organization had 300 support committees spread throughout France and 25,000 members.

Occitanian graffiti: "We want to live in our country." The regionalist call from the Midi is given an extra twist by the mass tourism which the area experiences each summer, and by the increasingly frequent practice of "foreigners" – that is, French as well as non-French – buying up second houses in the choicest areas, thereby sending up property prices.

Another form of cultural politics to emerge strongly in the 1970s and 1980s was the regionalist movement, which was increasingly shaking off its reactionary and Pétainist aura. But the change from an agrarian way of life in many French regions had dealt a heavy blow to their indigenous cultures – in particular their languages. Many regional dialects and patois, for example, were dying out with the disappearance of older inhabitants: the Franche-Comté patois, the romance language of Lorraine and Occitanian in the Tarn and Cantal were all cases in point by the late 1980s. The historical drive towards one unified French language initiated their decline, but the process was hastened by the development of the spoken and visual media.

When government accepted the need for a regionalist economic programme, particularly from the 1980s, new life was breathed into these linguistic traditions. The state threw its support behind the learning of Alsatian, Flemish and Breton in schools in those areas, while Basque and Catalan also revived in association with the linked groups in the Iberian peninsula. Even prior to that, regionalism had been becoming a left- rather than a right-wing concern. A good illustration was the response to government plans in the late 1970s to extend a military camp on the Larzac plateau in the

Cévennes. When local peasants protested against the loss of their livelihoods the Left orchestrated massive, nationwide support. Big solidarity marches and demonstrations were held in Paris and throughout France. One of Mitterrand's first acts on becoming president was quietly to shelve the military camp project.

Within this movement inspired by Larzac was a strong current of ecologically minded post-1968 *gauchisme*. Indeed the Massif Central had become a favoured spot for ex-militants to "drop out" and pursue alternative lifestyles. This was one element within the development of a strong Green movement, which tapped into the guilty conscience of a consumerist, increasingly urban society. The first political impact of the Greens came in 1974 when the distinguished economist René Dumont stood for president of the republic on this ticket. The movement gathered strength in the late 1970s and early 1980s, and its support was buttressed by voters' loss of enthusiasm for government-style Socialism after 1984. Elections to the European parliament allowed the ecological movement to make links with and gather strength from the strong Green movements in other countries, notably Germany. Slow but steady progress at the polls was rewarded in 1988 when Mitterrand, less sure of the Communists as his political allies, and looking for other supporters on the Left, appointed Green leader Brice Lalonde (who had stood in the 1981 presidential elections) as minister for the environment. The Greens made strong progress in the legislative elections of 1993, drawing many normally Socialist voters into their camp.

PROBLEMS OF CULTURAL IDENTITY

Politics and culture have since 1789 at least been inextricably intertwined in France. Social and cultural solidarities, bound up with geographical region, family outlook and choice of profession, have long tended to dictate specific forms of political identity. The Vendée, for example, was indelibly marked by its treatment at the hands of the infant First Republic in 1793/4, and thereafter was pro-Church, anti-republican and Right-voting. The liberal professions, in contrast, were one of the social groups to lead and to do best out of the Revolutionary experience; they have tended to be anti-clerical and to vote for Radicals and Socialists. For much of the nineteenth and twentieth centuries the "party of reaction" faced the "party of movement", and a definable line between the two sides could be drawn on most major issues – whether these were lay schooling, colonial issues or constitutional arrangements.

This long-established fusing of political and social identity appeared to be breaking down in the last quarter of the twentieth century, under the pressure of social, economic and cultural change. Two countervailing developments seemed at work. First, there was the way in which all conventional party formations accepted and worked within the constitutional framework. Such stability was both a rare bird and a new arrival in recent French history. Second, and by contrast, a more diverse and colourful political scene was emerging outside or marginal to the parliamentary arena. Many of these unconventional groups offered new models of political engagement and new styles of cultural politics. "Left" and "Right" seemed suddenly to count for less than "green", "gay", *gauchiste* or whatever. So just as Left and Right had for the first time since 1789 managed to agree to work within the same constitutional framework, new cultural and political forms appeared, questioning the very terms in which debate was framed.

It is too soon to understand the reasons for these shifts of political and cultural identity in the Mitterrand years – or to gauge their likely impact. We can, however, explore generally how these forms developed. It seems clear, for example, that the new fluidity in political and cultural expression owed much to changes in access to information technology and telecommunications. Public access to information has always been a key issue for the French state. This has sometimes been restricted through censorship or, more typically with republican regimes, shaped through emphasis on lay schooling and freedom of speech. The early history of the Fifth Republic was marked by bitter debate about state control over information, notably radio and television. De Gaulle's famous scorn for the journalistic profession ("scribblers, wanglers and crawlers") was echoed in Pompidou's more guarded comment: "French television is thought of as the voice of France, at home and abroad." Many of the sharpest barbs in May 1968 were directed against government control of the media. News, it was held, was little more than the general addressing the nation.

State monitoring of the media, however, was greatly relaxed from the 1970s on, as the regime became more settled and as new information technologies came on stream. Giscard d'Estaing made moves in this direction, but it was Mitterrand's presidency which saw the biggest changes. From the early 1980s audio-visual freedom was proclaimed; private radio stations were permitted; an independent broadcasting authority was established to keep government at arm's length; private TV channels were authorized (the first, *Canal Plus*, opened in 1984); and cable and satellite broadcasting started to make advances.

The increased freedom of television was particularly significant in that the medium had become the means by which French people derived information, and it constituted a widespread form of popular leisure – to the nation's detriment, some felt. Opinion polls in the late 1980s found that while, on average, French people spent twenty minutes a day reading newspapers, they spent two hours listening to the radio and three hours watching television. The decline in newspaper reading was a particularly dramatic component in this story. A century earlier, at the time of the Dreyfus affair, France was the world's leading consumer of newsprint; as the end of the millennium approached, it found itself in eighth position within Europe and twenty-seventh in the world, on a par with Korea and Singapore. Competition from the electronic media was largely responsible for this decline. It is noticeable, too, how the *minitel* took over the role formerly played by the newspaper small-advertisement in addressing individuals' wants and needs.

The changes detectable in the news media reflected the growth of consumerism within French society. News had become a commodity to be consumed like cars, video-players or blue jeans. This commodification of culture began to have a noticeable impact on the way French history itself was viewed. As we have suggested, the French

"My French is rich," a headline from *Libération*, 24 February 1994. This incomprehensible phrase alludes to a stock construction of school English: "My tailor is rich." The headline announces a revival of the government attack on foreign terms (especially from Britain and the United States) being used where a French term was available. The laws against franglais were created in 1977, but have rarely been used.

past has long been a critical component of civic identity: the story of "the nation" constituted one of the ways in which individuals asserted their own political and cultural identities. How history was written and how it was read thus proved a particularly interesting yardstick by which late twentieth-century social and cultural change could be registered.

When that last quarter of a century began, in 1975, the national bestseller list was headed by two history books: Emmanuel Le Roy Ladurie's *Montaillou*, an account of the Cathar heresy in a Pyrenean village of the same name in the fourteenth century; and amateur historian Pierre Jakes Helias' *Le Cheval d'orgueil* ("Horse of Pride"), an account of traditional Breton peasant culture. Their lead position was not as exceptional as it might appear – history was a market leader among academic books throughout the 1970s and 1980s. Such commercial success reflected the quality and the orientation of the French historical method in the wake of the so-called *Annales* "school" – the historians associated with the famous journal of that name. The *Annalistes* had endeavoured to revolutionize historical writing. Shifting the focus away from the traditional chronicle of kings, queens and battles, they sought to recreate a "total history", which examined broader time patterns – the *longue durée*, as master *Annaliste* Fernand Braudel called it. Furthermore, they attempted to build bridges between history and the other social sciences – sociology, economics, demography, linguistics,

The weekly television show, *Apostrophes*, was a cultural trendsetter in the 1970s and 1980s. Its host Bernard Pivot became a kind of literary impresario and cultural ringmaster. Among his guests here are Jacques Attali, sometime personal aide to Mitterrand, disgraced president of the European Development Bank, and writer and historian.

anthropology (as in *Montaillou*), oral history (as in *Le Cheval d'orgueil*) and so on. The result was innovatory forms of history writing which by the 1960s had conquered the academic establishment in France and turned the French historical method into a world leader.

Yet this can hardly explain its popular success, any more than the fact that both the 1975 bestsellers were brilliantly written. One must bear in mind that history was traditionally viewed in France as an intellectual crossroads where cultural identity was transacted. Both Le Roy Ladurie and Helias in their different ways evoked lost worlds – rural civilizations that were grounded, for all their manifest faults and problems, in enduring values. In this way history writing addressed a nostalgic itch, which other historians too numerous to mention capitalized upon. Agrarian life could be experienced by ever fewer French people; but it could be consumed vicariously by millions. Historians became chat-show guests, television presenters, newspaper columnists. History became a means by which the entrails of a changing society could be read. This "new history" caused political as well as social debate. There were those on the republican Right, in particular, who resented the disappearance of "event history", with its attendant dates and "facts", and school syllabuses were brought back hurriedly into line.

The phenomenon reached its high point with the bicentenary of the French Revolution of 1789. The event was bound to raise political disputes along well-worn lines: thus the pro-Church Right, marshalled by maverick Protestant historian Pierre Chaunu, attempted to conflate 1789 with the alleged "genocide" meted out by republican armies in the Vendée in 1793/4. Similarly there was ritual sniping between President Mitterrand and Mayor of Paris Jacques Chirac over the form the celebrations on 14 July 1989 in Paris should take. Beyond what might have been expected, however, three features of the celebrations shone out.

First, it was noticeable how virtually the whole political nation engaged in the events positively and constructively. This underlined the extent to which the republican values embodied in 1789 provided the established framework for political debate and civic affirmation. Second, the enthusiasm which the commemoration evoked in towns and villages was also most remarkable. Huge numbers of local bicentenary committees were established, and many, encouraged and shepherded by professional historians, proved eager to find out about local history in the Revolutionary epoch. The bicentenary, then, prompted a search for origins and fuelled a quest for local identity that both chimed with the shift to a new cultural politics of the grassroots and highlighted a sense of uncertainty about cultural identity.

The third striking feature of the bicentenary was the extent to which Revolutionary culture was being commercialized. While historians held their Revolutionary conferences and wrote their Revolutionary books, radio and TV producers produced Revolutionary programmes and entrepreneurs fabricated their Bastille tee-shirts, guillotine earrings and tricolour underpants. This element was captured in its purest form in the massive procession organized on the evening of 14 July in Paris. Bastille ing of Eurodisney suggested a similar anxiety over cultural identity. So too did a worrying resurgence of anti-gay opinion in the wake of the appearance of AIDS.

All developed nations towards the end of the twentieth century were grappling – some with greater success than others – with the problems and difficulties of multi-culturalism. France boasted a more distinguished record than most in integrating minorities: on numerous occasions the republic had risen to the challenge of bringing socially and culturally marginalized groups into the political fold. Yet integration had worked best when notions of French identity were relatively stable, and when economic circumstances were propitious. In the mid 1990s, with economic recession proving difficult to shake off, and with the uncertain venture of European integration looming, neither condition applied. With the grounds of political and cultural identity seemingly in flux, the French republic faced a considerable challenge, as the *fin de millénium* drew nigh.

Afro-American opera singer Jessye Norman, massively draped in the tricolour, performs "The Marseillaise". One of the high spots of the bicentenary celebrations held in Paris on 14 July 1989.

Chronology

c. 2,000,000 BC Early hominid societies.

c. 30,000 BC Old Stone Age.

c. 10,000 BC End of Ice Age.

c. 6,000 BC New Stone Age.

c. 1,800 BC Age of Metal.

700 BC Celts present throughout Gaul.

125–121 BC Roman colonization of southern Gaul.

58–51 BC Rome conquers Gaul.

177 First Christian martyrs at Lyon.

406 Major barbarian raids and settlement.

476 Roman Empire in west falls; Franks develop empire.

511 Paris established as Frankish capital by the Merovingian Clovis.

732 Arab forces defeated at Poitiers.

751 Carolingians assume power.

771 Charlemagne sole ruler.

800 Charlemagne crowned Emperor in the west.

843 Treaty of Verdun divides Carolingian empire.

987 Hugh Capet becomes king, establishing Capetian dynasty.

1095 First Crusade called by Pope Urban II.

1159 "First Hundred Years War" (to 1299).

1214 Battle of Bouvines.

1299 Treaty of Montreuil confirms end of "First Hundred Years War".

1302 Estates General convened.

1309 Papal residence established at Avignon.

1328 Philip VI succeeds to throne, establishing Valois dynasty.

1337 Hundred Years War between England and France (to 1453).

1346 English defeat French at Crécy.

1347 Loss of Calais to the English.

1348 Black Death breaks out leading to huge population losses.

1356 English defeat French at Poitiers.

1356 English capture King John II "the Good".

1358 Jacquerie rising in northern France.

1360 Peace of Brétigny signed between England and France.

1415 English defeat French at Agincourt.

1431 Joan of Arc burnt at the stake.

1438 Pragmatic Sanction of Bourges secures monarchy greater control over papacy.

1453 Battle of Castillon, the final battle of the Hundred Years War.

1470 First printing presses in France established in Paris.

1477 Death of Charles the Bold, duke of Burgundy.

1482 Treaty of Arras incorporates duchy of Burgundy into France.

1494 Italian Wars (to 1559).

1515 French victory at Marignano.

1516 Concordat of Bologna confirms king's rights over French Church.

1525 French defeated and Francis I captured at Pavia.

1534 Affair of the Placards pushes government into overt repression of Protestantism.

1534 Jacques Cartier leads expedition to Canada.

1539 Edict of Villers-Cotterets makes French the language of all legal and official documents.

1559 Treaty of Cateau-Cambrésis ends Italian Wars.

1561 French Wars of Religion (to 1598).

1572 Saint Bartholomew's Eve Massacre: prominent Protestants murdered in Paris.

1588 Day of the Barricades by Catholic League in Paris.

1589 Henry IV succeeds to throne, establishing Bourbon dynasty.

1594 Croquant peasants rise in the south-west (to 1595).

1598 Edict of Nantes ends Wars of Religion.

1598 Treaty of Vervins with Spain.

1618 Thirty Years War against Austria and Spain (to 1648).

1622 Peace of Montpellier reduces Protestant garrison towns to two.

1624 Richelieu enters royal council as principal minister (to 1642).

1630 Day of the Dupes consolidates Richelieu's hold on power.

1631 First national newspaper, the *Gazette*, established.

1639 Nu-Pieds revolt in Normandy.

1643 French victory over Spain at Rocroi.

1643 Louis XIV becomes king of France.

1648 Treaty of Westphalia ends Thirty Years War.

1648 Fronde (to 1652).

1659 Treaty of the Pyrenees concluded with Spain.

1661 Colbert, finance minister (to 1683).

1667 War of Devolution (to 1668).

1672 Dutch War (to 1678).

1685 Edict of Fontainebleau revokes the Edict of Nantes.

1689 War of the League of Augsburg (to 1697).

1701 War of Spanish Succession (to 1713).

1702 War of the Camisards in the Cévennes waged by Calvinist peasants (to 1704).

1713 Treaty of Utrecht ends War of Spanish Succession.

1715 Death of Louis XIV: parlement of Paris installs duke of Orléans as regent of Louis XV (to 1723).

1740 War of Austrian Succession (to 1748).

1756 Seven Years War: France suffers heavy losses at England's hands (to 1763).

1775 Flour War; rioting over grain shortages.

1778 War of American Independence: France joins rebel colonies against England (to 1783).

1783 Treaty of Versailles: France makes some colonial gains.

1788   Estates General convened to meet in May 1789.

1789   (20 June) Tennis Court Oath: the National Assembly swears not to disband until basis of a new constitution has been established.

1789   (14 July) Bastille stormed in Paris. French Revolution starts.

1789   (Autumn) Peasant revolution; the abolition of feudalism.

1792   Outbreak of war with Austria.

1792   Louis XVI overthrown and First Republic declared.

1792   September Massacres: vigilante gangs murder prisoners in Parisian gaols.

1793   The Terror (to 1794).

1795   Directory, a new constitutional regime, is established (to 1799).

1799   Napoleon overthrows Directory and creates Consulate.

1801   Pope and Napoleon sign Concordat, re-establishing Catholicism.

1804   Napoleon crowned Emperor: creation of First Empire.

1804   *Code Napoléon* (Civil Code) issued.

1808   Peninsular War in Spain begins.

1812   Napoleon defeated in Moscow campaign.

1814   Napoleon deposed and sent to Elba.

1815   Napoleon's "Hundred Days" end in defeat at Waterloo.

1815   Bourbon dynasty re-established on throne in person of Louis XVIII.

1830   French conquest of Algeria begins.

1830   *Trois glorieuses* (27–29 July) force Charles X to abdicate, ending Bourbon dynasty. Louis-Philippe, duke of Orléans, becomes king.

1848   July Monarchy falls.

1848   Second Republic is declared, Louis-Philippe abdicates and a Provisional Government is formed.

1848   "June Days"; repression of Paris radicals.

1851   *Coup d'état*: Louis Bonaparte seizes power.

1852   Second Empire, president Louis Bonaparte appoints himself emperor Napoleon III.

1870   Franco-Prussian War.

1871   Paris Commune; loss of Alsace and Lorraine to Germany. Third Republic declared.

1898   Emile Zola publishes "J'accuse": the Dreyfus Affair.

1905   *Entente Cordiale* between France and Britain.

1914   First World War (to 1918).

1914   Battle of the Marne.

1916   Battle of Verdun.

1919   Treaty of Versailles; Alsace and Lorraine reincorporated into France.

1924   Dawes Plan for German reparations.

1925   Locarno Treaties between France, Germany and other powers.

1929   Decision to build Maginot Line.

1934   The Stavisky Affair.

1936   Popular Front government unites Communists, Socialists and other Left groups.

1938   Munich agreements signed by Daladier.

1939   World War II (to 1945).

1940   *Etat français*. End of Third Republic; establishment of Pétain's Vichy France.

1944   D-Day Allied landings.

1944   Overthrow of Vichy regime.

1946   Fourth Republic established.

1954   Algerian War begins.

1954   Vietnamese defeat French at Dien-Bien-Phu.

1957   Treaty of Rome establishes the Common Market.

1958   Deadlock in Algeria leads to constitutional crisis: the Fourth Republic gives way to the Fifth.

1962   Evian agreements grant Algeria full independence.

1968   May Events; students and unions stage massive anti-government protests.

1981   François Mitterrand elected president (re-elected 1988).

1994   Official opening of the Channel Tunnel.

Picture Acknowledgements

The following abbreviations have been used:

BN: Blbliothèque Nationale, Paris
BL: British Library, London
Bridgeman: Bridgeman Art Library, London
Coll: Collection
DO: G. Dagli Orti, Paris
Giraudon: Giraudon, Paris
HJ: Hubert Josse, Paris
JLC: Jean-Loup Charmet, Paris
MC: Musée Carnavalet, Paris
pc: Private Collection
RMN: Réunion des Musées Nationaux, Paris
RV: Roger-Viollet, Paris.

Half title page Keystone/Sygma. Title page RV. 11 Coll: BN. Photo: HJ. 15 René Burri/Magnum. 16 Coll: Musée de l'Homme, Paris. 18 Ministère de l'Education nationale et de la Culture, Direction du Patrimoine. Photo: A. Chêne (C.N.R.S., Centre Camille Jullian). 19 & 22 Eric Lessing/Magnum. 23 Coll: Soprintendenza delle Marche, Ancona, Italy. Photo: DO. 24 left Coll: Musée Massey, Tarbes. Photo: ALPY, Tarbes. 24 right Coll: Musée de la Vieille Charité, Marseille. Photo: Giraudon. 26 Coll: Musée Archeologique, Châtillon-sur-Seine. Photo: DO. 26 below Coll: Musée Archeologique, Châtillon-sur-Seine. Photo: HJ. 27 Coll: Musée de la Civilisation Gallo-Romaine, Lyon. Photo: DO. 28 Coll: Musée de Saint-Germain-en-Laye. Photo: RV. 31 Collection & photo: BN. 32 Photo: RV. 34 Photo: DO. 35 Coll: Musée Bargoin, Clermont-Ferrand. Photo: Lauros-Giraudon. 37 Coll: Maison Carrée, Nîmes. Photo: Lauros-Giraudon. 38 above Coll: Jean Vinchon, Paris. Photo: DO. 38 below Photo: Fototeca Unione, Rome. 40 Collection & photo: Musée Calvet, Avignon inv. 16.273. 42 Collection & photo: © Musée d'Aquitaine, Bordeaux-France. 43 Coll: Musée de Saint-Germain-en-Laye. Photo: JLC. 45 Photo: Landesmuseum, Trier. 46 Coll: Saint-Germain-en-Laye, Musem of National Antiquities. Photo: RMN. 50 Coll: BN Grandes Chroniques de France. Photo: HJ. 51 left Collection & photo: BN Cabinet des Medailles. 51 right Collection & photo: BN Cabinet des Medailles. 54 Collection & photo: The Metropolitan Museum of Art, New York, The Cloisters Collection, 1925. 55 Coll: Bibliothèque Municipale, Poitiers. Photo: DO. 57 Photo: RV. 58 Collection & photo: BN Ms Lat. 12135. fol.1.v. 59 Collection & photo: BN. 62 Coll: Staatsbibliothek zu Berlin. Photo: Preussischer Kulturbesitz Hanschrifteabteilung. 63 Coll: Treasury of Reims Cathedral. Photo: Caisse Nationale des Monuments Historiques, Paris © DACS 1994. 65 Coll: Treasury of the Abbey Church at Conques. Photo: DO. 66 Coll: Musée du Louvre, Paris. Photo: HJ. 70 Collection & photo: The Bayeux Tapestry – 11th Century, by special permission of the City of Bayeux. 72 Collection & photo: BL Ms Add. 37768 fol.4r. 75 Coll: Musée Tessé, Le Mans. Photo: HJ. 79 Collection & photo: BL Ms D XI fol.134 v. 80 Photo: Lauros-Giraudon. 82 Collection & photo: BN Ms Lat. 17716 fol.91. 83 Photo: Adam Woolfit/Robert Harding Picture Library, London. 86 Coll: BL. Photo: Bridgeman. 87 Collection & photo: BN Ms Fr. 13568 fol.83. 88 Coll: Archives Nationales, Paris. Photo: JLC. 90 left Photo: RV. 90 right Coll: BN Grandes Chroniques de France. Photo: HJ. 91 Photo: RV. 92 Photo: Yan, Toulouse. 95 Coll: Arsenal Ms 5080 fol.373. Photo: JLC. 97 Collection & photo: BN Ms Lat. 9187 fol.30 v. 98 Collection & photo: BN Ms Fr.18437 fol.2. 100 Collection & photo: BL Ms Royal 20 CVII fol.48. 101 Coll: BN. Photo: HJ. 103 Collection & photo: Bibliothèque Municipale, Dijon Ms 170 fol.41. 105 Coll: Archives Nationales, Paris. Photo: JLC. 107 Coll: BN Ms Lat. 1118 fol.112 v. Photo: Giraudon. 108 Coll: Escorial Library, Codex provençal fol.215 v. Photo: DO. 111 Photo: Hirmer Fotoarchiv, Munich. 112 Coll: University Library, Heidelberg. Photo: DO. 115 Collection & photo: BL Ms Royal 20.C.VII

fol.72 v. 116 TAX picture 117 Collection & photo: BL Ms Royal 22 C VII fol.212 v. 118 Coll: BN. Photo: HJ. 119 Coll: BN Ms Fr. 2030 fol.1 v. Photo: JLC. 121 above Coll: Musée de l'Histoire de France, Paris. Photo: JLC. 121 below Collection & photo: © Musée d'Aquitaine, Bordeaux-France. 122 Collection & photo: BN Ms Fr. 87 fol. 138. 124 Photo: Paul M.R. Maeyaert, Zelzate, Belgium. 125 Collection & photo: Blbliothèque Royale Albert Ier, Brussels. Ms 9242 fol.1 r. 126 Collection & photo: BL Ms Harley 4431 fol.3. 128 Eric Lessing/Magnum. 129 Coll: BN. Photo: RV. 132 Photo: Giraudon. 134 Photo: JLC. 135 Coll: Bibliothèque des Arts Décoratifs, Paris. Photo: JLC. 137 Coll: BN. Photo: JLC. 138 Coll: Château Musée de Blois. Photo: DO. 139 Coll: MC. Photo: RV. 142 Coll: BN. Photo: JLC. 145 Coll: Château Musée de Versailles. Photo: RMN. 146 Coll: BN. Photo: Giraudon. 148 Coll: MC. Photo: JLC. 150 Coll: MC. Photo: Giraudon. 152 Photo: HJ. 155 Coll: Bibliothèque des Arts Décoratifs, Paris. Photo: JLC. 156 Coll: BN. Photo: RV. 157 Coll: Bibliothèque des Arts Décoratifs, Paris. Photo: JLC. 159 Coll: BN. Photo: RV. 160 Coll: MC. Photo: Musées de la Ville de Paris © DACS 1994. 161 Coll: Bibliothèque des Arts Décoratifs, Paris. Photo: JLC. 162 Photos: HJ. 165 Photo: Calmann & King Archives, London. 167 Coll: Schloss Charlottenburg, Berlin. Photo: Bridgeman. 168 Coll: BN. Photo: JLC. 170 Coll: Musée des Bades, Moulins. Photo: RV. 171 left Photo: JLC. 171 right Coll: BN. Photo: JLC. 172 Coll: BN. Photo: JLC. 174 Coll: Château de la Malmaison. Photo: HJ. 177 Collection & photo: Le Centre Départemental de Documentation Pédagogique de Tarbes, Hautes Pyrénées. 178 & 179 Coll: BN. Photo: JLC. 180 Coll: MC. Photo: HJ. 181 Coll: MC. Photo: RV. 182 Coll: MC. Photo: JLC. 183 Coll: Giraudon-Lauros/Bridgeman. 184 Coll: MC. Photo: JLC. 185 Coll: Musées Royaux des Beaux-Arts de Belgique. Brussels. Photo: Giraudon/Bridgeman. 187 Coll: BL. Photo: Bridgeman. 188 Coll: Musée d'art et d'histoire de Cholet. Photo: Studio Golder, Cholet. 190 Coll: MC. Photo: Giraudon/Bridgeman. 192 Coll: Bibliothèque des Arts Décoratifs, Paris. Photo: JLC. 194 Coll: Château de Malmaison, Paris. Photo: Lauros-Giraudon/Bridgeman. 197 Photo: Fotomas Index, Kent. 199 Coll: Palais de Tau, Reims. Photo: Caisse Nationale des Monuments Historiques, Paris © DACS 1994. 202 Coll: Musée du Louvre, Paris. Photo: RMN. 204 Coll: BN. Photo: JLC. 205 Coll: BN. Photo: JLC. 206 Coll: Bibliothèque des Arts Décoratifs, Paris. Photo: JLC. 208 Coll: BN. Photo: JLC. 209 Photo: Léonard de Selva-Tapabor, Paris. 210 Coll: BN. Photo: RV. 213 Coll: Archives Départementales du Haut-Rhin, Musée d'Unterlinden, Colmar. Photo: Christian Kempf. 214 above Coll: Musée du Palais de Compiègne. Photo: JLC. 214 below from L'Illustration, Paris, March 13, 1869. Photo: Keystone/Sygma 215 Collection & photo: Museum Folkwang, Essen. 218 & 220 Photo: JLC. 222 Coll: MC. Photo: JLC. 223 Photo: JLC. 226 Coll: MC. Photo: JLC. 227 pc. Photo: JLC. 229 Photo: JLC. 230 Coll: BN. Photo: JLC. 231 pc. Photo: JLC. 232 Coll: Musée d'Histoire de la Médecine, Paris. Photo: JLC. 234 both Coll: BN. JLC. 236 Coll: Musée de la Police, Paris. Photo: JLC. 239 pc. Photo: JLC. 240 Photo: Giraudon. 243 Photo: RV. 244 Coll: Musée des Deux Guerres Mondiales, Paris. Photo: JLC. 245 Coll: Bibliothèque Forney, Paris. Photo: JLC. 246 Coll: Musée d'Histoire Contemporaine, Université de Paris – BDIC/Archipel © Spadem. 249 Photo: RV. 250 pc. Photo: JLC. 251 pc. Photo: JLC. 252 Photo: RV. 254 René Magritte, Je ne vois pas la Femme Cachée dans la Forêt, collage, published in La Revolution Surréaliste (No 12), December 1929 © ADAGP, Paris and DACS, London 1944. 255 Photo: JLC. 256 Photo: JLC. 257 Popperfoto, London. 258 Photo: RV. 260 Photo: RV. 262 David Seymour/Magnum. 263 Henri Cartier-Bresson/Magnum. 265 Photo: RV. 267 pc. Photo: Giraudon. 269 Photo: RV. 270 Photo: RV. 271 Photos: JLC. 272 Photo: Keystone/Sygma. 275 Robert Capa/Magnum. 277 left pc © DACS 1994. 277 right Sergio Larrain/Magnum. 278 Robert Capa/Magnum. 280 David Seymour/Magnum. 281 Collection & photo: Alan Gesgon, Paris. 283 Robert Capa/Magnum. 284 Nîcolas Tikhomiroff/Magnum. 285 Photo:

Magnum. **287** Nicolas Tikhomiroff/Magnum. **291** Keystone/Sygma. **292** Photos: Citroën, Neuilly-sur-Seine. **293** Collection & photo: Vintage Magazine Co. Ltd., London. **294** Guy Le Querrec/Magnum. **296** Bruno Barbey/Magnum. **297** Bruno Barbey/Magnum. **298** Gérard-Aimé, Paris. **299** Henri Cartier-Bresson/Magnum. **301** J.C. Martel/Archipress, Paris. **304** Raymond Depardon/Magnum. **307** Bruno Barbey/Magnum. **310** Leonard Freed/Magnum. **311** Photo: Sygma. **314** Steve McCurry/Magnum. **316** © Plantu, Paris. **318** Dominique Aubert/Sygma. **319** S. Couturier/Archipress, Paris. **322** Dominique Aubert/Sygma. **323** Abbas/Magnum. **326** Bisson/Sygma. **327** Photo: RV. **330** S. Bassouls/Sygma. **332** Regio Bossu/Sygma. **335** Yves Forestier/Sygma.

Bibliography

General Works

Atlas historique de la France contemporaine, 1800–1965. Paris: A. Colin, 1966.

B.S. Anderson and J.P. Zinsser, *A History of Their Own: Women in Europe from Prehistory to the Present*, 2 vols. New York: Harper & Row, 1988.

J. Ardagh and C. Jones, *Cultural Atlas of France*, Oxford: Facts on File, 1991.

P. Ariès *et al.* (eds), *History of Private Life*, 5 vols. Cambridge, Mass.: Belknap, 1987–90.

L. Bergeron, *Paris: Genèse d'un paysage.* Paris: Picard, 1989.

G. de Bertière de Sauvigny and D.H. Pinkney, *History of France.* Arlington Heights: Forum Press, 1977.

M. Bloch, *French Rural History: An Essay on Its Basic Characteristics.* London: Routledge Kegan Paul, 1966.

M.J. Boxer and J.H. Quataert (eds), *Connecting Spheres: Women in the Western World: 1500 to the Present.* New York: Oxford University Press, 1987.

F. Braudel, *The Identity of France*, 2 vols, New York: Harper & Row, 1986 and 1988.

F. Braudel, *Civilisation and Capitalism*, 3 vols. New York: Harper & Row, 1982–4.

F. Braudel and E. Labrousse (eds), *Histoire économique et sociale de la France*, 4 vols. Paris: PUF, 1970–82.

F. Brunot, *Histoire de la langue française des origines à 1900*, 12 vols. Paris: A. Colin, 1905–53.

A. Burguière and J. Revel (eds), *Histoire de la France*, 3 vols. Paris: Seuil, 1989 and 1990.

H. Clout, *Themes in the Historical Geography of France.* New York: Academic Press, 1977.

R. Collins, *The Basques.* Oxford: Blackwell, 1986.

R. Dion, *Les Frontières de la France.* Paris: Hachette, 1947.

——————, *Le Paysage et la vigne.* Paris: Payot, 1990.

G. Duby (ed.), *Histoire de la France*, 3 vols. Paris: Larousse, 1982.

——————, *Histoire de la France urbaine*, 5 vols. Paris: Seuil, 1980–5.

——————, *A History of Private Life*, 5 vols. Cambridge, Mass.: Belknap, 1987–90.

G. Duby and M. Perrot (eds), *A History of Women in the West*, 5 vols. Cambridge, Mass.: Belknap, 1992–3.

G. Duby and A. Wallon (eds), *Histoire de la France rurale*, 4 vols. Paris: Seuil, 1975–6.

J. Dupâcquier (ed.), *Histoire de la population française*, 4 vols. Paris: PUF, 1988.

J.B. Duroselle, *Europe: A History of Its Peoples.* London: Viking 1990.

P. Goubert, *The Course of French History.* New York: Watts, 1991.

A. Guérard, *France: A Modern History*, 2nd edn. Ann Arbor: University of Michigan Press, 1969.

H. Le Bras, *Les Trois France.* Paris: O. Jacob, 1986.

H. Le Bras and E. Todd, *L'Invention de la France.* Paris: Seuil, 1981.

E. Le Roy Ladurie, *Times of Feast, Times of Famine: A History of the Climate Since the Year 1000.* New York: Doubleday, 1971.

R. Mettam and D. Johnson, *French History and Society: The Wars of Religion to the Fifth Republic.* London: Methuen, 1974.

L. Mirot, *Manuel de géographie historique de la France*, 2nd edn, 2 vols. Paris: Picard, 1947 and 1950.

J.R. Pitte, *Histoire du paysage français*, 2 vols. Paris: Tallandier, 1983.

X. de Planhol, *Géographie historique de la France.* Paris: Fayard, 1988.

R. Price, *A Concise History of France.* Cambridge University Press, 1993.

E. Todd, *The Making of Modern France.* Oxford: Blackwell, 1991.

——————, *The Causes of Progress.* Oxford: Blackwell, 1987.

P. Wolff (ed.), *Univers de la France et des pays francophones* (multi-volumed series, covering histories of individual provinces and cities). Toulouse: Privat, 1967–.

Introduction

Annales: Economies, Sociétés, Civilisations (appears six times per annum)

J. Ardagh and C. Jones, *Cultural Atlas of France.* Oxford: Facts on File, 1991.

R. Barthes, *Mythologies.* Paris: Seuil, 1957.

M. Bloch, *The Royal Touch.* London: Routledge, 1973.

F. Braudel, *The Identity of France*, 2 vols. New York: Harper & Row, 1986 and 1988.

R. Cobb, *A Second Identity.* Oxford University Press, 1969.

E. James, *The Franks.* Oxford: Blackwell, 1988.

——————, *The Origins of France: From Clovis to the Capetians 500–1000.* London: Macmillan, 1982.

J.R. Pitte, *Histoire du paysage français.* Paris: Tallandier, 1983.

X. de Planhol, *Géographie historique de la France.* Paris: Fayard, 1988.

E. Weber, *Peasants into Frenchmen: The Modernization of Rural France 1870–1914.* Stanford University Press, 1977.

Before the Middle Ages (Chapters 1–3)

a) Before the Romans

P.G. Bahn and J. Vertut, *Images of the Ice Age.* Oxford: Facts on File, 1988.

J.L. Brunaux, *The Celtic Gauls: Gods, Rites and Sanctuaries.* London: B.A. Seaby, 1987.

J.G.D. Clark and S. Piggott, *Prehistoric Societies.* New York: Knopf, 1965.

J. Guilaine, *La France d'avant la France: du néolithique à l'âge de fer.* Paris: Hachette, 1980.

——————, *La Préhistoire française.* Paris: CNRS, 1976.

J.J. Hatt, *Celts and Gallo-Romans.* London: Barrie & Jenkins, 1970.

R. Joffroy, *Le Trésor de Vix: Histoire et portée d'une grande découverte.* Paris: Hachette, 1962.

A.P. Phillips, *The Prehistory of Europe.* Bloomington: Indiana University Press, 1980.

S. Piggott, *Ancient Europe*. Edinburgh University Press, 1965.

S. Piggott, G. Daniel and C. McBurney (eds), *France before the Romans*. London: Thames & Hudson, 1973.

T.G.E. Powell, *The Celts*. New York: Praeger, 1958.

M. Ruspoli, *The Caves of Lascaux*. London: Thames & Hudson, 1987.

N. Sandars, *Bronze Age Cultures in France*. Cambridge University Press, 1957.

C. Scarre (ed.), *Ancient France: Neolithic Societies and their Landscapes, 6000–200 BC*. Edinburgh University Press, 1983.

A. Sieveking, *The Cave Artists*. London: Thames & Hudson, 1979.

D. Trump, *The Prehistory of the Mediterranean*. New Haven: Yale University Press, 1980.

b) The Romans

T. Cornell and J. Matthews, *Atlas of the Roman World*. New York: Facts on File, 1982.

J.F. Drinkwater, *Roman Gaul: The Three Provinces, 58 BC–AD 260*. Ithaca, New York: Cornell University Press, 1983.

P. Garnsey and R. Saller, *The Roman Empire: Economy, Society and Culture*. London: Duckworth, 1987.

C. Goudineau, *César et la Gaule*. Paris: Errance, 1990.

P. Grimal, *Roman Cities*. Madison: Wisconsin University Press, 1983.

A.H.M. Jones, *The Decline of the Ancient World*. London: Longman, 1966.

A. King, *Roman Gaul and Germany*. Berkeley: California University Press, 1990.

F. Millar, *The Roman Empire and Its Neighbours*, 2nd edn. London: Duckworth, 1981.

M. Pobé, *The Art of Roman Gaul*. Toronto University Press, 1961.

A.L.F. Rivet, *Gallia Narbonensis: Southern France in Roman Times*. London: Batsford, 1988.

R. Van Dam, *Leadership and Community in Late Antique Gaul*. Berkeley: California University Press, 1985.

E.M. Wightman, *Gallia Belgica*. Berkeley: California University Press, 1985.

A. and P. Wiseman, *Julius Caesar: The Battle for Gaul*. Boston: Godine, 1980.

c) The Merovingians and Carolingians

B.S. Bachrach, *A History of the Alans in the West*. Minneapolis: Minnesota University Press, 1993.

D. Bullough, *The Age of Charlemagne*, 2nd edn. New York: Puttnam, 1973.

G. Duby, *The Early Growth of the European Economy: Warriors and Peasants from the 7th to the 12th centuries*. Ithaca, New York: Cornell University Press, 1974.

P. Galliou and M. Jones, *The Bretons*. Oxford: Blackwell, 1991.

P.J. Geary, *Before France and Germany: The Creation and Transformation of the Merovingian World*. New York: Oxford University Press, 1988.

W. Goffart, *Barbarians and Romans AD 418–584: The Techniques of Accommodation*. Princeton University Press, 1980.

R. Heer, *Charlemagne and His World*. New York: Macmillan, 1975.

R. Hodges and D. Whitehouse, *Mohammed, Charlemagne and the Origins of Europe*. London: Duckworth, 1983.

G. Holmes (ed.), *The Oxford Illustrated History of Medieval Europe*. Oxford University Press, 1988.

E. James, *The Franks*. Oxford: Blackwell, 1988.

————, *The Origins of France: From Clovis to the Capetians, 500–1000*. London: Macmillan, 1982.

R.M. McKitterick, *The Frankish Kingdoms under the Carolingians, 751–987*. London: Longman, 1983.

P. Périn and L.C. Feffer, *Les Francs: A la conquête de la Gaule*. Paris: A. Colin, 1987.

M. Todd, *The Early Germans*. Oxford: Blackwell, 1992.

J.M. Wallace-Hadrill, *The Barbarian West, 400–1000*, 3rd edn. London: Hutchinson, 1967.

————, *The Long-Haired Kings*. New York: Barnes & Noble, 1962.

S. Wemple, *Women in Frankish Society: Marriage and the Cloister, 500–900*. Philadelphia: Pennsylvania University Press, 1981.

The Middle Ages and the Early Modern Period (Chapters 4–6)

C. Allmand, *The Hundred Years War*. Cambridge University Press, 1989.

M. Barber, *The Two Cities: Medieval Europe, 1050–1320*. London: Routledge, 1992.

C. Beaune, *The Birth of an Ideology: Myths and Symbols of Nation in Late Medieval France*. Berkeley: California University Press, 1985.

J. Bergin, *The Rise of Richelieu*. New Haven: Yale University Press, 1991.

M. Bloch, *Feudal Society*. Chicago University Press, 1962.

————, *The Royal Touch*. London: Routledge, 1973.

F. Bluche, *Louis XIV*. Oxford: Blackwell, 1990.

R. Bonney, *Society and Government under Richelieu and Mazarin: 1626–61*. London: Macmillan, 1981.

R.M. Briggs, *Communities of Belief: Cultural and Social Tensions in Early Modern France*. Oxford: Clarendon Press, 1988.

————, *Early Modern France: 1560–1715*. Oxford University Press, 1977.

P. Burke, *The Fabrication of Louis XIV*. New Haven: Yale University Press, 1992.

J. Calmette, *The Golden Age of Burgundy*. New York: Norton, 1962.

R. Chartier, *Cultural Origins of the French Revolution*. Durham: Duke University Press, 1991.

N.Z. Davis, *Society and Culture in Early Modern France*. Stanford University Press, 1965.

G. Duby, *France in the Middle Ages, 987–1460: From Hugh Capet to Joan of Arc*. Oxford: Blackwell, 1991.

J. Dunbabin, *France in the Making: 843–1180*. Oxford University Press, 1985.

R. Fossier, *The Cambridge Illustrated History of the Middle Ages: 350–950*. Cambridge University Press, 1989.

J. Gillingham, *The Angevin Empire*. New York: Holmes & Meier, 1984.

P. Goubert, *The Ancien Régime*. New York: Harper & Row, 1971.

P. Goubert and D. Roche, *Les Français et l'Ancien Régime*, 2 vols. Paris: A. Colin, 1984.

M. Greengrass, *The French Reformation*. Oxford: Blackwell, 1987.

————, *France in the Age of Henry IV*. London: Longman, 1984.

E.H. Hallam, *Capetian France*. London: Longman, 1980.

————, *Occupied France: Collaboration and Resistance, 1940–4*. Oxford University Press, 1985.

T. Kemp, *The French Economy, 1913–39*. New York: St Martin's Press, 1972.

A. Kriegel, *The French Communists: Profile of a People*. Chicago University Press, 1972.

J. Lacouture, *De Gaulle*, 3 vols. London: Collins Harvill, 1984–6.

M. Larkin, *France Since the Popular Front, 1936–86*. Oxford: Clarendon Press, 1988.

J.F. Macmillan, *Twentieth-Century France: Politics and Society, 1898–1991*. New York: Macmillan, 1992.

M. Marrus and R.O. Paxton, *Vichy France and the Jews*. New York: Basic, 1981.

H. Mendras, *The Vanishing Peasant*. Cambridge, Mass.: MIT Press, 1970.

H. Mendras and A. Cole, *Social Change in Modern France: Towards a Cultural Anthropology of the Fifth Republic*. Cambridge University Press, 1991.

A. Milward, *The New Order and the French Economy*. Oxford: Clarendon Press, 1970.

E. Mortimer, *The Rise of the French Communist Party, 1920–47*. London: Faber & Faber, 1984.

M. Ophuls, *The Sorrow and the Pity: Chronicles of a French City under the German Occupation*. New York: Dutton, 1975.

R.O. Paxton, *The Vichy Régime: Old Guard and New Order*. New York: Knopf, 1972.

A. Prost, *In the Wake of War*, New York: Berg, 1992.

J.P. Rioux, *The Fourth Republic, 1944–58*. Cambridge University Press, 1987.

G. Ross *et al.*, *The Mitterrand Experiment*. New York: Oxford University Press, 1987.

J.F. Sweets, *Choices in Vichy France: The French under Nazi Occupation*. New York: Oxford University Press, 1986.

J.M. Winter, *The Experience of World War I*. New York: Oxford University Press, 1988.

V. Wright, *The Government and Politics of France*. New York: St Martin's Press, 1989.

V. Wright (ed.), *Continuity and Change in France*. London: Allen & Unwin, 1985.

T. Zeldin, *The French*. New York: Pantheon, 1983.

Index